MEDITERRANEAN
SUBMARINES

MEDITERRANEAN SUBMARINES

Michael Wilson
&
Paul Kemp

CRÉCY

Published in 1997 by
Crécy Publishing Limited,
Southside, Manchester Airport, Wilmslow,
Cheshire SK9 4LL, United Kingdom

ISBN 0 947554 57 2

Typeset in Monotype Baskerville by
Ace Filmsetting Ltd, Frome, Somerset

Printed by
Biddles Ltd, Guildford and King's Lynn

The tides of war flow up the beach and at the ebb they leave behind tales, countless as the drying grains of sand, tales that must be told.

Anon.

Contents

Acknowledgements

The authors wish to acknowledge the great help they have received from a great many different sources and in naming names apologise in advance should anyone have been inadvertently omitted.

They are indebted to Commander Richard Compton-Hall, MBE, RN, the Director of the Royal Navy Submarine Museum and Mr Gus Britton, the Archivist, who were as usual a mine of information and hospitality: Captain A J Wale, RN, for his help with technical matters; both Mr N J M Campbell and Mr T H King, the curator of the Naval Ordnance Museum at Gosport, for their help with tracing the gun armament fitted at various times to the British submarines in the Mediterranean; Mr Alan Francis of the Naval Historical Branch who willingly helped in tracing documents, Brian Head and Mr Rod Suddaby, Keeper of the Department of Documents at the Imperial War Museum.

They are grateful to Mr N A M Rodger for permission to quote from the Navy Records Society's Volume 1 of the Keyes Papers, to the Controller of HMSO for permission to quote from official papers at the Public Record Office and to the Archivist of the Churchill College Archives Centre, University of Cambridge to quote from the papers of Admiral Tomkinson.

We also wish to acknowledge the assistance generously given by the following individuals and institutions abroad: Service Historique de la Marine, Paris; Peter Jung and Susanne Neuwirth of the Kriegsarchiv, Vienna; Dr Achille Rastelli; Ufficio Storico delta Marina Militare, Rome; Berd Langensiepen; Erwin Sieche; Museum of the Black Sea Fleet, Sevastopol, and Professor Antonov of the Black Sea Fleet Museum, Varna.

Preface

Mention of submarine warfare during the Great War, or First World War as it is now more generally known, and thoughts will instantly turn to the German U-boat offensive against allied shipping in the Atlantic. For the British submariner it will bring thoughts of the hours spent in the Heligoland Bight with too few targets, the danger of mines and the terrible weather found all too often in that part of the ocean.

Few people would be bold enough to claim that the naval war in the Mediterranean was anything but a side-show. Yet it is of great interest since it was the only theatre where the new weapon of war, the submarine, could be found in operations by the navies of six of the eight major navies of the world possessing them: Britain, France, Germany, Italy, Austria and Russia with only Japan and the USA being absent. Despite the 'side-show' label it must not be forgotten that the three German commanding officers with the highest total of tonnage sunk all operated in the Mediterranean, while four British commanding officers received the award of the Victoria Cross. The German U-boats operating from Constantinople were sent either southwards into the Mediterranean or north through the Bosporus into the Black Sea, and for that reason it is logical that the operations of both the Russians and the Germans in the Black Sea should be included in this story of submarines in the Mediterranean. This book then is designed to bring together the operations of all these submarines.

The submarines of the Austro-Hungarian navy were originally just known by their number, which was then written in Roman numerals, viz.: VI. Later a 'U' (for *Unterseeboot*) was added as a prefix, and finally sometime in 1915 the same method of numbering as their German allies was adopted, namely the letter U followed by a number in Arabic numerals. For the sake of uniformity, and it is hoped ease of reading, a standard method of naming has been used throughout using the latter way. In any cases of doubt as to whether a German or Austrian boat is being referred to then a descriptive adjective has been added. To the purist we apologise and can only say that this has been done with the best of intentions.

There is always a problem with names of places in areas where there has been great political change in the years following the events described. In general we have used the names of places currently in use at the time with spelling taken from the Admiralty 'Pilots'. Similarly when dealing with the names of places in Turkey and Russia where the difference in the written script make exact translation impossible the Admiralty 'Pilot' has been taken as a base.

In any book which is devoted to the actions of submarines there comes a time when a decision has to be made on how much space has to given to other operations. Some is undoubtedly necessary; in any book on the Mediterranean war it is obvious that the escape of the two German ships to Turkey in the first days of the war, or some description of the Dardanelles Campaign is vital to the understanding of events.

CHAPTER ONE

The Road to War

On 28 June 1914, when Gavrillo Princip and his fellow conspirators of the Serbian Black Hand extremist secret society murdered the Austrian Archduke Franz Ferdinand, the heir to the throne of the Austro-Hungarian Empire, and his wife, they set Europe on the road to a war that was to affect the lives of many millions throughout the world. But although the assassination was carried out by Serbs and took place in the city of Sarajevo, in the Austrian province of Bosnia-Herzegovina, the main centres of the fighting in the war to follow were away from what is now Yugoslavia and the littoral countries of the Mediterranean and the Adriatic. Yet the Mediterranean area was to play an important role, both naval and military, in the chronology of the war beginning from those days immediately before hostilities were formally declared.

By contrast, on that June day most of Europe was outwardly calm; the Balkan States recovering from the disastrous wars of the immediately preceding years; Russia still not recovered from the turmoil of the Japanese war at the start of the century and the internal unrest that accompanied it; the French President about to set off on a goodwill visit to the Tsar; and the British Navy paying a courtesy visit to its German counterparts and to the Kaiser in Kiel.

Politically the war-time line up of the Nations of Europe had begun to form when in 1871 the Prussian armies had smashed those of France, and the policies of the newly created German Empire had been shaped by the Chancellor, Prince Otto von Bismarck. He fashioned the alliances between the Kaiser and his fellow Emperors in Austria and Russia, then saw the Russians withdraw over rivalry with the Austrians in the Balkans. Italy too joined this alliance, guaranteeing Italian neutrality in the event of war between Austria and Russia, as well as Italian assistance should Germany be attacked by the French. At the same time a rider allowed for Italy to remain neutral in the event of war with Britain. France remained isolated until 1891 when she concluded financial and military agreements with Russia. Two years later this was expanded into a more formal military assistance pact with both countries pledged to come to the aid of the other if attacked by either Germany or Austria. Britain's first major peacetime alliance was concluded with Japan in 1902, which incidentally enabled the Japanese to strike against Russia in 1904 without fear of a third power interfering. In this case the advantage to Britain was that she no longer had to maintain a large fleet in the Far East thus releasing more ships to be kept at Home to face the threat of the Germans. The French came to an agreement with the Italians over their respective areas of interest in North Africa. More importantly the British and French tried to overcome centuries of mistrust and signed the Entente Cordiale – though this was no formal alliance – which in turn was followed by the Anglo-French naval agreement allowing each to concentrate their fleets in particular areas.

Of the main combatants in the forthcoming war only Turkey remained unaligned to any of the other Powers. For years the sickly Ottoman Empire had been supported by both Britain and France, mainly against the unwelcome attentions of the Russians. With the French then in alliance with the Russians it was left to the British to try and keep the Turks friendly and to this end they despatched a Naval Mission to Constantinople in 1910. However, in 1913 the Turkish army was the recipient of a Mission from the Germans!

The peace of Europe had been broken when in September 1911 Italy declared war on Turkey with the stated intention of seizing the province of Libya, countering French expansion in Tunisia. The war was soon over leaving the Italians with not only their objective in Libya but also in possession of the Dodecanese Islands, while the Italian navy had had the chance to show its ability though against a foe that was ill-armed and poorly trained. The Turkish ships found outside the Dardanelles were virtually annihilated in a series of engagements, and by the end of the war the Italian ships even appeared off the Dardanelles itself.

Taking advantage of the Turks' preoccupation with Italy, a league of Bulgars, Serbs and Greeks, with the later addition of Montenegro, attacked the European mainland portion of the Ottoman Empire in the autumn of 1912. Although the Balkans was an area traditionally regarded by the Russians as within their sphere of influence they were powerless to intervene, weakened as they were by their own humiliating defeat by Japan. Indeed, secretly, they were only too pleased to see the Turks being defeated by the Slavs and Greeks. The Turks were pushed back nearly all the way to Constantinople before suing for peace in May 1913.

It is of interest that during the fighting a submarine of the Greek navy made the first ever torpedo attack on an enemy ship in war. At 8.30 am, on 9 December 1912, the new French built submarine *Delphin*, based on the recently captured island of Tenedos, sighted the Turkish cruiser *Medjidieh* leaving the Dardanelles with five escorts. An hour later Lieutenant Paparrigopoulos gave the order to fire the torpedo at a range of only 50 yards. It failed to function correctly and the Turkish ship escaped unscathed; it was a failure that was to recur all too often for the pioneer submariners.

Later in 1913 the victorious Balkan states fell out among themselves, leaving the unfortunate Bulgars to face a new alliance of their erstwhile allies. The Romanians also joined in as did the Turks who were anxious to recover what they had lost earlier in the year. By August the new war was over. Large areas of the Balkans were devastated, the Nations themselves were bankrupt and had suffered countless thousands of casualties while Turkey was the main loser of territory.

The province of Bosnia-Herzegovina, with its capital at Sarajevo, had been occupied militarily by the Austrians since 1878 with the tacit agreement of its titular owners, the Turks. Then in 1908 the Austrians declared the formal annexation of the province, to the fury of the Serbs who regarded it as being properly within the kingdom of Serbia, as most of the population were Serbs. Austrian policy was against the growth of the Slavic states in the Balkans as this only increased pressure from the many ethnic groups within the Empire which, in the long run, would tend to lead to its break up. Serbia itself was regarded by the Austrians as an anathema whose King had come to the throne by dubious means and the whole country was a mass of intrigue and corruption.

At the time of the assassinations in Sarajevo the British and German navies were making a show of friendship at Kiel where the British had been invited for the official reopening of the Kiel Canal by the Kaiser, having been enlarged to take the new German battleships, and for the annual yachting regatta. When the news from Sarajevo was received the celebrations were brought to an abrupt end as the German court went into mourning and the British ships left to return home.

Surprisingly, events in the Balkans remained relatively calm for some time after the assassinations as the Austrians considered the situation, although it has been suggested that the Austrians did not want to provoke a crisis until after the harvest had been gathered. In Vienna, where almost any incident would have been used to spark off a row with Serbia, any suggestion that the Serbian Government was innocent as a whole to the plot in its execution, if not its existence, was not well received. The Chief of the Austrian General Staff, General Franz Conrad von Hotzendorf, wanted war with Serbia and was determined that it should happen, regarding it as his country's last chance to assert herself in the Balkans and to put down the Serbs in the process. He expected a short war, and did not expect Russian interference as she was still militarily weak after the war with Japan a decade earlier. In those circumstances he reasoned the Serbs could not expect support from any other country.

It took until the 23 July, a month after the assassinations, before Vienna sent its harsh ultimatum to Belgrade. It was an ultimatum that would have been difficult for any nation to accept, whatever its degree of guilt, without loosing its self-respect and independence. Even so the Serbs went as far as they could in accepting most of the terms to appease the Austrians, but to no avail. On the 28th Austria declared war on Serbia and Austrian artillery began to bombard Belgrade.

With the declaration of war by Austria events then moved in a certain fateful pattern, as if nothing could stop the apparent inevitability of war. Russia began to mobilise in support of Serbia, Germany acted in support of her ally Austria and ordered Russia to stop mobilisation, and then Germany and Russia were at war. Inevitably this drew in France in response to her alliance with Russia while Britain hovered on the brink until Germany invaded Belgium to outflank the French armies. Britain, a guarantor of Belgium's neutrality, sought an assurance that German troops would withdraw from that country immediately, and when this was not forthcoming Britain and Germany too were at war.

In its heyday, in the early years of the century, the Royal Navy's Mediterranean Fleet could boast of 14 battleships plus supporting cruisers and destroyers. In the years following the Anglo-French Entente Cordiale the size of this fleet was progressively run down as an act of policy. Staff talks between had led to an understanding that the French fleet would concentrate in the Mediterranean leaving the British to deploy in strength in the North Sea, where it was considered that the main threat arose from the emergent German navy. However, the Foreign Office were to point out in 1912 that this was only an 'understanding' not an 'agreement', as measured in diplomatic language, and they opposed Churchill, then First Lord of the Admiralty, in his plan for too great a withdrawal from the area. As a compromise it was decided that the fleet should be large enough so that, when added to the French, the combined force would be equal to that of Austria and Italy combined, and hopefully large enough on its own to deal with any one power other than France.

During the crisis period, following the Austrian ultimatum to Serbia, the Admiralty had sent a telegram to all British Commanders-in-Chief and Senior Officers abroad warning them that the political situation was such that 'war was by no means impossible'. This message was received by Vice-Admiral Sir Archibald Berkeley Milne, the British Commander-in-Chief in the Mediterranean, who at that time was in his flagship, HMS *Inflexible*, visiting Alexandria with most of his fleet. This consisted of the 2nd Battlecruiser Squadron of the *Inflexible* (17,373 tons, $25\frac{1}{2}$ knots, 8 x 12 inch and 16 x 4 inch guns), HMS *Indomitable* and *Indefatigable*; the 1st Cruiser Squadron of four armoured cruisers, with in addition four light cruisers, a destroyer flotilla of 16 destroyers and their depot ship. There were also six elderly and obsolete submarines of the 'B' class, of which three were at Malta and the others at Gibraltar. One of the cruisers, HMS *Defence*, and a destroyer were detached and were at Durazzo where they formed part of an international squadron watching the situation in Albania where a crisis, whose origins lay in the recently concluded Balkan Wars rather than at Sarajevo, was causing concern.

While the French concentration of their fleet in the Mediterranean left them more than a match for the individual Italian or Austrian fleets, there was considerable worry over the situation should they combine, and the Italian stance in the crisis was by no means a foregone conclusion. The Commander-in-Chief, Vice-Admiral Boué de Lapeyrère, flew his flag in the *Courbet* (22,189 tons, $21\frac{1}{2}$ knots, 12 x 305 mm guns), but his only other modern dreadnought, the *Jean Bart*, was hastening back from Russia with the French President after his official visit to the

Tsar. Two other dreadnoughts had yet to join the fleet after building, though one, the *France*, was even then at sea with the *Jean Bart*. His other battleships were the six *Danton* class (18,318 tons, 19½ knots, 4 x 305 mm and 12 x 240 mm guns), all completed in 1911 but regarded as only semi-dreadnoughts, and five even older ships. There were six armoured cruisers, but these were slow (28 knots at best), under-armed with only 190 mm guns, and had large crews.

The French also had several flotillas of destroyers and torpedo boats, though the older destroyers were too small for efficient work with the fleet at any distance from their base or in bad weather being of only about 300 tons, while the latter had little fighting value. Newer ships of the *Spahi* and subsequent classes were little better at 450 tons, leaving only the nine ships of the 800 tons *Bouclier* class and most of the slightly smaller *Bisson* class serving in the Mediterranean which could be regarded a modern destroyers. Yet, they too had their faults being lightly constructed they found it impossible to maintain a high speed it rough weather, while their fire control equipment was not of the same quality as that fitted in the destroyers of their allies.

France had led Europe in pioneering submarine construction and by 1914 had built 89, of which 79 were still listed and 34 were in commission. Of these about half were in the Mediterranean based at Toulon and Bizerta. Yet few of these were of modern design and many relied on steam propulsion when on the surface and were fitted with torpedoes in external cradles rather than torpedo tubes where it could not be fired with the submarine on the surface and making it susceptible to damage in bad weather.

The *Kaiserlich und Königlich* (K.u.K.) – Imperial and Royal, the designation applied to the navy and other official arms of the dual Monarchy of Austria-Hungary – *Kriegsmarine* was the chief potential opponent of the Franco-British fleet in the Mediterranean. Yet, it had no base in the open Mediterranean and had only some 370 miles of friendly coastline along the eastern shore of the Adriatic. Potentially allied with Italy in the Triple Alliance it could then form a strong combined force to test the strength of the French and would not be liable to any of the constraints that the limited access to the Adriatic implied. However, historically the Italians were not friendly to the Austrians since the claimed large areas of Austrian territory where there was a predominantly Italian population.

In the early years of the new century the Austrian navy was involved in internal wrangling over whether to build a strong coast defence force or to build up an even stronger 'blue water' navy, and in a bitter struggle for funds with the army. The dispute came to a head in 1904 when the Navy's budget was cut by 25 million Crowns whereas that of the army was cut by only 5 million. Admiral Spaun, the Commander-in-Chief resigned in protest, but a more serious consequence of the affair was that between 1905 and 1909 there was no new capital ship construction, though work continued on the three semi-dreadnoughts of the *Radetzky* class which were completed between 1910 and 1911 (14,508 tons, 20½ knots, 4 x 305 mm guns and 8 x 240 mm guns). Spaun's successor, Admiral Rudolph Graf von Montecuccoli, was more successful politically, and under his leadership and aided by the patronage of the Archduke Ferdinand the Austrian navy underwent considerable expansion, although the problem of extracting funds from a reluctant Parliament remained. When both Austrian and Hungarian elements of the Imperial Parliament refused funds for the construction of four new dreadnoughts Montecuccoli took a personal credit of 32 million Crowns to enable construction to begin on time. Three of the four of these dreadnoughts of the *Tegetthoff* class (20,013 tons, 20 knots, 12 x 305 mm guns) were completed before the outbreak of war. Another four dreadnoughts were due to be laid down in the latter half of 1914 onwards, but the project was abandoned because of the war. Besides a number of old pre-dreadnoughts and coast defence ships there were two old armoured cruisers, two fast light cruisers, some older cruisers and several flotillas of destroyers and torpedo boats. There were six submarines with a seventh boat built but not accepted by the Austrian Navy. There were five more building in German yards.

Two submarines each had been built to three different designs, although all were similar in size they had markedly different capabilities. Two, with good diving qualities were hampered by having petrol engines, two more had poor diving qualities and were fitted with the German 'Korting' paraffin engines which tended to produce clouds of dark exhaust smoke and sparks which would betray the submarines' presence by day or night. The final pair also suffered by being fitted with petrol engines.

There was an additional problem for the Austrians in that there were eleven ethnic groups within the Empire each with its own language and customs. Officers were required to be fluent in three of the Empire's languages while ratings were expected to understand orders given in German whatever their language of birth. Despite the efforts made to combat the language problem it cannot have helped foster efficiency. Presumably the Russian Navy faced similar problems although there is no evidence as to how they dealt with the situation.

There was only one other navy of consequence in the Mediterranean itself – the Italian. Despite their political alliance the ships of the Italian navy had been designed rather as a counter to the Austrians than the French. Even so, if allied to the Austrians they would have provided a sizeable reinforcement which would have been of considerable concern to the Anglo-French fleet. The pre-war building programme was ambitious and beyond the capacity of Italian industry to fulfil. Of the six dreadnoughts planned only three were available in July 1914, two of these being of the *Cavour* class (22,992 tons, 21½ knots, 13 x 305 mm guns). There were also four pre-dreadnoughts, seven armoured cruisers, three light cruisers, 33 destroyers and a large number of torpedo boats of varying military usefulness. There were 20 submarines with others building.

The Turkish navy had suffered badly in the war with Italy and,

despite the efforts of a British Naval Mission, since 1910 they presented little serious threat. As part of the post-war naval reconstruction two
battleships were building in Britain and in August 1914 they were
almost complete, in fact the crews had arrived ready to commence
training and to take the ships back to Turkey. There were no submarines either in commission or actually building, although four boats
had been ordered in April 1914, two from Britain and two from France.
There was no submarine experience within the Turkish navy though, in
the 1880s, the Turks had arranged for two submarines to be built by
Nordenfelt, on the Thames in England, to a design by the Reverend
Garrett. They were then shipped out to Constantinople in sections. One
was re-assembled and began trials, which were not a success, and there
the matter rested with neither boat ever being commissioned.

The presence of any units of the German navy in the Mediterranean
at the outbreak of war was almost fortuitous. In 1912 with the victorious Bulgar army was almost at the gates of Constantinople the Turks
appealed for help to the signatories of the Congress of Berlin in 1878
to avoid a situation whereby the Turks would lose control of the city
and, perhaps worse in British eyes, the Russians would at last gain their
outlet to the open sea. Nine nations – strangely including Russia –
decided to send warships to protect their interests, and those of
Turkey. The British sent two cruisers, but the Germans had no ships in
the area to match this move, much to the chagrin of the Kaiser. It was
suggested that *Goeben*, the latest battlecruiser even then on sea trials after
building, and the new light cruiser *Breslau*, which had just completed
hers, should be sent. The idea appealed to the Kaiser and the two ships
sailed from Germany within days. Within weeks the need for an international squadron off Constantinople had passed, but the two ships
remained in the Mediterranean.

The *Goeben* (22,616 tons) with her main armament of 10 x 280 mm
guns and a maximum speed of 27 knots presented a threat to any similar British or French ship that might be encountered while she could
outrun any superior force. Her guns though of smaller calibre than
those mounted in the British ships fired at a higher muzzle velocity, and
being mounted on a broader beamed vessel with better range finders
gave her the advantage. Indeed, a full ten gun broadside from the
Goeben weighed 6,600 pounds compared to the 6,800 pound broadside
from the British battlecruisers. The lightly armed *Breslau* (4,570 tons, 12
x 105 mm guns) could also outrun any of the British or French cruisers.

It had been intended that the *Goeben* should return to Germany in the
Autumn of 1914 being relieved by her sister ship the *Moltke*. However,
following the assassinations at Sarajevo it was thought prudent to send
her to the Austrian base at Pola to have repairs carried out on her
defective boiler tubes, the work being carried out by specialist dockyard
workers sent from Germany to add a sense of urgency to the more easy
going attitude of the Austrian dockyard labour force. Meanwhile the
Breslau had been detached to join the International Squadron at

Durazzo – formed as a result of squabbles arising from the end of the Balkan Wars – where she occupied an adjacent anchor berth to HMS *Defence*.

The Russians had no direct access to the Mediterranean for their Black Sea Fleet, being constrained to pass through the Turkish controlled Dardanelles. No great hardship in times of peace though perhaps hurtful to national pride, but in time of war it meant that the Russians were cut off from their allies. Nevertheless in any study of the naval war in the Mediterranean it is necessary to review the state of this Russian fleet in that summer of 1914 and, later, to consider the operations in the Black Sea.

The Russo-Japanese War of 1904/5 had virtually wiped out the Russian Far East and Baltic Fleets and left morale within the entire navy at a low ebb, weakened even more by the revolutionary period through which the country had gone in 1905. Funds for a new navy were delayed by the Duma and when these were indeed voted it left insufficient time for the inadequate industrial capacity of Tsarist Russia to complete the new ships before war broke again in 1914. The Black Sea Fleet was the least affected by the debacle in the Far East, and in 1914 had only an even weaker Turkish fleet to counter. Three dreadnoughts were ordered for the Black Sea Fleet under the 1911 Programme, but although all were launched before the outbreak of war the first, the *Imperatritsa Mariya* (22,180 tons, 21 knots, 12 x 305 mm guns), was not in service before 1915. For the early months of the war the Russians were therefore forced to rely on pre-dreadnoughts built around the turn of the century or earlier. Of these the *Evsrafi* (12,840 tons, 4 x 305 mm and 4 x 203) had been launched in 1906 and was the fleet flagship, while the *Pantelimon*, launched in 1900, is better known as the 'Battleship *Potemkin*' which had been renamed after the mutiny of 1905.

It was the custom of naval authorities in 1914 to compare the strength of fleets by relative numbers of dreadnoughts and semi-dreadnoughts and the weight of each side's broadsides. Numbers of cruisers was of less importance, while destroyers and other craft were merely considered as being present to protect the big ships from torpedo attack from like vessels. The question of submarines and their performance was ignored, such vessels being considered of little importance in the days of the 'big gun' navy. It was left to events in the war to follow which would show how the balance of power was being changed with more and more importance being required for both the submarine and anti-submarine fleets of warring nations.

Of the naval commanders in the area, Vice-Admiral Sir Archibald Berkeley Milne, has already been mentioned, but Admiral Sir John (Jacky) Fisher, soon to be reinstated as First Sea Lord, had described him in most unflattering terms to Winston Churchill. Known throughout the navy as 'Arky Barky' his advancement had been due more to influence than ability. His second in command, Rear Admiral Ernest Troubridge, had had experience of war when, as Naval Attaché in

Tokyo, he had witnessed some of the action in the Russo-Japanese War. He was no doubt a natural seaman but was to take most of the blame for the events which followed.

Vice-Admiral Augustin-Emmanuel-Herbert-Gaston Boué de Lapeyrère was over 60 years old in 1914 and had been in command of France's Mediterranean Fleet (*1ère Armée Navale*) since 1911 and, consequently, was titular Commander-in-Chief of the combined French and British fleet after the outbreak of war. Earlier he had served in the political post of Minister of Marine where he had been responsible for creating the conditions for French naval superiority in the area. He cut an impressive figure being of large frame and sporting a greyish beard. His manner was gruff, taciturn, but with a reputation for hard work which he expected to be matched by his men who knew him as the 'Seawolf'.

Rear Admiral Wilhelm Anton Theodor Souchon, who had taken command of the two German ships in October 1913, was a much younger man than his French counterpart. He had held several commands at sea besides being known for his good work as a staff officer. He was a hard working officer with a generally cheerful manner that brought him the respect of his subordinates. Now, in the Mediterranean on the brink of war and cut off from his own country by many miles of hostile waters, he was going to need these qualities to the full.

The Commander-in-Chief of the Austrian Navy was Admiral Anton Haus. The 63 year old Admiral enjoyed a high reputation although he was troubled by ill health, indeed he had had a major surgical operation in 1913 not long after taking office. He was a sharp man who did not suffer fools gladly, although his often irascible behaviour may now be attributed to the side effects of pain killing drugs. Haus' headquarters were at the main Austrian naval base at Pola where he had used a yacht as his flagship, but on 24 August 1914 he moved his flag to the dreadnought *Viribus Unitis*. Under Haus two other flag officers, the easy going and ineffectual Vice-Admiral Maximilian Njegovan and Rear Admiral Franz Lofler, commanded the sea-going squadrons into which the fleet was divided.

Vice-Admiral Andrei Augustovich Eberhard who commanded the Russian Black Sea Fleet at the outbreak of war remains a rather shadowy figure. He was a Russian of Swedish extraction who had spent many years in the Russian navy where he had built up a reputation as an efficient leader in a navy where efficiency was not common. It would seem that he was a very able administrator, though, not surprisingly, this is not the view taken by Soviet writers. But, as a fleet commander, he was not the equal of his able colleague Vice-Admiral Otto von Essen who commanded in the Baltic. Yet despite the mutinies of 1905 and 1912, the efficiency of the Black Sea Fleet was apparently high and morale was better than in many units of Russia's armed forces.

CHAPTER TWO

1914: The Opening Moves

With the outbreak of war imminent Vice-Admiral Boué de Lapeyrère was faced with two problems. First he had to ensure that the reinforcements for the French army, some 40,000 men, which had to travel from their Empire in North Africa to mainland France were able to do so without interruption. It was accepted by the French that as speed was paramount the troop-ships should sail as soon as they were ready, and that no effort would be made to form escorted convoys. The risk was considered acceptable. The threat to their safety came not only from the two German ships, but also from the entire Austrian fleet which might well sortie from the Adriatic. Secondly, there was the question of the attitude of the Italians. Under the terms of her alliance with Germany and Austria Italy did not have to take action in support of her allies in the event of a war caused by the aggressive actions of either of those Powers. Would she take an active role alongside Germany and Austria or would she remain neutral? It began to appear that she was unlikely to declare war, and it was therefore most important that no action by de Lapeyrère, or his British counterpart, should provoke them.

Berkeley Milne at Malta, having gone there from Alexandria on receipt of the Admiralty's warning telegram, found that he was in the awkward position of being bound to co-operate with the French in the event of war but unable to contact them. The fallacy of pre-war planning was laid bare in that any 'understanding' with the French had not been converted into any joint plans, and although joint signal books had been issued they had had not been tested, nor had any communications been exercised between the two fleets. Indeed, he had to wait for authority from the Admiralty before even making any moves to contact his opposite number.

The International Squadron at Durazzo soon began to feel the effects of the deepening crisis. The Russian gunboat *Teretz* was the first to head for more friendly waters leaving on 27 July, only the day before the Austrian attack on Serbia. HMS *Defence* and her escorting destroyer were ordered to leave and join the remainder of the fleet at Malta on the 29th, while the French armoured cruiser *Edgar Quinet* similarly left for Toulon. The *Breslau* left at the end of the month to rendezvous with the *Goeben*, while the Italian *San Marco* and Austrian *Admiral Spaun* then left for their respective bases with the Squadron no longer effective, or necessary.

Even before the outbreak of war Milne was ordered by the Admiralty to find and shadow the two German ships, with the intention that he would then be in a position to bring them to battle as soon as war was declared. It was 3 August before he managed to get a message to de Lapeyrère and, in reply, was asked to watch the Adriatic for movements of the Italian, Austrian and German ships while the French were busy in the Western Mediterranean covering the movements of their reinforcements for the army.

Souchon took the two German ships to Messina in Sicily on 2 August where it had been planned that he would join with the Italian and Austrian ships in the event of war. He found that there was every indication that the Italians would remain neutral, and were even making difficulties in supplying the limited stocks of coal which were available for his ships. It was unlikely too that the Austrians would venture outside the Adriatic at that time. He was on his own. Indeed it was to become an added complication in an already confused situation that Austria was not at war with either Britain or France until 12 August. Souchon considered that his immediate task was to cause damage on the Algerian coast and intercept the lines of communication between North Africa and Toulon or Marseilles. That night he sailed with his two ships to be ready to execute this plan in the event of war between Germany and France, an event which was to become fact at 6.00 pm on 3 August. Early the next morning the ports of Philippeville and Bône were bombarded by the two German ships. It was a brief action scarcely lasting ten minutes and doing little damage.

However, during the night prior to this action Souchon at last received his orders from Berlin – to proceed at once to Constantinople, though Souchon allowed himself the luxury of continuing with his planned bombardment before carrying them out. It is strange that it had taken the German Admiralty so long to give him any orders in what must have seemed a very lonely and confused situation. What can have been expected of him? With the Italians almost certain to remain neutral was he to join the Austrians at Pola after disrupting the French reinforcement traffic from North Africa? To break out into the Atlantic, and then try to return to Germany? When they came the orders were a surprise for Souchon, as they were for the British, for at that time Turkey was neutral and under International Law such a move could only mean internment for these two valuable ships and their crews. The reasons for this order lay partly in the actions of Winston Churchill in Britain, and partly with a secret agreement between Germany and Turkey signed only on 2 August.

After the crushing defeats suffered first in the war with Italy and then against the Balkan states the Turks took great interest in the building of two battleships in Britain. They had been ordered through the British Naval Mission and paid for by a nation-wide public subscription involving great sacrifice by many of the population. In July 1914 the first of the two ships, *Sultan Osman I*, was nearly complete and some 500 officers and men of the Turkish navy were in England for training and

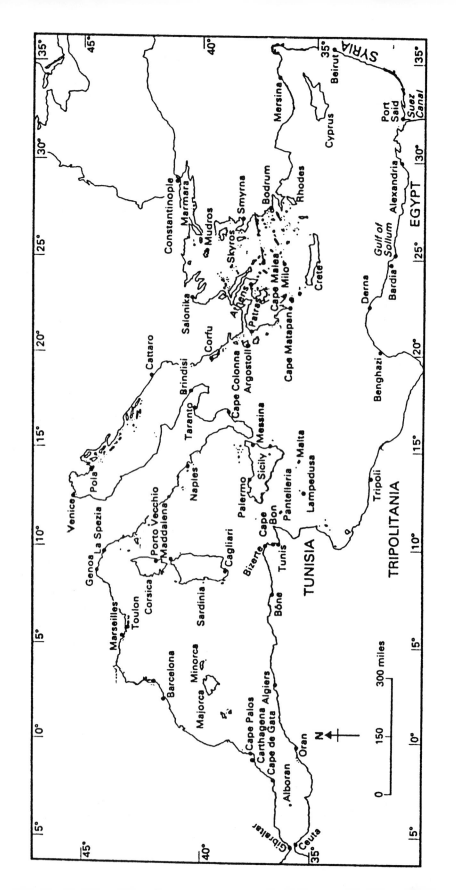

OPPOSITE:
Map 1. The Mediterranean.

were then to sail the ship back to Turkey. The second ship was due for completion soon afterwards. However, with the signs that the European crisis could end in war Churchill was acutely conscious that the Royal Navy had a superiority over the Germans of only seven dreadnoughts in Home Waters. On the eve of war both ships were taken over for the Royal Navy, and assurances of compensation and promises that they would be returned after the war did nothing to mollify the anger of the whole Turkish nation. Whatever the rights and wrongs of Churchill's action – and, after the signing of the secret agreement of the 2nd, how easy it could have been for the Turkish crew to sail just across the North Sea and present their new allies with a brand new battleship – it provided the Germans with the opportunity they wanted to supplant the British in Turkey. For the Germans saw that the arrival in Turkey of the *Goeben* and *Breslau* could be used to increase German influence there.

It is not necessary to follow in detail the moves of the next few days as both the British and French fleets failed to catch Souchon, and his two ships, and bring them to battle. It is a humiliating story that they were able to reach Constantinople in safety, an event for which both Milne and de Lapeyrère must bear responsibility and for which Troubridge was subsequently relieved of his command and court-martialled on his return to England, though eventually acquitted.

The passage of the German ships through the Dardanelles to Constantinople was followed by immediate diplomatic protests to the Turkish Government. The official reply stated that the ships had been bought by the Turks, a statement that only added to the fears that the Turks would soon be openly joining Germany. Yet in Turkey there was a power struggle taking place with the 'Young Turks' led by Enver Bey and Talaat Bey, the Minister for War and the Minister of the Interior respectively, being sympathetic to the Germans, while the more traditionalist Grand Vizier, Kemal Pasha, wanted to keep Turkey neutral in what he saw as primarily a European war in which the Turks had no part. Rear Admiral Limpus, as head of the British Naval Mission, was told that the ships would be placed under his control and would be used to counter the Greeks in an attempt to regain islands in the Aegean lost in the recent wars. In fact Limpus and his mission only lasted a short time longer, their position had become intolerable. Souchon's officers were soon to replace the British while Souchon himself became the Commander-in-Chief of the Turkish Navy. Despite this set back diplomatic moves were continued to try and ensure that nothing further was done that would drive the Turks into open hostilities and on the side of the Germans. Up to this time the British and French had been acting independently, though in co-operation with each other. Now, with the *Goeben* and *Breslau* in Turkish waters, and nominally part of the Turkish navy though still manned by their German crews, the general direction of operations in the Mediterranean came under the orders of the French, while many of the British ships were deployed for service elsewhere, as had been agreed in the Anglo-French Naval Convention signed on 6 August. Sir Berkeley Milne, being senior to de Lapeyrère, was ordered home. Rear Admiral Sackville Carden, the Admiral Superintendent at Malta, thus by chance became the senior British naval officer in the Mediterranean and was promoted at the end of August. Troubridge was left with a handful of ships to watch the Dardanelles in case the German (or were they Turkish?) ships tried to leave. De Lapeyrère took the French ships to Malta from where he could best operate against the Austrians. The French also became responsible for protecting allied commerce throughout the Mediterranean and guarding the Straits of Gibraltar. There was one bonus in this unfortunate start to wartime operations in that the entire French army corps in North Africa had reached the mainland without loss.

On 10 September Troubridge also left, to return home to face the enquiry into his conduct in allowing the German ships to reach Constantinople. In his place Churchill wished to appoint Limpus who had finally left Turkey. The Foreign Office, who were still trying to woo the Turks, persuaded the Prime Minister that such an appointment would be regarded as the 'unduly provocative', and Churchill had to accede. Carden was therefore sent from Malta to take command while Limpus, a much more able officer, went to Malta as the Admiral Superintendent. Carden's Orders were quite explicit:

From Admiralty
To Vice-Admiral Carden, Malta.
21 September.
Assume command of the squadron off the Dardanelles. Your sole duty is to sink the *Goeben* and *Breslau*, no matter what flag they fly, if they come out of the Dardanelles. We are not at war with Turkey but German Admiral Souchon is now C-in-C Turkish Navy and Germans are controlling and largely manning it. Turks have been told that any Turkish ships which come out with the *Goeben* and *Breslau* will be equally attacked by us. You are authorised to act accordingly without further declaration or parley.

In Constantinople Souchon saw it as his task to ensure that the Turks entered the war on the side of Germany. However, first the Turkish Government as a whole had to be convinced that this was the best course for them despite their recent secret treaty with Germany. Meanwhile Souchon had the chance to take a look at the state of readiness of his new command. Despite the efforts of the British Naval Mission since 1912 there was little to give cause for satisfaction. To make matters worse, the best of the Turkish personnel had not yet returned from England where they had been sent to collect the two, now requisitioned, battleships. Soon he had assessed the situation and was able to signal Berlin.

Think it possible [to] break out of Bosporus if Turkish Government can be successfully deceived beforehand. Ambassador thinks operation in Black Sea premature at present. Ambassador lays great weight on presence Goeben and Breslau inside Narrows now until Turkish mobilisation further progressed and political situation clarified. Hold this view correct in light of general war purpose.

So Souchon played a waiting game while the 'Young Turks' prepared the ground for him politically, for the Grand Vizier still held a majority in the Government who favoured a neutral stance. Souchon took his fleet into the Black Sea for training exercises, while in late September an incident between British forces in the Aegean and a Turkish destroyer gave Enver the excuse to close the Straits to all shipping thus cutting off any trade with the Russians in the Black Sea.

It was the end of October before all was ready and Enver gave Souchon secret orders to attack the Russian fleet and achieve naval supremacy prior to any declaration of war. Souchon himself informed Berlin of what he was doing adding that he was entering the Black Sea under the guise of an exercise. On the morning of 29 October the *Goeben*, now nominally renamed *Sultan Yavuz Selim*, with the destroyers *Tasoz* and *Samsun* appeared off the main Russian base at Sevastopol, the *Breslau*, under the Turkish name *Midilli*, was directed to the Kerch Strait and then to Novorossisk, the Turkish cruiser *Hamidieh* to Feodosia while the destroyers *Gairet-i-Watanije* and *Muavenet-i-Millet* went to Odessa. The main units of the Russian fleet consisting of seven battleships, three cruisers, five destroyers and four submarines with some smaller vessels were all in Sevastopol, the surface ships all coaling after returning from exercises. Further up the coast three destroyers on patrol off Eupatoria were the only units at sea.

The destroyers at Odessa opened the attack, prematurely. The gunboat *Donetz* was torpedoed and sunk, and some other damage was done to both ships and shore facilities by gunfire. News of the attack was sent from Odessa to Sevastopol but there was no time to alter the readiness for sea of the fleet though some of the shore batteries were alerted. The *Goeben* approached the base from the northward and opened fire at a range of about four miles, firing a total of 47 280mm (11 inch) rounds from her main armament, and 12 from the secondary armament. Although a number of fires were started ashore none of the ships were hit. The range was closer than had been intended and well within range for the shore batteries which replied and scored three hits on the *Goeben* causing some minor damage and a number of casualties before she retired out of range.

The *Breslau* laid some mines in the Kerch Straits and then went on to bombard the oil fuel tanks at the base at Novorossisk, leaving some large fires burning as she headed back towards the Bosporus. The following day two ships were sunk in the Kerch minefield.

As the *Goeben* sailed away from Sevastopol she sighted the three Russian destroyers which had been on patrol off the coast and were now steaming south to give support to the minelayer *Prut*, a converted merchant ship, on passage to Sevastopol. The destroyers decided to attack but were driven off without further damage to the *Goeben* and with the *Lieutenant Pushchin* badly damaged. The *Prut*, with a cargo of over 700 mines was unable to escape. After the *Goeben* had opened fire the crew opened the seacocks to scuttle the ship and then took to the lifeboats. The captain and 74 of the crew were picked up by the Turkish destroyer *Samsun*. The remainder of the crew were later rescued from the other lifeboat by the old submarine *Sudak* and taken to Sevastopol.

Justifying his actions Souchon first claimed that after leaving the Bosporus with his ships the Russians had disrupted his exercises and entered into hostilities to which he had been obliged to reply. This was in line with the opening paragraph of the Operation Order which stated that 'various reports lead to a conclusion that the Russian Black Sea Fleet is planning a surprise attack'. In fact the only Russian ship they had seen had been one merchant ship off the Bosporus patiently hoping to be allowed through to the Mediterranean, although the Dardanelles had been closed for a month. Later this outrageous untruth was changed to the effect that the *Prut* had been met with outside the Bosporus about to lay mines – an act of war – and had therefore been sunk. In fact, as has been related, the *Prut* was sunk after the attack on Sevastopol and the merchant ship met off the Bosporus was harmless. These versions of the outbreak of hostilities were meant as much for the Turkish Government, where a final struggle for power was taking place to ensure the country's entry into the war, as for the rest of the world.

The political effect was all that Souchon had hoped, though militarily he failed to achieve the aim of so damaging the Russian fleet that he would attain superiority in the area. In the words of nearly thirty years later it was no 'Pearl Harbor'. Any hope that the neutralists in the Turkish Government would be able to smooth things over was lost when the British, French and Russian Ambassadors asked for their passports to leave, while in addition the British Ambassador presented a final ultimatum. The Turks were given 12 hours to agree to sending all the German officers and men home and to demobilise. Not unexpectedly this was ignored. The Russians declared war on 2 November, while on the following day the British and French ships shelled the forts at the entrance to the Dardanelles to emphasise their determination and to influence the Turks to accede to their demands. Naturally it had the opposite effect and both Britain and France declared war on the 5th.

From Admiralty
To Vice-Admiral, *Indefatigable*
1 November
Without risking the ships a demonstration is to be made by bombardment on the earliest suitable day by your armoured ships and the two French battleships against the forts at the entrance to the Dardanelles at a range of 14,000 to 12,000 yards. The ships should keep under way, approaching as soon after daylight as possible. A retirement should be made before the fire from the forts becomes effective.

With that one bombardment completed the allied fleet resumed their waiting watch for any attempt by the enemy to emerge from the Dardanelles.

In September the allied fleet watching the Dardanelles had been augmented by the three British submarines from Malta, HMS *B9*, *B10* and *B11*, together with their depot ship, the old converted merchant ship *Hindu Kush*. They were joined in November by two French submarines *Faraday* and *Le Verrier*, and for a short time by the *Circé*, although she was soon withdrawn for operations in the Adriatic. The French boats had no depot or accommodation ship of their own, nor did they make use of the limited facilities in the *Hindu Kush*. Instead they used the destroyer depot ship HMS *Blenheim* where they were made welcome.

In the rapidly changing world of submarine development the three British boats, completed in 1906, were already obsolete. Indeed, they were to become, with their three sisters at Gibraltar, the oldest British submarines to see active service during the war. At 140 feet overall length they were nearly 40 feet longer than the even earlier 'A' class, and had a displacement of 287 tons on the surface, 316 tons dived. A 16 cylinder petrol engine gave a maximum speed on the surface of 12 knots and an endurance of 740 miles. When the class had been built there was little alternative to the petrol engine for surface propulsion though the dangers from petrol fumes were well known. The main motor used when dived or manoeuvring worked on a nominal 100 volts from the submarine's main battery which consisted of 159 chloride cells. Two 18 inch torpedo tubes comprised the armament and four torpedoes could be carried. The complement was two officers and 13 ratings. However, the living conditions for even this small sized crew were little better than primitive, though it was not anticipated that they would be required to live onboard for more than two or three days at a time. There were no dividing bulkheads and any seating, tables or sleeping accommodation was portable and normally stowed. Of necessity ventilation was provided for the battery, but not for the crew's space, and there could be little free circulation of fresh air. Fumes from the engine would have mixed with the aroma of any cooking, slops and normal body smells. Tame mice were carried to detect any dangerous build-up of carbon monoxide within the boat from engine exhaust.

Both *Faraday* and *Le Verrier* were boats of the *Brumaire* class completed in 1911 and 1912. Unlike the single hulled British boats these were of the double hull type, with the main ballast tanks external to the pressure hull. With a length of 171 feet they displaced 397/551 tons. Two diesel engines gave a maximum speed of 13 knots on the surface, while the two electric motors provided up to eight knots dived. There was only one 450mm (17.7 inch) internal torpedo tube in the bow for which a single reload was carried. A further six torpedoes were carried outside the pressure hull; four in Drzewiecki drop collars (an early but notoriously unreliable alternative to the torpedo tube from which a torpedo could be angled and fired) and two in straight forward cradles abreast the conning tower. These external torpedoes could only be fired with

the submarine on the surface and the torpedoes themselves were highly susceptible to damage in bad weather. Their complement was 29 officers and ratings.

From September when the British boats arrived their routine had been two days at sea followed by one in harbour alongside the *Hindu Kush*. With the arrival of the French that routine had been modified to give them two days in harbour after each trip to sea. With no shore base their time in harbour was limited in value for there could be no shore leave to help break the tedium.

It was recognised that none of the submarines present were capable of penetrating the Dardanelles and entering the Sea of Marmara – their endurance was just too limited – but it was considered that one might be able to proceed as far as Chanak and attack any shipping that might be met. The boat would then still have sufficient battery capacity to be able to return safely to the Aegean. HMS *B11*, commanded by Lieutenant Norman Holbrook, RN, had recently been fitted with a new battery, and was thought to be the submarine with the best chance to try out this daring scheme. It would, in any case, be a way of breaking the seemingly endless monotony of short profitless patrols around the entrance to the Dardanelles waiting for an enemy that appeared unlikely to emerge.

Before sailing the staff of HMS *Blenheim* fitted the submarine with guards around the hydroplanes to protect them from picking up the mooring wires of any mines, such an action might well drag the mine down onto the submarine with fatal consequences. To some the 13th may not seem an auspicious day on which to sail, but nevertheless on that day in December Holbrook and his crew took the *B11* to sea and headed northwards from Tenedos towards the Dardanelles and then Chanak.

Almost immediately fate took a hand and the submarine was forced to stop when one of her own mooring ropes was caught in one of the new hydroplane guards, but the crew freed it within minutes. Creeping to within a mile of Cape Helles at the southern end of the Gallipoli peninsula Holbrook dived before dawn and began his approach to Chanak keeping close to the European shore and hoping to make good about two knots. With Cape Helles abeam he went to 60 feet to avoid any mines. But at that depth there was no way of checking his position and he had to return to periscope depth from time to time for this purpose.

After four hours Holbrook was eventually rewarded by the sight of the old Turkish battleship *Messudieh* (9,200 tons and launched as long ago as 1874) lying at anchor near the shore on the Asiatic side by the town of Chanak. Although her main armament was inoperative and had been landed she had been sent to the area to act as a floating battery with her 150mm secondary armament to reinforce the shore forts. It had been intended that she should be moored in shallow water alongside the quay at Chanak, but this had not been possible and she was anchored further out, but still under the protection of the guns ashore.

To reach her Holbrook had to turn to starboard and take the *B11* across the main stream of the current, increasing speed to help Lieutenant Winn, the First Lieutenant, maintain the trim as the current again affected the submarine's trim. Fifteen minutes after first sighting his target Holbrook fired the starboard torpedo at the Turkish ship and was immediately caught by a fierce eddy of current which swung the submarine violently off course and prevented the firing of the second torpedo. As Holbrook and Winn tried desperately to control the submarine the Turks sighted their periscope and opened fire on it, then the B11 went aground on a shoal leaving the conning tower exposed to the fire of the Turkish guns. Here the current came to their aid for as they were straddled by the gunfire they slid off into deeper water before they were hit. The *Messudieh* was hit aft and sank in about ten minutes leaving some of the wreck above water.

Holbrook now had the task of returning down the Dardanelles to the open sea and safety with the Turkish defences thoroughly alerted. The submarine's battery was rapidly becoming exhausted and the helmsman had trouble maintaining a course. Not only was the current still affecting the submarine but the prisms which reflected the position of the magnetic compass needle from outside the boat (where they were less influenced by the magnetism in the hull) to the helmsman were misted over and hard to read. The air inside the submarine became more and

The wreck of the Turkish coast defence battleship Messudieh *sunk on 13 December 1914 by the British* B11. (IWM 14379)

more foul and less easily breathed by the minute. Eventually at 2 o'clock Cape Helles was once more abaft the beam and they could surface.

Nine days later Holbrook received the award of the first naval Victoria Cross of the war, Winn received the Distinguished Service Order (DSO) and the whole crew received Distinguished Service Medals (DSMs).

The current in the Dardanelles was to play an important part in subsequent submarine operations and it is worth noting Holbrook's own comments on the subject when he wrote to Commodore Roger Keyes, who at that time was Commodore (Submarines) at Harwich.

Before going up the Dardanelles I took particular care in trimming etc. To start the boat dived very well taking little helm to keep her at any depth. As soon as I got inside the Dardanelles she took full dive helm and 300 on two [amps on two of the armatures] to keep her down at 60 feet. Often she came up as far as 40 feet and then went down again without altering speed or helm. When I wished to bring her up I had to give full rise helm and speed up to 500 [amps] on two, and even then I sometimes remained at 20 feet for a quarter of an hour or more, before she would come up the remaining five feet to see. When I sighted the *Messudieh* I altered eight points to starboard to attack her, the boat immediately sank to 80 feet and remained there and nothing would bring her up till I blew two auxiliaries [tanks] for five minutes. I think the cause of this was the sudden change of tide from ahead to abeam. Up to the time of firing the diving was very erratic, the depth varying from 15 to 40 feet. On firing the boat sank to 40 feet and I took some time with 500 on three [full speed] before she came up, then she refused to dive till I flooded the auxiliaries that I had previously blown.

The following month the French submarine *Saphir* attempted to copy Holbrook's exploit. The *Saphir*, fresh from a refit in Bizerta, had arrived to replace the *Circé*. Built in 1908 she was, like the British boats, a single hull design of 392/425 tons displacement with twin diesel engines and a crew of 23 officers and ratings. She was more suited to operations in the Dardanelles in that her armament of 6 x 450 mm torpedo tubes (four forward and two aft) were internal to the hull. During her refit she had been fitted with a new battery which nearly doubled her dived endurance and she seemed an ideal choice for the task ahead.

Commanded by *Lieutenant de Vaisseau* Henri Fournier the *Saphir* had been fitted with the same type of hydroplane guards as the B11 at Malta while on passage to the Aegean where she arrived to join the allied force on 9 January 1915. Morale onboard was high and the crew confident that they could achieve a success to equal that of the British; the torpedo men had even painted on their torpedoes the words 'A souvenir of Bône and Philippeville' in a reference to the attacks made by the *Goeben* and *Breslau* in the first days of the war. On 15 January she sailed for the Narrows diving off Kum Kale. Nothing more was heard of her until three days later the Turks announced that she had been mined, her loss being confirmed by the American Ambassador in Constantinople when he reported that some of her crew had been taken prisoner. But a mine was not to blame.

At first all seemed to go well and the *Saphir* passed successfully through the minefields with the mine mooring cables being heard scraping along the hull. By 11.30 am she was through the minefields and proceeded towards Nagara Point. It was there that she went aground just before midday. Fournier immediately ordered the motors to full astern and the ballast blows. While this was being done the boat came free but plunged straight down to a depth of over 200 feet. Her hull had been damaged in the grounding and she began to take in water which contaminated the battery cells and polluted the air with dangerous chorine gas. While the level of water in the boat rose it was only after Fournier had ordered the drop keels to be released, though only one of three fell away, that the boat began to rise with the tanks being blown with the last of the compressed air and the motors going full astern. As the *Saphir* broke surface she was greeted by the gunfire of the forts on the Asiatic shore and of two Turkish gunboats. With the release of even one of the drop keels and with her ballast tanks blown Fournier was unable to dive the boat, where in any case the air was rapidly becoming unbreathable, and he decided to scuttle in as deep water as possible where she could not be salvaged. About a mile from the Asiatic shore the crew began to abandon the submarine while still under fire from the Turkish guns. The First Lieutenant, *Enseigne de Vaisseau* Cancel, stayed below to destroy the last of the secret documents and to check that the main vents were opened. He was the last to leave the stricken boat imploring his captain to save himself, in vain. Only 13 of her complement were picked up, neither Fournier nor Cancel being amongst them.

Although both the Turks and Russians carried out several operations in the Black Sea in the closing months of 1914 none of them involved submarine activity, so that Holbrook in the *B11* achieved the only success of the year in the war against Turkey. In the Aegean the British and French ships and submarines continued their wait for the *Goeben* and *Breslau* to emerge, perhaps with some of the Turkish fleet, while north of the Bosporus the Russians waited for their new ships to complete.

CHAPTER THREE

The Adriatic 1914–15

The early stages of the naval war in the Adriatic were almost a private campaign between the French and the Austrians, with the British concentrated at the eastern end of the Mediterranean watching the *Goeben* and *Breslau* while the Italians remained neutral. It was a campaign in which the Austrians enjoyed numerous advantages. The main base for their navy was at Pola at the northern end of the Adriatic, a large port in a protected anchorage well equipped with dry docks and repair facilities. There were also a number of smaller ports all the way down the Dalmatian coast: Fiume, Spalato, Ragusa, and above all Cattaro where a series of three inter-connected deep water fjords were protected from the sea and storms by high mountains.

The Austrians possessed the smallest submarine fleet of the principal Mediterranean powers engaged in the war. They had not rushed into developing their own submarine preferring to let others undertake the development work. It was not until 1904 that the Navy's technical committee (MTK) was ordered to produce a design for an Austrian submarine. However, neither private proposals nor a MTK design were considered suitable, and it was decided to buy three different foreign designs, two boats of each, which would then be competitively evaluated. The *U1* and *U2* (actually at that time known merely as *I* and *II*) were built to the design of the American, Simon Lake. They were of 229/248 tons displacement and armed with two bow 45cm torpedo tubes and a single stern tube. The *U3* and *U4* were built by Germania at Kiel and were 240/300 tons displacement but with only two bow 45cm torpedo tubes. Finally, Whitehead's at Fiume built the *U5* and *U6* to a design by the other great American pioneer, J P Holland, these boats being of 240/273 tons displacement and again had two 45cm torpedo tubes. Subsequently, a further five boats were ordered from the Germania yard, tentatively numbered *U7* to *U11* but on the outbreak of war they had not been delivered and as it was felt that they had little chance of reaching an Austrian port from Germany they were taken over by the German navy. There was one other boat. Whiteheads had built a third boat as a speculative venture to roughly the same specifications as the *U6*, but this had not been accepted by the navy, being retained by the Company and known as the *SS3*. On the outbreak of war she was incorporated into the Austrian navy as the *U12*.

The Austrian submarine service was headed by *Korvettenkapitän* (later

Fregattenkapitän) Franz *Ritter* von Thierry. Relations between Thierry and his Commander-in-Chief were not cordial and much of Haus' disdainful attitude towards submariners stems from the bad feeling between the two men. Thierry was often brusque to the point of rudeness and had little time for staff officers with little or no knowledge of submarines. He once pilloried one of Haus' Flag Lieutenants who had the temerity to ask if one could see aft through a periscope. For his part Haus found Thierry to be 'more confusing than convincing' and unwilling to risk his few submarines against French warships in the Straits of Otranto. However, although relations between the two were often strained Thierry was retained in command of the Austrian U-boats for the whole war.

If the Austrian U-boat arm was the smallest of the Mediterranean powers then the French, their principal opponents during the early months of the war, was one of the largest with 34 submarines in commission on 2 August 1914. Fifteen of these submarines were allocated to the *Armée Navale* in the Mediterranean. The *1ère Escadrille* consisted of the *Monge*, *Gay-Lussac*, *Ampère*, *Papin*, *Messidor*, *Cugnot*, and *Fresnel*, supported by two destroyers. The *2eme Escadrille* consisted of the *Joule*, *Faraday*, *Coulomb*, *Bernouilli*, *Arago*, *Le Verrier*, *Curie* and *Circé*, supported by three destroyers. Both Escadrilles were under the command of *Capitaine de Vaisseau* Moulle whose broad pennant flew in yet another destroyer, the *Dehorter*. The development of the French submarines had been marked with typical Gallic flair but the impressive number of hulls available for service hid serious deficiencies. Between 1898 and 1909 the French Navy had suffered from a series of ministerial overlords whose chief preoccupation was the destruction of the work of their predecessor: the so called *Naufraugeurs de la Marine*. During this period there was no coherent naval policy, and the French submarines had suffered in that too many had been built too quickly before the lessons of previous designs had been fully digested.

If the Austrians possessed numerous advantages in the Adriatic, then the French had none at all. They had no bases in the area, and since Italy was neutral, they depended on the goodwill of the Royal Navy for the use of Malta – so much so that Malta became, in the words of one British officer, 'an extension of Toulon dockyard'. Even then distances were considerable, it being 480 miles from Malta to Antivari on the Albanian coast. Further away still was the French base at Bizerta in North Africa, about 32 hours steaming at 15 knots.

The first objective of the French in the Mediterranean had been the safe transport of their Army Corps from North Africa to France itself. Once this had been achieved, and with the *Goeben* and *Breslau* out of the way in Constantinople, then Vice-Admiral Boué de Lapeyrère could concentrate his forces at Malta for operations against the Austrians, against whom the British and French did not declare war until midnight on 12 August. There was no shortage of ideas as to how the French should proceed against the Austrians, ranging from attacks on Pola and 'demonstrations' off Trieste to a combined assault on the heavily fortified base at Cattaro. Most ideas were impractical because of the logistic problem of keeping the fleet at sea so far from its base. However, de Lapeyrère was not content to wait at Malta for the Austrians to come out from Pola, and within hours of the declaration of war had sailed on the first of series of sorties into the Adriatic with the dual aim of surprising Austrian ships enforcing their blockade of Montenegro and of covering merchant ships taking supplies to the Montenegran forces. The small Kingdom of Montenegro occupied strategic positions on the high mountains overlooking the Austrian base at Cattaro and thus was able to provide the French with considerable intelligence regarding the Austrian movements. As a result, on 16 August the French, joined by a British cruiser squadron, succeeded in sinking the small Austrian cruiser *Zenta* off Antivari, though a torpedo boat in company succeeded in escaping.

The French then established a blockade of the Adriatic with a cruiser patrol in area between Cape Santa Maria di Leuca on the heel of Italy and Fano island in the south, and in the north between Cape d'Otranto and Cape Linguetta near Valona in Albania.

French submarines were also planned to operate in support of the cruiser patrol, although the ever present problem of a lack of a base near the operational area placed severe restrictions on their activities. On 27 August six submarines of the *2eme Escadrille* departed from Malta in company with the *Foudre*, an old cruiser launched in 1895 but then acting as a depot ship, anchoring in Greek waters to the west of Corfu. The following day the *Joule* and *Le Verrier* sailed for patrol off Cattaro. The former had an unpleasant time being hunted by Austrian torpedo boats while being unable to manoeuvre into an attacking position. The latter spent a quiet patrol between Cattaro and Antivari seeing nothing of interest. Both boats returned to the *Foudre* on the 30th suffering from damage caused by bad weather – which necessitated their return to Malta for repairs. The same fate befell the next two boats to go out, the *Faraday* and *Bernouilli*, making it clear that the numerous external fittings which festooned the hulls of French submarines were very vulnerable to weather damage. The *Foudre* was not able to act as a proper repair ship, and in any case she was withdrawn from the Adriatic in November to join the French ships off the Dardanelles, so repairs had to be undertaken at Malta or Bizerta, thus removing submarines from the patrol line for longer periods. The situation eased somewhat with the arrival of the old battleship *Marceau* which was anchored at Navarino on the Peloponnesian coast to act as a depot slip. Nevertheless the problem of lack of proper repair facilities was not to be solved until after Italy entered the war in May 1915 and her bases became available for the French.

The considerable amount of French activity at the southern end of the Adriatic represented a tempting opportunity for the seven Austrian submarines. Yet they were slow to take advantage of the chance, and when they did move south luck was not on their side. Haus had retained the Austrian boats in the north as a defensive measure in the

Map 2. The Adriatic.

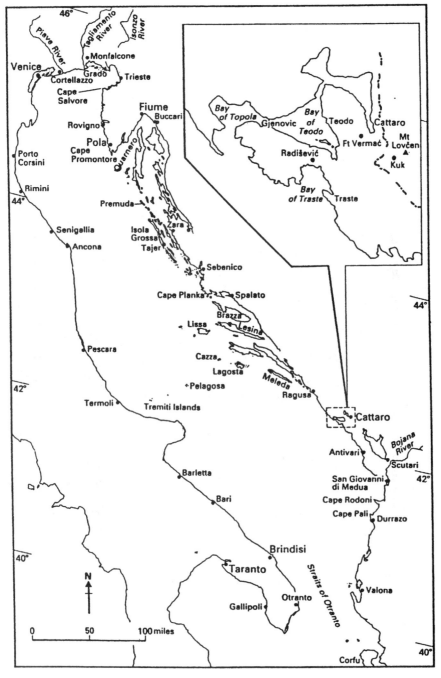

Korvettenkapitän *Franz* Ritter *von Thierry (*seated centre*), senior submarine officer in the* KuK Kriegsmarine *with* Linienschiffsleutnant *Egon Lerch, commanding officer of* U12 *(left) and* Fregattenleutnant *Ernst Zaccaria,* U12*'s executive officer. Lerch and Zaccaria were killed on 12 August 1916 when* U12 *tried to enter the harbour at Venice.* (Kriegsarchiv, Vienna)

event of a French attack on Pola and it was not until 20 September when he allowed two submarines, the *U3* commanded by *Linienschiffsleutnant* [*LSL*] Eduard Hubner and *U4* (LSL Herman Justels) to proceed under tow of two torpedo gunboats to Cattaro where they became based on the depot ship Gaa, a former liner. They were followed on 21 October by *U5* (*LSL* Friedrich Schlosser) and *U6* (*LSL* Nikolaus Halavanja).

It was not until 17 October that the Austrians had their first chance of action. The French fleet entered the Adriatic escorting the merchant ship *Liamone* carrying urgently needed food to Antivari for the Montenegran army. While the *Liamone* was unloading the fleet patrolled off Cattaro to prevent the Austrians interfering with the operation. The *U3* with the *TB13* and the *U4* with the destroyer *Uskoke* slipped out of Cattaro to a position west of the harbour and to the west of Molenta respectively, with the intention that the surface ships would lure the French towards the submarines. The French cruiser *Waldeck Rousseau*, some 25 miles north west of Cattaro, had already been attacked unsuccessfully by a flying boat when she fell into the Austrian trap and turned towards the *TB13*. The *U3* steered towards the cruiser until, when about 4,000 yards off she broke surface to entice the cruiser on. The *Waldeck Rousseau* opened fire and increased speed hoping to ram the submarine, but the *U3* dived again and the cruiser turned away and headed south, avoiding attack. The *U4* also managed to place herself in the cruiser's line of advance but she too did not fire.

The next chance came on 3 November when the *U5* sighted the entire French battlefleet of three battleships and seven cruisers. Schlosser's attack on the cruiser *Victor Hugo* was thwarted by poor torpedo maintenance. The flooding valves on the torpedoes had been left open and when fired both torpedoes were full of water and sank like stones. Schlosser did not attempt a second shot, and for this was severely criticised by Haus who noted 'this trembling heart is, according to Thierry, Number One!'

If luck did not favour the Austrians then the French were equally frustrated. Patrolling off Cattaro proved to be a fruitless business since the Austrians rarely appeared and their battlefleet remained safe in the north protected by geography and the defences of Pola. Admiral Haus was not prepared to risk a major engagement against a superior French fleet when the attitude of Italy was so uncertain. Yet without proper repair facilities the French struggled to maintain a presence off Cattaro but the best they could manage was to keep a submarine on patrol for one day in three. The weakness of the blockade was shown when the Austrians were able to bring the old pre-dreadnought *Radetzky* down from Pola without hindrance and into Cattaro where she was able to use her guns against the Montenegran positions overlooking the Austrian base.

If the Austrians would not come out then the French submariners would have to go in. The *Fresnel, Monge* and *Ampère* each penetrated the outer defences of Cattaro and fired at torpedo boats without success. The *Cugnot*, a steam driven submarine of 398/550 tons built in 1909 and with four torpedoes in external launching cradles and two in Drzewiecki drop collars, went even further and succeeded in penetrating the great harbour of Cattaro itself.

Under the command of *Lieutenant de Vaisseau* [*LV*] Dubois, the *Cugnot* passed through two minefields and an anti-submarine net to enter the Gulf of Cattaro. As she passed the battery at Porto Rose heading towards Castelnuovo her periscope was spotted by a sentry onboard the torpedo boat *TB57* who gave the alarm. As the *Cugnot* moved towards

Castelnuovo she was fired on by the old cruiser *Krönprinz Erzherzog Rudolf* but although the range was only some 800 yards the submarine was not hit. Four old torpedo boats were then ordered to block the entrance to the inner harbour while other units pursued the *Cugnot* firing guns and even torpedoes. In this fashion Dubois spent three hours exploring Topla Bay looking for any major units but finding only light craft. He was unable to penetrate the inner harbour where the *Radetzky* was lying, so with the situation around him becoming decidedly lively he made his escape without firing a single torpedo. Admiral Haus paid Dubois a back-handed compliment when he wrote afterwards.

> . . . when one hears what our own submarine commanders consider as being dangerous then you can only declare the feat of the French submarine commander who went into Cattaro on 29 November as madness [*verrueckt*].

The French were planning more 'madness'. The *Cugnot's* success in penetrating the formidable defences of Cattaro led de Lapeyrère to ask his commanding officers if one would be prepared to attempt to enter Pola where the bulk of the Austrian fleet lay at anchor. Selected for the attempt was another of the *Brumaire* class, the *Curie* under the command of *LV* Gabriel O'Byrne.

On 16 December the *Curie* left Navarino and proceeded up the Adriatic, being towed as far north as Pelagosa by the cruiser *Jules Michelet* in order to save fuel. O'Byrne spent the 18th and 19th studying the defences of Pola before deciding to make his entry the next day. Then just after midday he dived to 60 feet and headed for the harbour entrance. It was not long before the crew all heard the noise of chains and nets scrapping along the hull, and when they ceased O'Byrne thought that he was safely through and ordered the *Curie* to be brought to periscope depth. As the submarine rose her periscope fouled a second barrier and she was caught.

O'Byrne tried every manoeuvre possible to free his submarine: he ordered the motors alternately full speed ahead and then astern; he ordered violent changes in depth, but without effect and it seemed his efforts merely served to worsen the *Curie's* predicament as the wires became wrapped around the propeller shafts. Eventually both electric motors burnt out under the strain leaving the boat without power. The air became foul and the crew's reactions more and more dulled while their mascot, a small mongrel dog, collapsed and died. At about 4.30 pm the *Curie* suddenly took on a 30° bow down angle. With acid spilling out into the bilges to mix with sea water and give off chlorine O'Byrne now had no alternative but to try and surface and then abandon the submarine.

Naturally the *Curie's* violent attempts to free herself had not gone unnoticed. The shore battery at Punta Christa had spotted the disturbance in the water and had alerted the gunboat *Satellit* which was engaged in routine harbour patrols. The *Satellit* went to the spot indi-

The French submarine Cugnot *which made a number of daring attempts to enter the Austrian port at Cattaro.* (Marius Bar)

cated by the battery and was joined by three torpedo boats and two armed auxiliaries. At about 5 o'clock when the *Curie* broke surface she was immediately fired on by all the Austrian ships and the shore battery. O'Byrne led his crew out onto the casing, having first opened all the main vents, leaving the *Curie* settling in the water. Seeing that the crew were abandoning the submarine the order to cease fire was given, though one of the last shots from shore struck the submarine aft of the conning tower and she sank. All the survivors were picked up though one, Quartermaster Mariage Lebon, was fatally wounded and died that night. It was a miracle that casualties were so light considering the hail of fire that had swept over the *Curie* as she surfaced. The crew were made prisoners of war, and in a chivalrous gesture O'Byrne's wife was later allowed to visit him in hospital when he was ill. As for the *Curie* she was soon salvaged, refitted and commissioned into the Austrian Navy as the *U14*.

Worse was in store for the French. On 20 December the merchant ships *Tidjitt* and *Voltaire*, carrying supplies for the Montenegrans, were escorted to Antivari by the French fleet. The battleships remained cruising along a line between Brindisi and Cape Linguetta while the light forces covered the transports all the way into Antivari. On the same day the Austrian *U12* (*LSL* Egon Lerch) left Cattaro for an offensive patrol in the southern Adriatic. At 6.30 am on 21st Lerch sighted smoke and dived to attack. What Lerch had seen was the main French fleet, lead by the dreadnought *Jean Bart* flying the flag of Vice-Admiral de Lapeyrère himself, steaming slowly at 14 knots with no escort. Eventually Lerch was less than ½ mile away from the French flagship which was beam-on to him. He fired both bow torpedoes, one of which hit the *Jean Bart* forward while the other missed. Nevertheless the great French ship was badly hit and was nursed back to Cephalonia and then to Malta for repairs. The occasion marked the last sortie into the Adriatic of the French battlefleet since the dangers from submarine attack were now considered too great.

During the winter of 1914/15 the submarines of both sides were active in patrolling the Otranto Straits. The *U4*, *U5* and *U6* all carried out patrols in the southern Adriatic or the Ionian Sea without result. The French submarines were equally unsuccessful while the considerable distance between their bases and the patrol areas meant that they could only spend two days on station out of six days at sea. On 2 April the *U5* (*LSL* Schlosser) spent three and a half days off Corfu looking for the French, but without sighting anything, returning to Cattaro with most of the crew sick and complaining of the foul air in the boat.

But the *U5* was to have better luck later in the month after Schlosser

The French submarine Curie in dock at Pola following her gallant but unsuccessful attempt to enter the harbour on 20 December 1914. She subsequently, enjoyed a new lease of life as the Austrian U14. (Kriegsarchiv, Vienna)

had turned over command to *LSL* Georg Ritter von Trapp, a submariner of some experience who had joined the navy in 1894 and whose first submarine command had been the *U6* in 1911. The *U5* left Cattaro on 24 April for a patrol in the southern Adriatic with the specific aim of attacking French warships on patrol. Trapp was well aware that French cruisers patrolled across the entrance to the Adriatic and so took the *U5* through the Otranto Straits at night to an area off Lefkimos where he waited for a suitable target. Next morning smoke was sighted and Trapp dived the submarine and began to make an attack on what he later identified as a cruiser of the *Victor Hugo* class, but in the mirror calm sea his periscope was sighted and the enemy turned away at speed. Shortly after midnight he again sighted the cruiser but once again was unable to make an attack. After recharging the submarine's batteries Trapp made plans to attack the cruiser again the following night using the information that he had gained on her movements, which appeared to be routine and predictable. Before midnight he was in position off Cape Santa Maria di Leuca, with the *U5* stopped and trimmed down waiting for her target to appear silhouetted against the moon.

Sure enough just after midnight in the early minutes of the 27th the cruiser came in sight. The *U5* was on her starboard bow as Trapp dived to close the range. When 3000 yards away and with the cruiser going at an estimated speed of only 4½ knots she was seen to start a slow turn

The Austrian U5 *enters the Bocche di Cattaro on 24 August 1915. The boat's commanding officer Linienschiffsleutnant* Georg *Ritter* von *Trapp, is standing on the conning tower.*

to starboard. Trapp brought the submarine round so that he was on the cruiser's port quarter, and at a range of under 500 yards Trapp fired one torpedo at the after group of funnels followed ten seconds later by another torpedo at the forward group. After 25 seconds the first explosion was heard followed by a second. According to Trapp's report his crew broke into spontaneous applause.

The stricken ship was the 12,550 tons cruiser *Leon Gambetta* which had been steaming at 6½ knots without an escort, a little further north than usual since de Lapeyrère had anticipated Austrian activity in the southern Adriatic as a result of the diplomatic activity which was to lead to Italy's entry into the war. The first torpedo struck on the port side in the dynamo room and the second in the after boiler room leaving the cruiser with an almost instant 35° list. Despite some splendid rescue work by two Italian destroyers which happened to be nearby only 137 ratings survived, the Admiral, Captain and all the officers were among those that perished. Trapp and the *U5* returned that evening to a hero's welcome at Cattaro.

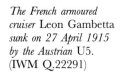

The French armoured cruiser Leon Gambetta *sunk on 27 April 1915 by the Austrian* U5. *(IWM Q.22291)*

The loss of the *Leon Gambetta* showed that the French had learnt nothing from the disaster inflicted by the German *U9* on the Royal Navy in the North Sea the previous September when three cruisers were sunk

while moving slowly and without zigzagging. It also had a tremendous effect on French naval activity in the Adriatic for de Lapeyrère ordered that in future no French cruisers were to operate north of Cephalonia except for specific important operations which would be conducted at high speed and with a heavy escort. He also considered that the submarine base off Navarino was insecure and since he lacked ships for a proper defence he moved the French submarines back to Malta, with all the disadvantages that such a move involved. For the price of two torpedoes Trapp had succeeded in turning the Adriatic into a virtual Austrian lake.

The next development in submarine warfare in the Adriatic was to be the arrival of the *Kaiserliche Kriegsmarine*. The Germans had long been concerned about the level of Anglo-French naval activity off the Dardanelles and successive appeals to their Austrian allies for help had met with no response. Consequently the Germans resolved to send some of their own boats to the area, either direct from Germany or overland to Pola. The story of the *UB3*, *UB7* and *UB8* as well as the *U21*'s epic voyage from Germany belongs in another chapter, but provided the answer to Austrian demands for compensation for the five large U-boats building for them in Germany and taken over by the *Kriegsmarine* after the outbreak of war. As a start Admiral von Tirpitz announced that the *UB1* and *UB15* would be sent by the overland route to Pola and transferred to the Austrians once the necessary crews had been formed and trained. Moreover, the two mine-laying submarines, the *UC14* and *UC15* (168/183 tons, with 12 UC120 mines in external vertical chutes) would also be sent to Pola although these would be retained by the Germans for operations off Malta or in Turkish waters. Thus the foundations were laid for future German involvement in the war in the Adriatic.

The Adriatic was quickly becoming the focus of considerable naval activity. Inevitably both sides began to pay careful attention to whether Italy would remain neutral, or could be persuaded to declare war on one side or the other. The *Regia Marina* was a potent factor in these negotiations for with four dreadnoughts in commission and another two nearing completion they could tip the balance of naval power in the whole Mediterranean. The Italians thus found themselves in the fortunate position of being courted by both sides. Germany offered Austrian territory in the Tyrol and around Trieste if the Italians would, at least, stay neutral, to the understandable fury of the Austrians. Britain and France offered much more if Italy joined them, an offer that carried the day. On 26 April 1915 the Italians concluded the Treaty of London by which they undertook to enter the war within a month. The Italian Chamber of Deputies, hitherto in favour of neutrality, obediently voted for war after a mob, organised by pro-war agitators, threatened to storm the Parliament building. On 24 May Italy formally declared war on Austria – but not Germany. Under the terms of the Anglo-French-Italian Naval Convention of 10 May 1915 Britain undertook to send a squadron of four pre-dreadnought battleships and a light cruiser squadron to join the Italian fleet. The British ships would be commanded by Rear Admiral Cecil Thursby, who rejoiced in the acronym RABAS (Rear Admiral Commanding British Adriatic Squadron) flying his flag in HMS *Queen*, but would be part of an allied fleet based at Taranto under the overall command of the Italian Commander-in-Chief, Vice-Admiral the Duke of Abruzzi. The French were to provide a force of seven submarines to this allied fleet, the *Monge*, *Ampère*, *Messidor*, *Cugnot*, *Fresnel*, *Aigrette* and *Papin*, supported by the depot ship *Marceau*, which would work from Brindisi. No British submarines were immediately available, but later six 'B' class were to be sent to Venice.

In terms of submarines the Italians had 21 boats in commission. Seven were based at Brindisi, one at Ancona and 13 at Venice. Although the first Italian submarine, *Delfino*, had been built in the 1890s it was not followed by a successor until 1905 when the first of the five *Glauco* class (157/161 tons, 2 x 45 cm bow torpedo tubes, 3 x 45 cm tubes in *Glauco*) had been laid down. These five submarines were followed by the *Foca*, of similar dimensions, and then the eight boats of the *Medusa* class (248/252 tons, 2 x 45 cm bow tubes) which were the mainstay of the Italian submarine fleet at the outbreak of war, although by then there had been another six completed. Of these the most interesting was the *Argonauta* (255/306 tons, 2 x 45 cm tubes). She had originally been ordered by the Russians as an improved unit of the *Medusa* class, and been named *Svyatoy Georgi* being launched in July 1914. While fitting out at La Spezia she had been seized by an Italian naval officer who intended to take her into the Adriatic and attack Austrian shipping thus forcing Italy into the war! The Italians were duly thankful when the French intercepted the submarine off Corsica and returned her to the builders. In 1915 when there was no hope of her being delivered to her Russian owners she was purchased by the Italians and renamed.

The first fruits of co-operation between the French and the Italians were shown when the French submarines *Messidor*, *Monge* and *Fresnel* patrolled off the entrance to Pola during the move of the Italian IV Cruiser Division from Brindisi to Venice. But, submarines were to play no other part in these early moves in the Adriatic. The Austrians had lost no time in getting to grips with their new adversary. They were well aware of the Italian move towards hostilities and only hours after the declaration of war on 24 May the Austrian fleet bombarded Ancona, Porto Corsini (near Ravenna), Rimini and Senigallia on the Italian Adriatic coast. Considerable damage was done ashore while the destroyer *Turbine* was sunk by gunfire from the cruiser *Helgoland*. Later the British Naval Attaché was to write that.

> In four months the Austrian fleet has established a moral ascendancy in the Adriatic, and had played the part of the weaker force with conspicuous success. Not only has it succeeded in weakening the Italians fleet but it has immobilised a force very considerable superior to itself.

Once the allied fleet had gathered at Taranto it began to exercise
manoeuvres which might be necessary in the event of action with the
Austrian fleet. The results were hardly satisfactory, 'God help us if we
have to tackle the Austrian battle fleet' wrote one frustrated British officer. But the Admirals at Taranto were preparing for an eventuality that
was not to occur. The real action would involve cruisers, destroyers, and
above all, submarines. Nevertheless a series of raids against the
Dalmatian coast were planned. On 1 June HMS *Dublin* and the Italian
light cruiser *Quarto* demolished the signal station at Lissa, while on the
5th the *Dublin* destroyed a lighthouse at Glavat. Abruzzi was pleased
with these operations as a start and felt that the best protection against
submarine attack lay in the speed of his ships. He was to be proved very
wrong in the coming months.

On 8 June HMS *Dublin* (Captain John Kelly) escorted by four Italian
and three French destroyers left Brindisi for a sweep off the Albanian
coast, making a rendezvous early the following morning with the Italian
Nino Bixio and a further six destroyers. After a reconnaissance of San
Giovanni di Medua they all retired towards Brindisi, steaming at 18
knots and zigzagging. The *Dublin* had the three French destroyers ahead
and two Italians on either beam.

At the same time the Austrian *U4* (*LSL* Rudolf Singule) was coming
to the end of a patrol off Cape Pali when she found herself on the
Dublin's port bow. Singule coolly allowed the French destroyers to pass
over him and then closed to 500 yards before firing both bow tubes at
the British cruiser. At the last moment his periscope was sighted and
the *Dublin* altered course and opened fire at the spot where the
periscope was last seen. But it was too late. One of the torpedoes missed
but the other struck on the port side in Number One stokehold as the
ship was turning, and tore a large hole in her side. The escorts closed
around the stricken cruiser while her crew dealt with the damage.
Eventually the *Dublin* got under way and was later able to work up to
17½ knots, arriving at Brindisi without further incident. The *Dublin* was
a smart ship with an efficient well trained crew whose prompt actions
had undoubtedly saved the ship from sinking while casualties were limited to 13 men killed. The *U4* was able to get away unmolested and
return to Cattaro.

The story of the Italian occupation of the small island of Pelagosa,
lying roughly in the middle of the Adriatic, provided ample work for
the submarines of both sides. The occupation was carried out on 11
July by the Italians as the first stage of an operation to set up a series
of observation and signal stations on islands off the Dalmatian coast,
only two terrified lighthouse keepers found hiding in a cave provided
the Austrian garrison. The next stage should have been to move east-
ward to take Lagosta but the Italians dithered despite aggressive reconnaissance carried out by French destroyers which indicated the island
was unoccupied. Submarines covered the operation with the Italian
Vellela off Pelagosa itself, the *Nereide* off Cape Planka and the French
Monge off Cattaro.

Linienschiffsleutnant *Rudolf Singule, commanding officer of the Austrian* U4, *who attacked and damaged the British cruiser* Dublin *on 9 June 1915 and sank the Italian cruiser* Giuseppe Garibaldi *on 18 July 1915.* (Kriegsarchiv, Vienna)

But Austrian reaction was not slow in coming. On 13th a flying boat flew over Pelagosa and this was followed by a bombardment carried out by the destroyer *Tatra*. By this time the French *Fresnel* (*LV* René Jouen) had taken over the patrol off the island. Jouen manoeuvred for an attack but was spotted and unsuccessfully bombed by the flying boat before he could get into position.

While both sides were considering what to do about Pelagosa, *LSL* Singule of the *U4* scored another success on 18 July when he sank the 8 110 tons Italian cruiser *Giussepe Garibaldi*. The *Garibaldi* was the flag-

ship of the V Cruiser Division and in company with two other cruisers she had sailed from Brindisi during the evening of 17 July for a bombardment of a bridge carrying the railway between Ragusa and ˙ˑh had only just been repaired following an earlier bom-
ˑidge had once again been destroyed while the escort-
ʰot up a barracks and a railway marshalling yard.
ˑo at 2.0 am on the 18th to search for an aircraft
ʳn from a raid Brindisi the previous evening. At
lookouts sighted smoke, and after closing the
ʰe was in contact with the three cruisers of
ˑon, another cruiser and some destroyers. Closing
still further Singule's periscope was sighted but ignoring the fire which was directed at him he pressed on and fired two torpedoes, being rewarded 30 seconds later by the sound of an explosion. The old cruiser was hit amidships and sank in three minutes.

Singule took the *U4* to 60 feet to avoid the escorts, but could not resist coming back to periscope depth 20 minutes later to examine the results of his handiwork. Once again his periscope was spotted by a destroyer who turned towards to try and ram. Singule knew that his torpedoes were set too deep for a successful attack, so once again went deep and crept away from the scene. He finally surfaced at 5.30 am and continued his search for the airmen, but by then they had been found by the Italians and taken prisoner.

To have damaged a modern light cruiser and sank an armoured cruiser in little over a month was no small achievement. Singule must have been most upset to have been publicly criticised by Admiral Haus in front of all his fellow submarine commanding officers at a meeting on 25 July. Haus betrayed a remarkable lack of understanding of the capabilities of the submarines under his command by criticising Singule for sinking only the *Garibaldi* when he had the entire Cruiser Division spread in front of him.

On 27 July the Austrians returned to Pelagosa, this time in force. The cruisers *Helgoland* and *Saida* with six destroyers and two torpedo boats first bombarded the island and then landed a party of armed sailors who met with unexpectedly strong resistance. While the fighting was in progress the landing party was withdrawn. A torpedo fired by an enemy submarine had narrowly missed the destroyer *Balaton*, and though it had missed it had brought the operation to a halt, and the Austrians thought that lying off the island they were too vulnerable. The landing party was re-embarked and the whole force returned to Cattaro. The submarine was the French *Ampère* under the command of *LV* Leon Henri Devin.

The intervention of the *Ampère* brought home to the Austrians the value of submarines in the defence of the island. Austrian boats were then ordered to patrol off the island to seek any French or Italian boats. On 5 August the Italian submarine *Nereide* (built in 1913, 225/320 tons displacement and 2 x 45 cm torpedo tubes) was on patrol off the island when she was attacked and sunk by the *U5* under the command of von Trapp who had sunk the *Leon Gambetta* in April. Trapp had left Cattaro

on 2 August and was approaching a position off the south east end of the island when just after 5 o'clock in the morning he sighted the distinctive red, white and green Italian ensign against the land, the *Nereide* had just hoisted her colours. Trapp immediately dived and altered course to achieve an attacking position. The Italians ashore had seen the *U5* and warned the *Nereide*. The Italian submarine fired a torpedo ineffectively in the general direction of the Austrian's periscope, but Trapp was not to be distracted and fired both his torpedoes. The *Nereide* was hit on the starboard side abaft the conning tower, broke in two, and sank.

The French submarine Fresnel sunk on 5 December 1915.

But the Austrians also had their share of losses. The 13 August saw the loss of the *U3* which had sailed from Cattaro on the 10th under the command of *LSL* Karl Strnad for a patrol in support of torpedo boats raiding the Italian coast north of Brindisi. After that she was given a patrol area before returning after about four days at sea. On 12 August she attacked the Italian armed merchant cruiser *Citta di Catania* between Saseno and Otranto, which successfully evaded the torpedoes fired at her, turned to ram the submarine and damaged Strnad's periscope. The *Catania*'s escorts then dropped some of the new depth charges in the area which caused more damage to the submarine. The two French destroyers were then joined by two Italian destroyers and the French destroyer *Bisson* (*LV* Le Sort).

It was not until early the next morning that the U3 was able to surface. As her conning tower broke surface she was seen by the *Bisson* less than 300 yards away. The *Bisson* immediately opened fire and her third round struck the submarine which started to sink. Strnad realised that there was no hope left so he gave the order to abandon ship and for the vents to be opened. One officer and eleven ratings were picked up ~~by the French. Strnad was not among them.~~

Commanding Officer could do but abandon the submarine and save his crew who became prisoners of war, while the boat was destroyed by gunfire.

Then, early on the morning of 29 December the Austrian cruiser *Helgoland* accompanied by five destroyers left Cattaro for a raid on the port of Durazzo on the Albanian coast where operations were in progress to evacuate the Serbian army. There were two French sub-

Lieutenant de Vaisseau *Roland Morillot, commanding officer of the French submarine* Monge, *who remained in the boat's conning tower to make sure it sank when she was rammed by the* Balaton *on 28 December 1915.* (Service Historique de la Marine, Paris)

marines on patrol off Cattaro at this time, *Archimède* to the north and *Liege* to the south. However, the former had been forced to retire following an attack in which she had torpedoed and sunk the transport *Kuma*, but had subsequently been damaged when attacked by an Austrian aircraft.

The *Monge* under the command of *LV* Roland Morillot had spent 28 December dived off Cattaro, retiring to the south west at night to charge her batteries. Shortly after 4 o'clock her lookouts reported the Austrian ships, and Morillot dived to begin his attack. He found himself in a good firing position for an attack on the *Helgoland* but was suddenly rammed by the destroyer *Balaton*. Morillot had been so engrossed in his attack that he had failed to see the destroyer's approach. The conning tower began to flood and the *Monge* began to sink with a large bow down angle, and went to nearly 200 feet before the drop keels were released and she returned to the surface. On breaking surface the Austrian ships opened fire and the submarine was hit again. Realising that the boat was doomed Morillot ordered his crew to abandon the submarine and saw them up through the conning tower one by one. The French were quickly picked up by the Austrians who were illuminating the scene with searchlights, all being rescued with the exception of Morillot who stayed below to ensure that his command did not fall into the hands of the enemy.

The Austrian ships carried on to the south where they bombarded Durazzo. In the course of the action a destroyer was mined and sunk, while a second, also mined, had to be taken in tow. The alarm having been raised British and Italian cruisers hastily left Brindisi to intercept

The French submarine Monge, sunk by the Austrian cruiser Helgoland on 28 December 1915. (Marius Bar)

to be able to provide him with some targets'.

But Thursby was to be disappointed for the *E21* (Lieutenant Commander Thomas C B Harbottle) had to abandon her first patrol on 21 December because of engine problems, and was forced to return to Malta for repairs. This time Thursby was constrained to write 'It looks so bad and makes them [the French and Italians] think all our ships are as unreliable as their own.' Thursby was in an unenviable position having to maintain British prestige with old and worn out units such as his own pre-dreadnoughts. But the criticism of the submarine activities of his allies – he described the French submarines as 'quite useless' – was unmerited and uninformed. Despite the bad start, the British contribution and total numbers of allied submarines operating in the Adriatic would increase in 1916 as operations in the Dardanelles were wound down. The Adriatic was becoming a truly international theatre of operations.

CHAPTER FOUR

Turkish Waters: The Submarines Gather

While the French and Austrian submarines were busy in the Adriatic, the submariners off the Dardanelles had started 1915 with the exhilaration of Holbrook's success in the *B11* in December, only for all their hopes for the future to be dashed by the loss of Fournier and half his crew in the *Saphir*. No further attempts to enter the Dardanelles and sink enemy shipping were planned for the time being, such operations were considered to be beyond the scope of the elderly submarines that were then available, both British and French, and would have to wait for some of the more modern boats still building. Nevertheless there were submarine reinforcements with the arrival of the British *B6*, *B7* and *B8* from Gibraltar in February, and later the French were to send another six boats.

However, the first of the modern submarines to arrive was Australian, the *AE2*. HMAS *AE2*, like her sister the *AE1*, were British 'E' class submarines built in England for the Australian navy, and both boats had sailed to Sydney in the summer of 1914 with crews made up of both British and Australian personnel. With the outbreak of war both had been sent to operate off the German port of Rabaul in the Bismarck Archipelago where the *AE1* was lost in an accident, the details of which are still not known. Once the Germans in that area had surrendered and any threat to Australia had disappeared with the defeat of Admiral von Spee's Asiatic Squadron at the Battle of the Falkland Islands in December 1914 the remaining submarine was available to be redeployed to a more active area. It had been expected that she would be sent to operate in the Heligoland Bight being based at Harwich, but instead she was sent to the Aegean. Under the command of Lieutenant Commander H G Stoker, RN, she sailed across the Indian Ocean with 19 troopships all carrying the troops of the second Australian and New Zealand contingent for Egypt. The *AE2* actually led this armada through the Canal to Port Said, the bridge of the submarine having to be especially protected for this last part of the trip for it was known that Turkish snipers were active in the desert, while the troops entrenched on the west bank were daily waiting a Turkish offensive. From there Stoker took his submarine up to Tenedos to join the other boats alongside the *Hindu Kush*, and to take part in the daily patrol off the entrance to the Dardanelles.

Lord, immediately drew up a plan for the Churchill's consideration and which could then be presented to the Cabinet. He proposed a combined military and naval operation. The army, with troops which would have to be withdrawn from France, would attack up the Gallipoli Peninsula with Greek participation while the Bulgars would open an offensive directly against Constantinople. The Navy would simultaneously attack up the Dardanelles. It was an ambitious plan but doomed from the start. Neither Lord Kitchener nor the French would countenance the withdrawal of troops from France while neither the Greeks nor Bulgars were at war with Turkey, so not only would they have to be persuaded to declare war but would then need time to mobilise. In any event the Russians would not agree to Greek participation.

By this time the problem had solved itself for the Russians had won a surprising but resounding victory in the Caucasus, and any proposed attack on the Dardanelles should then have been called off until it could be properly planned with all the necessary resources. Nevertheless, Churchill seized upon the last part of Fisher's plan and stated that the Navy would attempt to force the Dardanelles without support from the army and would go on to threaten Constantinople. It would be the chance for the Navy to be seen to be actively engaged, something for which his restless spirit continually pressed. He immediately signalled to Carden asking whether he considered the Dardanelles could be forced 'by the use of ships alone'.

Carden's reply indicated that he did not think that the Dardanelles could be rushed, but that it might be forced in stages in extended operations. This was what Churchill wanted to hear and Carden was ordered to prepare a more detailed plan. The upshot was that Carden's ships began an attack on the forts on the morning of Friday 19 February 1915, some six weeks after the Russians had asked for an urgent diversion to help their army in the Caucasus, and long after the threat there had been erased.

In early 1915 the defences of the Dardanelles included forts, mobile guns including howitzers, and minefields with shore batteries guarding

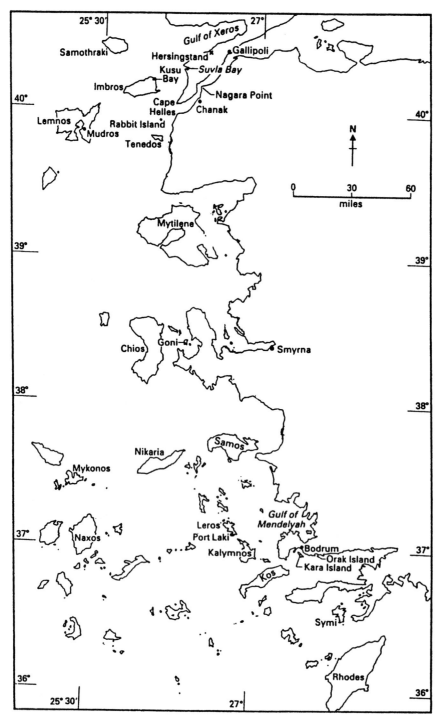

Map 3. Approach to the Dardanelles.

abandoned by the enemy. As the battleships advanced further into the Straits they were preceded by minesweepers, mostly converted trawlers and still manned by their civilian crews. All seemed to be going well and, on 2 March, Carden forecast that he hoped to be off Constantinople in 14 days.

Six days later the minesweepers had been halted by the fire of the Turkish guns and the bombarding battleships dared not go forward without them. Roger Keyes, who had been replaced in his appointment as Commodore (Submarines) at Harwich, had arrived in Malta in mid-February to become Carden's Chief of Staff. Now he was wholeheartedly supporting this operation to reach the Turkish capital and with the civilian manned minesweepers unable to go forward under fire he arranged for their crews to be replaced by naval volunteers from the fleet. Some progress was made but the cost was high in minesweepers and Carden called a temporary halt.

Urged ever onward by Churchill and thwarted by the stiffening Turkish resistance Carden's health broke and he was advised to return home on medical grounds. His second in command, Rear Admiral John de Robeck, took over the command of the force, with Keyes remaining as Chief of Staff. De Robeck ordered the attack to be resumed on 18 March and the first wave of British battleships led by the newly completed HMS *Queen Elizabeth* with her 15 inch guns opened a heavy fire on the forts. Then the French battleships joined in. As the third squadron was ordered up the second ship in the French line, the *Bouvet*, was mined, blew up and sank within minutes with the loss of over 600 men. Soon afterwards the battlecruiser *Inflexible* hit a mine and limped out of the line, eventually going to Malta for extensive repairs. When the old battleship *Irresistible* hit another mine the *Ocean* and *Swiftsure* went to her aid, but were unable to take her in tow. Later the *Ocean* too was mined and both ships eventually sank. By the end of the day when the action was called off both HMS *Agamemnon* and the French *Gaulois* had been also hit .

The following day a gale prevented a resumption of the bombardment, but when the weather cleared the fleet did not return to the attack. Keyes alone was ready to order another attempt but de Robeck felt that they should only continue if supported by the army. It was a view that was now to be taken by Kitchener too, despite his earlier rejection. The Gallipoli campaign became another step nearer. It is the benefit of hindsight that allows the historian to add that unknown to de Robeck the Turkish batteries were in a bad way with over half their ammunition expended and very little of what remained was armour piercing shell.

There was one other important development that took place during this phase of the Campaign. Until early March the Allied fleet was forced to use the uncertain anchorage off Tenedos as a base, with no harbour nearer than Alexandria in Egypt, or Malta. Then on the 7th the island of Lemnos was occupied by troops sent from Egypt. The island, like Tenedos, had been captured by the Greeks in 1912, now with the connivance of the pro-British Prime Minister, Venizelos, the Greek garrison was withdrawn. With the Greeks gone the island technically became Turkish again and could be occupied by the allies. Unfortunately, Venizelos' policies were too warlike and too pro-British for the King and he was replaced, but by that time Lemnos was occupied, and the fine natural harbour of Mudros became a valuable base for the fleet, and a jumping off place for the troops in their assault on the Gallipoli Peninsula.

One of the main worries for Carden, and later de Robeck, was that the Austrian submarines would leave the Adriatic and, working from some base in Asia Minor, attack the fleet off the Dardanelles. Indeed, Souchon signalled the Austrians asking that this be done. To no avail. The Austrians had started the war with only six submarines which were comparable with the obsolescent British 'B' class and Admiral Haus felt that they must be retained to guard the long coast line between the two Austrian bases of Pola and Cattaro, adding that only two were serviceable at the time of Souchon's request and that he doubted if they had an adequate range for the task. This prompted Souchon to signal to Berlin:

> Co-operation of submarines in defence of Dardanelles would promise great things and be very valuable. Austrian Admiral has refused my request to send submarines because unsuitable and required Adriatic.

It was a request that was supported the following day by the German Ambassador in Constantinople and also by Enver in separate messages to Berlin. Enver suggested that the Turks offer to buy three of the Austrian submarines and they could then sail to Turkey with German crews. As might be expected the idea of selling any of their submarines was rejected by the Austrians, for the same reasons that they had given for not sending any out of the Adriatic to help off the Dardanelles. Any support would have to come from the Germans themselves.

In October the Germans had approved new designs for two classes of small submarines that could be completed quickly, and an initial order had been placed for 17 coastal submarines of the UB type and

... . in the forward part of the hull. Because of their small size no torpedo tubes could be included in the design. One special feature of the design was that the boats could be broken down into three sections, each of which could then be transported on a railway wagon with the conning tower and battery on a fourth. Despite construction not having been started until late October the first of the UB boats had completed in March 1915, and they seemed the obvious choice of boat to use to try and reinforce Souchon.

The first submarine for the Mediterranean, the *UB8*, left Kiel by rail on 20 March and arrived in Pola on the 25th, with the *UB7* following behind. The task of reassembling the two boats began immediately and it was a remarkable feat that just over a month later *Leutnant* von Voigt had completed the sea trials of the *UB8* and was ready to set off for Turkey. The *UB7* was not so fortunate as she developed a leak while on trials and was delayed for a month while repairs were completed. As an aid to secrecy while the work was being carried out in Pola the Austrians let it be known that the two submarines were to become the Austrian *U7* and *U8* and that the German crews were only there to supervise the trials.

With the first submarine almost ready to sail from Pola there was the need to establish a base for them on the coast of Asia Minor, as well the need for them to refuel on passage. Arrangements were made for the submarines to call in at Bodrum on the Bay of Kos where a supply of fuel and other stores was collected nearby, opposite Orak Island. In addition the Greek steamer *Proton* was to be available to the south of Crete ready to transfer fuel to the small submarines. At the last moment it was decided that the *Proton* was not to be used to fuel the small submarines on passage from Pola as she was required for another task. Instead the Pola submarines would be towed for the first part of their passage so as to conserve fuel.

Having completed with stores and topped up with fuel at Porto Palazzo on Meleda Island (off the coast north of Dubrovnik and now known as Mljet) the met with the Austrian cruiser *Novara* on 4 May to be towed as far south as the cruiser could safely go, and hopefully through the Straits of Otranto. The *Novara*, under the command of

Linienschiffskapitän (Captain) Nikolaus Horthy, had already conducted towing trials with the submarine and a speed of 10 knots had been achieved, far better than the 6½ knots of the submarine under its own power. After some hours the bow of the submarine suddenly dipped and the boat began to dive. The Navigating Officer who was on watch on the bridge was unable to slip the tow and only at the last moment, before the whole submarine went under, was he able to throw the conning tower hatch shut. The *UB8* went down to 60 feet with water pouring in through the unclipped hatch while the three men who had been on watch on the bridge were left swimming. Luckily the accident had been seen from the bridge of the *Novara* and the cruiser's engines were stopped at once, and as the way came off the ship so the submarine returned to the surface. One man was drowned and von Voigt had to return to harbour to clean up and repair the minor damage. He was ready to sail again the next day.

Once again the *Novara* took the submarine in tow and this time all went well. The two ships passed through the Straits of Otranto on a dark moonless night untroubled by any of the allied patrols. The following morning when off the coast of Cephalonia Horthy sighted the funnel smoke of the patrolling French warships and had to slip the tow. The *Novara* turned north at high speed and returned to Cattaro leaving the *UB8* to continue alone, leaving the French unaware of her presence.

The passage for the *UB8* was not to be smooth however, for three days later the wind strengthened rapidly to force 8. The small submarine rolled so badly that von Voigt feared that the battery acid might spill and decided to heave to. With that the motion changed from violent rolling to a fierce energy sapping pitching with seas constantly washing over the conning tower. Now with the danger that the submarine's hydroplanes might be damaged by the force of the sea von Voigt felt that he must dive ride out the storm, but even at 60 feet the motion was noticeable, particularly to those with weak stomachs. As with many storms that blow up suddenly they moderate as quickly and the *UB8* was soon able to continue towards Bodrum on the surface, where they arrived safely on 11 May. Two days in harbour gave von Voigt's crew the chance to take some rest and top up with fuel and fresh provisions before they set off to begin operations against the fleet off Gallipoli, but the gyro compass soon broke down and with his magnetic compass unreliable von Voigt put into Smyrna for repairs.

The *UB7* (*Leutnant* Werner) left Pola on 11 May, and was towed through the Straits of Otranto on the night of 15/16th by the destroyer *Triglav*. They had a much more comfortable passage than the *UB8* and arrived safely at Bodrum on 20th. By this time a third boat had been made ready, the UB3 (*Leutnant* Siegfried Schmidt), but having been towed through the Straits of Otranto she was not seen again though reported herself some 80 miles from Smyrna on 23 May.

There was one other option open to the Germans – to send one of the larger U-boats direct from Germany. It was an indication of the advance made in the planning of submarine operations that such an

The main problem facing the Germans in such a voyage from Germany was fuel. Arrangements were made for him to meet with a German ship off the north coast of Spain where the submarine could transfer fuel. A similar operation was planned off the Balearics while later arrangements were made for Hersing to meet the Greek *Proton* off Crete, it being more important to use this ship for the *U21*'s needs than with the smaller boats sailing from the Adriatic. It was thus 25 April before Hersing set sail from Wilhelmshaven, his route taking to the north of Scotland and west of Ireland before effecting a rendezvous off Cape Finisterre a week later with the steamer *Marzala*. After a quick exchange of recognition signals the submarine followed the merchant ship into the Rio de Corcubin on the west coast of Spain where the merchantman anchored while Hersing brought the *U21* alongside. Working throughout the night they transferred 12½ tons of fuel to the submarine together with some lubricating oil and fresh provisions. By dawn Hersing was at sea again, with the Spanish authorities unaware of his visit in their waters, and with arrangements made to meet the *Marzala* again the next night to complete the transfer of fuel.

During the day Hersing discovered the awful truth that he had been supplied with the wrong sort of diesel fuel, and the 12½ tons he had taken inboard was totally unusable. He had left Germany with 56 tons and now had a mere 26 tons left, and was not half way to the nearest friendly port of Cattaro, let alone the new base at Bodrum. Hersing's decision was of extraordinary military significance and is best summed up as written in the *U21*'s log.

> Oil fuel onboard 26 tons. I decided not to go back but to try and reach Cattaro. This quantity will suffice with a little to spare at most economical speed [9 knots], provided it is not necessary to dive too often and too long. To return via the [English] Channel would be risky in view of the English defensive measures. By choosing the way back round Scotland more opposition is to be expected than by going on. The advantage in the slight difference [200 miles] if we went back would probably be rendered illusory by having to dive more often. Worse weather is also more probable in the north than in the

Mediterranean. Further, in the very worse case I am free to take in oil at a neutral port in the Mediterranean. Finally, to turn back would cause great delay in the undertaking.

At dawn on 6 May Hersing entered the Straits of Gibraltar, keeping close to the North African shore. Even so, that afternoon he was sighted by two old torpedo boats, HMS *TB92* and *TB96*, on patrol and was forced to dive, as one tried to ram him. The British report claims that the *TB92* evaded a torpedo fired at her, but there is no mention of this in the German account. The next day he was seen and later reported by the hospital ship *Delta* while on the 9th, in misty weather, he met with the French auxiliary cruiser *Corte II* and was again forced to dive. The French ship was almost abeam of the submarine when both must have sighted each other at almost the same moment, and as the former altered course as if to ram so Hersing dived. A final brush with allied patrols occurred south of Sicily when two French destroyers again forced the submarine to dive, with fire being opened momentarily on his periscope. The *U21* was brought triumphantly into Cattaro on 13 May without further incident but with only two tons of fuel remaining.

It was as well that Hersing had not relied on the other two oilers that had been arranged for him. The ship intended to rendezvous off the Balearics had been detained by the Spanish authorities on the grounds that the export of oil was prohibited. Meanwhile the *Proton* had attracted the attention of the British, had been arrested on the High Seas and taken to Alexandria.

By the time Hersing and the *U21* had arrived at Cattaro on 13 May, and with the *UB8* setting off from Bodrum, the *UB7* just leaving the Adriatic and the *UB3* preparing to do so, the British and French had already landed their troops on the Gallipoli Peninsula. There had been changes in the allied submarine force too. The French boats *Joule*, *Coulomb*, *Bernouilli*, *Topaze*, *Turquoise* and *Mariotte* had arrived in the Aegean in the spring, while the British had received reinforcements from Harwich in the shape of the depot ship HMS *Adamant* and the three 'E' class submarines *E11*, *E14*, and *E15*. These new British submarines, together with the Australian which had arrived earlier were destined for operations in the Sea of Marmara, as were some of the French boats.

The possibility of attack on the fleet off the Dardanelles by the Austrian submarines had always been a consideration for both Carden and de Robeck, and as early as January 1915 Holbrook mentions in a letter that there were many rumours of German submarine deployments to the area. One such was that there were five German boats in Constantinople which had come all the way from Germany by canal (sic) and that their engines and batteries had been put in on arrival. Another contemporary account mentions a report that six German submarines were being transported by rail to Turkey but they had been pilfered of their machinery while in transit in Rumania. These stories have a remarkable likeness to the UB class which by then were building, and tons. In company they left Mudros on 16 April and for nearly three weeks this old submarine kept a fruitless watch off Bodrum during the day, returning to lie alongside the *Gazelle* at night, and then only when conditions were suitable. It was an unprecedented length of time on patrol for this class of submarine whose pre-war limit had been three days, even taking into account the somewhat limited support that the ex-ferry could give the submarine. It was an unconventional patrol for a submarine as Gravener was to write in his report:

> *21 April*
> I observed Karada Island to be uninhabited except for two farms on the NE side and decided to lie off the SE shore of the island so as to be able to carry out a more efficient patrol of Bodrum during daylight. I laid out small moorings 600 yards from the shore in a position so that the lookout could see the Channel between Kos and the Dorian Promontory and between Kos and the mainland to the SE. I lay to these moorings during daylight. Before proceeding to the rendezvous [with *Gazelle*] I steamed into Bodrum harbour and examined it.

> *26 April*
> 9.00 am. I landed with the Coxswain, both armed, and climbed to the top of Karada and examined Bodrum harbour, returning at noon.

Such a landing became a regular occurrence of the *B10*'s patrol off Bodrum, although on one day they were fired on. A search revealed no sign of any enemy landing party, but the next day two local peasants, obviously over excited by the sight of these strangers, came down to the beach and waved a white flag. To make their peace they presented Gravener with a live goat and a large home made cheese, neither suitable gifts for a submarine, and Gravener omits to mention how he dealt with them!

The *B10* sailed again on 10 May, this time with another converted merchant ship, HMS *Hythe*, to patrol in the Doro Channel, returning on the 20th. The *B7* was also out at this time as were the French submarines *Coulomb* and *Bernouilli* in the Steno Pas . While returning to Mudros they sighted the *B6* with her escort, HMS *Carrigan Head*. With all this activity it is unfortunate that they all missed the arrival of the *UB7* at Bodrum on 20 May, though whether Gravener would have been any more fortunate if he had returned to his moorings off Karada Island can only be guessed.

Holbrook's *B11* had been sent to patrol off the entrance to the Gulf of Smyrna from 12 to 20 May, and he came nearest to intercepting the arrival of any of the U-boats. He was there when von Voigt was forced to take the *UB8* in with compass trouble, and actually sighted the German as he steamed in.

10.00 am. Sighted hostile submarine, apparently on motors about 4 miles from me proceeding towards Smyrna, and very close inshore. She looked very much like one of our later 'E' boats with a straight bow and more superstructure forward than aft, and with a conical shaped conning tower. I dived immediately to attack her. At 10.30 I came to the surface and discovered she was under way at full speed on engines, with a large bow wave. On sighting me she dived and I never saw her again.

Holbrook's sighting was the first confirmation that the Germans, or Austrians, had reached the eastern Mediterranean, though in this case he had hopelessly overestimated the size of von Voigt's small boat.

The task of keeping watch on the Dardanelles for any attempt by the German or Turkish warships to sally forth and attack the transports off the beaches of the Peninsula had to be kept up, and a B class submarine was sent daily to Cape Helles for this purpose. It was a boring task, and one of doubtful value should the enemy have decided to emerge, the submarine spending the day at a buoy especially laid for them. The patrol was not finally abandoned until August when two of the class were sent to Alexandria and the remainder to Malta.

The Aegean, where prior to 1914 two early Greek submarines represented the total deployment of this new weapon of war, had now become an international area for submarines The nine British boats were joined by an Australian and eight French ones, while on the other side there were two of the UB class already in Turkey, though perhaps not fully ready for operations after their long voyage from the Adriatic, while Hersing and his *U21* was preparing to leave Cattaro also to join the German naval forces – known as the Mediterranean Division – in Turkish waters.

the most serious threat to be faced by Vice-Admiral de Robeck's Anglo-French force off the Dardanelles. After his traumatic voyage from Germany he wasted no time in Cattaro and sailed again on 20 May. Four days later, south of the Bulgarian port of Dedeagach (now Alexandropolis), he sighted the Russian cruiser *Askold* lying at anchor, apparently a sitting target, but one that Hersing decided to forego so as to save not only his torpedoes but also the element of surprise for bigger and more important targets.

The following day was calm and windless with excellent visibility, and Hersing found three British battleships with numerous small craft off Cape Helles. He took the *U21* towards one of the battleships which was lying at anchor, in fact HMS *Swiftsure*, taking great care that his periscope should not be seen in the glass-like sea. A hospital ship, unaware of the submarine's presence, caused Hersing to go deep as it passed overhead, but despite his care he had been sighted and the great battleship began to manoeuvre on main engines while still at anchor so as to turn towards the threat and present as small a target as possible, at the same time opening fire with her 14 pounders in the general direction of where the periscope had been seen. Although not hit by this fire Hersing later reported that the noise of the shells striking the water nearby was quite noticeable in the submarine. By this time the range was less than 800 yards and he had to abandon the attack as destroyers became very active around him. It was a fortunate escape for the three battleships, but the lesson was not learnt.

A short while later he fired his stern torpedo at another battleship, the *Vengeance*, which was under way. The range was long (1,100 yards) and the torpedo was easily evaded as its track was clearly seen in the calm sea. Again Hersing was able to get away from the area unhindered and a few hours later he found the *Triumph* at anchor, but with her torpedo nets out and a destroyer circling slowly around her. Hersing fired just one torpedo from only 300 yards. There was no doubt as to the result. Despite the nets the great ship was holed and heeled slowly over and in half an hour was gone. The scene was described by an officer onboard the *Swiftsure*:

The unfortunate battleship lay with a heavy list and stricken to death.

Hersing claimed to have been hunted determinedly by the destroyers in the area, and made good his escape only by taking the *U21* under the sinking battleship. Perhaps a melodramatic exaggeration, and certainly risky, but much of the assumed hunt was caused by ships rushing to the battleship's aid and to take off survivors. Even so, *U21* was unmolested leaving the scene and remained dived until after nightfall, by which time they had been dived for 21½ hours.

The following day the *U21* returned to the place where the *Askold* had earlier been seen at anchor, but by then she had gone. His next success came on the 27th when once again with a single torpedo he sank the battleship *Majestic*. And once again the ship had been lying at anchor with torpedo nets in place, relying on them and on the presence of some protective destroyers circling the anchorage. These losses following the sinking of another battleship, the *Goliath*, earlier in May by the Turkish torpedo boat *Muavenet* caused de Robeck to order all the remaining battleships to leave the area except for specific tasks. It left the troops ashore without the comforting presence of the big guns of the fleet, and was a blow at morale. For the cost of three torpedoes, of which one missed, Hersing had given the defenders of Gallipoli a handsome bonus.

He next took the *U21* to the island of Imbros where Kephalo Bay had been turned into an advance base by the British. On the morning of 29 May he tried to get into a position for firing at a battleship which he could see lying in the anchorage. While doing so he became entangled in the net barrage guarding the entrance to the Bay, and it was with some difficulty that Hersing was able to extract the *U21* and abandon the attack. His efforts to free the submarine were not observed, and when he surfaced later that afternoon his crew took an hour to remove bits of broken net which stretched over the submarine. After two more fruitless days he decided to go to Bodrum where he arrived on 1 June.

Hersing allowed his weary crew just one night's rest, and after receiving information about a safe route into the Dardanelles he sailed again the next morning. Despite being caught in the same eddies that were to trouble the British and French submariners on their way to the Sea of Marmara he entered the Dardanelles without other incident and after surfacing was escorted to Constantinople by a Turkish torpedo boat. Both Hersing and later the other German submarine commanders had to take their submarines into the Dardanelles where their own allies were busy making the same waters as hazardous as possible for British and French submarines. A route close in on the European side was marked as unobtrusively as possible with small barrel buoys near the minefields. Additionally of course the German commanders had the advantage, once inside the Straits and safe from British patrols, of being able to proceed on the surface under the protection of the Turkish guns.

By this time the repairs to the *UB8* had been completed and von Voigt was able to sail from Smyrna towards the Dardanelles early on 29 May, leaving the Gulf undetected by any British patrols. After Hersing's earlier successes targets were fewer and it was dusk the following day when he made his first attack, firing just one of his two torpedoes at a large three funnelled ship heading towards Mudros. Voigt claimed a hit abreast the after funnel, but did not see his target sink. Because of the failing light he did not identify his target which in fact was the British merchant ship *Merion*. It was an unfortunate omission as the merchant ship was just one of several which had been rigged with dummy superstructure, funnels and even wooden guns to resemble warships to deceive the enemy as to the whereabouts of the real ship, in this case the battlecruiser HMS *Tiger*. Voigt then took the *UB8* to the north of Mudros into the Gulf of Xeros, down the west coast of the Gallipoli Peninsula before entering the Dardanelles on 2 June.

At this time the *UB7* (*Oberleutnant zur See* Werner) was also at sea. After arriving at the Bodrum base from Pola, on 20 May, Werner topped up with fuel and stores before heading towards Imbros to search for enemy shipping. On the 23rd he found that his main engine was defective, stopping as soon as the clutch was engaged to the propeller, and he was forced to rely on his electric motors, even on the surface, for propulsion and using the main engine only for charging – hardly a satisfactory state of affairs in a war zone. It meant the greatest economy with the battery, at one time involving hoisting a sail, as much to assist the electric motors as perhaps also to give a measure of disguise, and when dived trying to maintain a 'stopped trim'. Werner even experimented with suspending the *UB7* from a large buoyant barrel! After over two days of hard work the engine was repaired and the submarine was able to approach Kephalo Bay hoping to attack some of the ships lying there at anchor. Like the *U21* earlier so the *UB7* too became entangled with the net defences, though less seriously so, and in getting free was sighted by the guard ship. Werner retired safely to seaward and back to Smyrna on the 29th, firing a torpedo, which missed, at a British destroyer on patrol at the entrance to the Gulf.

The *UB7* remained at Smyrna until 12 June for a thorough overhaul of her engines, with German maintenance personnel being sent to the port from Constantinople to help the submarine's own small crew. Werner then took the boat to sea with the intention of attacking any shipping off the Dardanelles. During the morning of 17 June he fired two torpedoes at a merchant ship near Cape Helles, but no explosion followed, Werner blaming his bad luck on the poor weather at the time with rough seas which made the small submarine roll even at a depth of 40 feet. Two days later with the sea by then like a mirror Werner decided to follow the other two submarines and head for Constantinople, which he reached on the 21st.

All three German boats now required considerable time in harbour to make good the many defects and to give the crews some rest. Hersing's *U21* had been at sea for 40 days when she arrived at Constantinople. For the commanding officers and crews of the small UB boats the strain had been even worse though the shorter time at sea far exceeded that expected of this class when they had been designed. Werner, for example, in the *UB7* was the only officer onboard with all that entailed for a submarine commander in war, or peace. Hersing was the first to be ready for sea, but by then it was early July.

The *U21* sailed from the Golden Horn dockyard in Constantinople on 3 July and passed down the Dardanelles the next day sighting a French battleship off the Asiatic coast, but having been set off course by the current Hersing felt it was hopeless to try an attack at this time. Later that day he attacked and sank the French merchant ship *Carthage* (5,600 tons) with one torpedo. The following day off Imbros the *U21* was attacked by some anti-submarine trawlers, one of which had seen Hersing's periscope. As the submarine was leaving the area there was a loud explosion close astern, possibly a mine, putting some controls out of action and breaking lamps and gauge glasses. It was not until Hersing surfaced early the next morning that he discovered that there was also damage to the diving tanks, at which point he decided to return once more. It was the *UB8*'s turn next, sailing on 14 July from Constantinople. During the passage of the Sea of Marmara the German boat was sighted by the British *E7*, but the *E7* was unable to attack. Von Voigt carried out two separate attacks but missed on both occasions. He then noticed a strong smell of chorine gas and found that this was coming from one of his battery tanks which had become flooded in recent rough weather. With this serious defect rectified the *UB8* returned to Constantinople.

Other German submarines were now beginning to appear in the area. The *UB4* had arrived in Pola in June, although the Germans were at that time concerned that the Italian declaration of war against Austria would threaten the railway line to Pola along which their reinforcement submarines travelled. Luckily for them the Italian army failed to break through and the threat never materialised. While carrying out trials off that port she had flown the Austrian ensign as the *U26*, though still with her German commanding officer, *Leutnant* Heino von Heimburg, and crew but with one Austrian liaison officer onboard. It was during this period that von Heimburg sank the Italian armoured cruiser *Amalfi*, justifying the deceit of pretending the submarine was Austrian, since Germany was not then at war with Italy.*

The *UB14* sailed for the Dardanelles on 16 July, and as had been the case with the earlier departures she was towed by an Austrian destroyer to a point well south of Cattaro. He reached Bodrum safely on the 24th after a passage which was far from uneventful: he had decided not to attack an Italian cruiser sighted not long after slipping the tow from the Austrian destroyer; his engine broke down while south of Crete and thereafter was not reliable; finally, he had to complete the final approach to the base with a defective compass. Once again the German maintenance team had to travel from Constantinople to help with repairs.

Two of the new UC class submarines were the next to arrive at Pola, the *UC14* being retained for minelaying in the Adriatic or nearby Mediterranean areas, while the *UC15* was converted into a transport to take much needed supplies to Admiral Souchon's ships at Constantinople. *Leutnant* von Dewitz arrived at Bodrum with the *UC15* on 20 July having suffered from an unreliable motor while on passage, and with an engine that needed an overhaul on arrival. All the war material that she carried, with the exception of four spare torpedoes and some casks of acetone, was unloaded and taken to Constantinople overland. It was a task that required the services of 50 camels between Bodrum and Smyrna where the cargo was transferred to the railway. As for the *UC15* she was bottomed close to the shore with only the top of the conning tower above water, the seaward side of which was painted to blend in with the colour of the shore. When the *UB14* arrived in Bodrum she was able to give some help and charged up the other's batteries and compressed air bottles.

Of the two crippled boats the *UC15* finished refitting and sailed on 9 August for Constantinople, while von Heimburg sailed from Bodrum with the *UB14* on 12 August, passing a fully lit hospital ship that night. The next morning another hospital ship was sighted followed by a large steamer sailing unescorted for Mudros from Egypt. She was the *Royal Edward* carrying about 1400 troops for Gallipoli and one torpedo fired from under a mile hit her stern, three minutes later the after deck was awash and in six the ship had sunk by the stern taking more than half the men onboard with her. Von Heimburg then returned to Bodrum with a defective compass, staying only a few days before sailing again on the 18th.

Meanwhile the *UB8* had sailed from the Dardanelles on 12 August and headed towards the anchorage off Suvla Bay where a number of warships were supporting the recent landings, but because of the defences he found it impossible to attack. His first attack was on a kite balloon ship, HMS *Manica*, but his torpedo fired from 500 yards passed under the shallow draught vessel, and two days later another attack on a similar type of vessel was just as unsuccessful. With his torpedoes

* See Chapter 7.

UB14 proceeding up the Dardanelles escorted by a Turkish torpedo boat in 1915. The submarine is flying Turkish colours but no German colours are visible. (IWM Q.48410)

expended von Voigt returned to Constantinople. Von Heimburg was fortunate to survive his next foray from Bodrum for off the Dardanelles the *UB14* became enmeshed in a steel net off the entrance. He tried going ahead and astern at full speed while working the rudder from one side to the other, going as deep as 150 feet in the process. With parts of the net caught round the propeller there was a danger of damaging the motor and the shaft. Eventually he was free and returned to Bodrum where two days' work was needed to free the propeller from the last of the wires. At sea again on 2 September he fired a torpedo at a troopship – the *Southland* – from 1400 yards on the beam, though the ship later reached Mudros. On the 4th he had reached safety at Chanak, and while there he heard that a British submarine had been caught in the net at Nagara. It was the *E7* and though her command-ing officer tried all the same tactics that von Heimburg himself had tried only a few days earlier he was unable to free the boat from the steel embrace. The end came after von Heimburg and a seaman from the *UB14* went to the scene and lowered a charge down to the submarine and exploded it at 130 feet. Although it did not fatally damage the British boat it convinced her commanding officer that the next one might easily do so, and he surfaced to allow his crew to escape before scuttling the submarine.

At Pola the *UC13* was completed and fitted out to take 30 tons of urgently needed arms and munitions to Turkey, the boat sailing on 17 August under the command of *Leutnant* Kirchner. After an uneventful passage they arrived at Bodrum nine days later. Off the entrance to the Bay a small sailing vessel was sighted flying Turkish colours, but on investigation proved to be Italian. Not wishing to compromise the secrecy of the base she was sunk rather than captured and her crew taken to Smyrna. From Bodrum the *UC13* went on to Constantinople, again enjoying an event free passage.

The *U21* lay in Constantinople until 28 August for the damage to her on her last patrol to be repaired. Passing through the Sea of Marmara he was warned to be on the lookout for any British submarines, and it must have been all the more annoying to him to be fired on by a Turkish shore battery. Once out of the Dardanelles he too sought out the shipping off Suvla Bay, but he too was thwarted by the net barrage and patrols, while an attack on a warship in the Gulf of Xeros was avoided. A visit to the Gulf of Salonika was also unrewarding and so he once again went back to the area off Mudros, where on 9 September he fired at long range just after dusk at a large four funnelled steamer but missed. Finding his return blocked by the same net defences that had nearly accounted for the *UB14* he made for Cattaro where he arrived on the 21st. From there the *U21* went on to Pola where she was taken in hand by the dockyard for a thorough refit. It was the last patrol into the Aegean for some time by one of the boats based on Constantinople.

The importance of the Mediterranean and the Suez Canal to British imports and to the war economies of both France and Italy was well known to the German Naval Staff in Berlin, the *Admiralstab*. In July with the *U21* undergoing repair in Constantinople and likely to be out of action for some weeks it was decided to send two more large U-boats to the area from Germany. It was considered that while the small UB boats already in Constantinople were hardly suitable for operations against shipping other than around the Dardanelles they would be better used in the Black Sea, while others from Pola or Cattaro could cover the Adriatic and Ionian Sea. The rest of the Mediterranean could then be covered by the larger U-boats or the improved UB type expected into service later in 1915. The *Admiralstab* decided to send the *U34* (*Kapitänleutnant* C Rücker) and *U35* (*Kapitänleutnant* W Kophamel) directly to Cattaro as part of the newly formed 'German U-boat Half Flotilla, Pola', and thus they did not come under the command of Admiral Souchon in Constantinople.

These two boats were similar to the *U21* but had a larger range which obviated the need for any attempts to refuel them on their passage out to the Mediterranean. They had one big advantage over the *U21* being fitted with two 88mm guns, one forward and the other aft of the conning tower though retaining the same torpedo armament of 4 x 50 cm torpedo tubes with six torpedoes. They finally sailed from Heligoland on 4 August, and though they sailed independently they

Members of the crew of U35 unloading spent cartridge cases at Cattaro in April 1917. (IWM Q.53011)

arrived at Cattaro within hours of each other on the 23rd. They had passed through the Straits of Gibraltar undetected and it was not until the end of the month that the Admiralty were able to inform the Senior Naval Officer at Gibraltar that they had arrived. However, they were also able to inform him that two more submarines were expected to pass through the Straits about 6 September.

As a result of the British landings at Suvla Bay in early August there were fresh pleas for even more German submarines to be sent out, and as a consequence the *U39* (*Kapitänleutnant* W Forstmann) and the U33 (*Kapitänleutnant* K Gansser) were prepared for deployment to the Mediterranean, sailing on the 27th and 29th of the month respectively. British intelligence of the U-boats' movements was quite accurate, for on 8 September the old torpedo boat HMS *TB91* sighted a U-boat, the *U39*, just to the east of the Straits which dived before an attack could be made. The following day this submarine sank three ships, the French *L'Aude*, the British *Cornubia* and finally the French *Ville de Mostaganem*, a total of nearly 7,000 tons. Early the next morning the British *Antilochus* was attacked off Algiers but drove off the submarine with her gun. The *U39* then proceeded direct to the Austrian base at Cattaro arriving on the 15th.

The *U33* left a trail of sunken ships stretching from the Faroes-Hebrides gap to the Spanish coast. Yet after passing through the Straits, where she was engaged unsuccessfully by another of the old torpedo boats on patrol, Gansser made no more attacks before reaching Cattaro on the 16 September.

The first of the new arrivals to go on patrol was the *U35*, Kophamel being ordered to sail on 31 August for operations in the southern Aegean. In three weeks he sank three ships, in all about 10,600 tons of shipping. The most important of these was undoubtedly the troopship *Ramazan* which was shelled and sunk on 19 September while carrying Indian troops to Mudros with the loss of about 300 soldiers. Another of Kophamel's victims was the French *Ravitailleur*, ex-Austrian *Gradac*, which was stopped and sunk by gunfire south of Crete, the lifeboats then being towed towards the island. Despite his apparent lack of success Kophamel brought back a lot of information with him, his report includes:

> There is no enemy patrol service in the Aegean Sea or on the routes leading there. From the entries in the logs of the British and French transports sunk conclusions could be drawn as to the number and type of warship assembled at Mudros, and they contained particulars of the routes for the transports in the Mediterranean.

The *U34* sailed the day after her sister also with orders to operate in the southern Aegean, returning on 22 September. Rücker's first success was stopping the *Natal Transport* after a chase west of Crete and then sinking her with a torpedo. Four days later off Crete he torpedoed and sank the small French armed merchant cruiser *Indien* at anchor off Rhodes. Although making one other torpedo attack on the way back to Cattaro Rücker had no further success.

The period from the end of September until the middle of October provided the Entente with a foretaste of the problems to come, the action beginning of 28 September when the *U39*, out for the first time from Cattaro, sank an oiler in the Channel between the north east of Crete and the Greek mainland, and then another ship on each of the following two days, including the Italian *Cirene* (3,236 tons) which was sunk by gunfire. Then south of Crete on 2 October another ship was sunk, while a liner, which had just picked up survivors from the other vessel, was stopped and then allowed to proceed. Forstmann then began to take the *U39* further east sinking another three ships, and then attacking the British armed transport *Ajax* but was driven off by French destroyers which had been called to assist. Before returning to Cattaro on 12 October the *U39* sank another supply ship off the Montenegran coast.

When the *U39* moved off to the south of Crete her place between Crete and the mainland was taken by Gansser in *U33*. After passing through the Otranto Strait and while still in the Ionian Sea he stopped the small Italian sailing ship *Tobia*, and then sank her with an explosive charge. On 1 October Gansser sank a French collier returning empty from the Dardanelles, and then off Cape Matapan unsuccessfully chased the large White Star liner *Olympic* (46,359 tons), with 5,500 troops aboard, which had originally stopped to pick up survivors from the French ship. The next day saw the sinking of a French supply ship from

Inside the torpedo compartment on a German U-boat. Daily maintenace routine is in progress on the left hand torpedo (IWM Q.50047)

the Dardanelles and then the liner Arabian which was carrying ammunition for the troops which were to land at Salonika. Despite extra patrol vessels being sent to the area by de Robeck the *U33*'s successes continued on the 3rd, 4th and 5th of the month. The following day having moved towards Malta when two more empty colliers were sunk as was the Greek *Demetrios Dandiolos* with a cargo of rice for London. On the 7th the French *Amiral Hamelin* was unable to save herself with her gun and was also sunk with heavy loss of life. Gansser returned to Cattaro on 9 October, and the two submarines had between them sunk 18 ships.

The loss of the *Arabian* and the chase given to the *Olympic* together with the other losses emphasised the urgent need for more anti-submarine patrols in the area to the south of Greece and in the Aegean and a flotilla of French destroyers had to be sent from the Adriatic and additional trawlers or drifters were planned for that area. The British submarine *H2* was also sent to the Aegean together with the minesweeper HMS *Clacton*, a converted steamer and now disguised as a tramp with her guns hidden, while the submarine patrolled nearby submerged.

It was then again the turn of the *U35* whose patrol was to last until 12 November. Her first victim was another Italian vessel the steamer *Scilla* which was sunk off one of the islands in the Sporades. Kophamel then went north to the Gulf of Salonika where he thought there would be plenty of shipping supplying the new Anglo-French expeditionary force, but found and sank only the British *Marquette*, loss of life being small among the thousand troops onboard. From there he went across to the Gulf of Xeros where at the signal station known as 'Hersingstand' he received orders to go to Bodrum.

Mention has been made of the new Anglo-French expedition at Salonika. It had come about following Bulgaria's General Mobilisation in late September 1915, in turn prompted by the lack of success of the Gallipoli campaign. With Bulgaria ready for war the Austrian and German armies renewed their offensive against Serbia, the Bulgars joining in to complete the rout and resulting in Serbia being completely overrun while the remnants of her army were evacuated to Italy through Albania. The Greeks evaded their own responsibility to assist Serbia since the Serbs, being pre-occupied with the Austrians, were unable to field the requisite sized force of 150,000 men against the Bulgars required by treaty. One way round the impasse was thought to be the sending of a combined French and British force to Salonika and thence up through Macedonia to help the Serbs, thereby assuming the responsibility for the force against Bulgaria and making the Greeks keep to their obligation. At the invitation of the pro-Allied Prime Minister Eleutherios Venizelos the first allied troops landed at Salonika on 5 October. But the move was not popular with King Constantine and his supporters who at the best wanted Greece to remain neutral and at worst were pro-German, and Venizelos was forced to resign. Nevertheless the allied troops remained in Salonika, a major maritime commitment to keep them supplied, while they were unable to help the Serbian army and remained fearful of attack from the Greeks until 1917. In fact they did little to influence the war until 1918. Bulgaria invaded Serbia on 11 October to complete the defeat of that country, while Britain declared war on Bulgaria on 15 October and France the next day.

Although the British and French fleets were fully committed in supplying the troops in Gallipoli there was the new worry that the Greeks might enter the war on the side of the Central Powers and threaten the troops already ashore at Salonika. There were even fears that the two Greek submarines might be ceded or sold to the Germans for use against the British and French ships. To cover these eventualities a fleet was formed under Vice-Admiral Le Bris, the French themselves providing four battleships, two armoured cruisers and destroyers, and two submarines, while three battleships were detached from the Grand Fleet and sent to the Mediterranean. In the event an ultimatum was sent to the Greek Government on 23 November, with the intention that if the reply was unfavourable or if there were any hostile acts against the allied troops or ships then there would be offensive action. However, the Note was accepted by the Greeks and the crisis was over.

Already a number of Italian vessels had been sunk by the German U-boats although officially the two countries were not at war, the worst case being the sinking of the *Amalfi*, though attacks against merchant ships were to cause more international concern. As long as the submarine remained dived the Germans could easily maintain the fiction that it was not one of their submarines but an Austrian one that had fired the torpedoes. In the case of surface attacks it was more difficult and the German U-boats had to fly the Austrian ensign while snaking their attacks. The Austrians were unwilling partners in this deception, and from time to time tried to restrain their ally from the worst of excesses, but even so the German boats were entered into the Austrian Navy List and even given a Austrian number. It was to remain a matter of international concern and of friction between the two allies until the declaration of war between Italy and Germany made further use of the ruse unnecessary.

As early as May 1915 there were signs that the Senussi living in the newly acquired Italian North African colonies of Tripolitania and Cyrenaica were being subjected to pressure from the Turks to rebel, and to cause trouble for the British in neighbouring Egypt. In August the Italians had warned the British that they had information that there would be attempts to smuggle arms to the dissidents, and sought British help in preventing this. The British Commander-in-Chief in that area, Vice-Admiral R H Peirse, who was also Commander-in-Chief East Indies Station and whose area had been enlarged to take in the Egyptian coast, also had information that Turkish officers and supplies were to be landed, possibly from Greek steamers or perhaps submarines. There were few ships that could be spared for any patrol along this stretch of coast, and no reinforcements could be expected to be sent out from Home Waters for the task. Admiral de Robeck could spare two of his old submarines and the *B6* (Lieutenant C G MacArthur) and *B11* (Lieutenant N Holbrook) were sent from Mudros to Alexandria where they arrived on 13 August. They sailed the next day in company with the armed boarding steamer *Heroic* acting as a sort of depot ship.

On 16 August the two submarines had anchored at 8.0 am about 700 yards offshore not far from Cape Lukka, the *Heroic* being out of sight further to seaward. Not long afterwards a party of Arabs with some officers in European uniform were seen on the shore with a flag of truce. Holbrook, the senior of two commanding officers, pulled towards the shore in the small boat carried by the submarine. From a short way out he stopped and tried to parley with one of the party who asked if he were English and then invited him to go ashore. However, Holbrook became suspicious and suspected the man to be armed so began to return to the submarine. When Holbrook was nearly back to the submarines the group ashore opened fire sinking the boat but leaving Holbrook, at that stage unscathed, to swim the remaining distance. The submarines headed seawards at speed with their casings and bridge screens riddled with bullets. No one was hurt on the *B11* except for Holbrook himself who was hit on the face from a ricochet, but on the *B6* it was a different story. The Chief ERA was hit in the chest, killed instantly and fell overboard, while the other ERA was hit in the back and badly wounded, and the Coxswain slightly so. The submarines met with the *Heroic* to whom the wounded were transferred before the *B6*

was sent back to Alexandria under the command of the First Lieutenant, Lieutenant Rendel, while MacArthur took over the *B11* from the wounded Holbrook.

The situation could have become much more serious but for the tactful negotiations by Lieutenant Colonel C L Snow of the Egyptian Coastguard and the matter was closed with the acceptance of the Senussi's apologies. They claimed that they were not aware that the two submarines were British and assumed them to be Italian, the Arabs being hostile to them, while the British submarines had strayed westward of the frontier at Sollum and were in fact off Italian coast!

The *U35* on her patrol in the northern Aegean had called in at the signal station on the Gulf of Xeros and been ordered to Bodrum. There she picked up ten Turkish officers and supplies for the Senussi. Kophamel also had to escort two sailing vessels, carrying arms, supplies and 150 Turkish soldiers towards the North African coast, taking them in tow if they became becalmed On 3 November, while south of Crete he sank the *Woolwich* (2,936 tons) by gunfire, arriving in Bardia the next day after an uncomfortable passage with the submarine hot and overcrowded.

Kophamel wasted no time in Bardia and the next day was off Sollum where he sank the armed boarding steamer *Tara* with a torpedo, all the crew being towed in their boats back to Bardia where they were handed over to the newly arrived Turks as prisoners of war, who in turn handed them over to the Senussi. He then returned to Sollum where

Kapitänleutnant *Lothar von Arnauld de la Perière (centre) and the crew of* U35. *de la Perière was the highest scoring submarine captain of the First World War with 194 ships totalling 453,716 tons to his credit.* (IWM Q.24034)

he found the Egyptian Coastguard cutters *Abbas* and *Nurelbahr*, sinking the former by gunfire and damaging the other.

For the crew of the *Tara* their ordeal had hardly begun. The Senussi were to receive more aid from the Germans and Turks, brought to them by submarine, and it was not until 26 February 1916 that they were decisively defeated in a battle near Sidi Barani, and Sollum which had been evacuated in November was re-occupied on 15 March. It was then learnt that the survivors of the *Tara* were being held 120 miles to the west at Bir Hacheim. They were finally rescued after an amazing 14 hour dash across the unmapped desert by a convoy of armoured cars and ambulances of the Duke of Westminster's Armoured Car Squadron – a unit originally formed in 1914 by the Royal Navy Air Service (RNAS) to protect their airfields in France and Belgium, but which had been transferred to the army in early 1915 and moved to North Africa. The half starved survivors were taken to Sollum, four had died during their captivity.

Her task in North Africa complete the *U35* then headed towards Crete, operating to the south of that island before returning to Cattaro, having fired his last torpedo, arriving after 31 days at sea. Soon after his return Kophamel was promoted and left the *U35* to take command of the flotilla. He was relieved by *Kapitänleutnant* Lothar von Arnauld de la Perière.

By this time the *Admiralstab* had approved a sixth large U-boat being sent to the Mediterranean, hoping that this would ensure that at least two could always be kept at sea. The *U38*, *Kapitänleutnant* Max Valentiner, was directed to sail for the Mediterranean and left Heligoland on 20 October. The submarine had a rough passage through the Atlantic and reached the Straits of Gibraltar on 3 November. There she met with the steamer *Woodfield* during the afternoon not far from Gibraltar itself. The British ship tried to escape and fought back with its gun which unluckily was soon put out of action, at which stage the Master stopped and abandoned. A boarding party from the submarine managed to find the secret routing instructions for merchant ships which had not been destroyed and these were taken back to the submarine, after which the ship was hit by gunfire and helped to the bottom by a torpedo. Another ship did manage to escape the submarine, the *Mercian*. One of the first shells from the submarine destroyed the ship's radio and it was only her superior speed which enabled her to outrun the German and the providential arrival of a patrol boat that saved the British ship. Yet only a few hours later the Japanese *Yasukuni Maru* was stopped and sunk by gunfire.

The next day Valentiner stopped and sank another four ships, one of them being Italian, and another the *Calvados*. The latter was carrying Senegalese troops to France and there was heavy loss of life. By the 5th the *U38* was off Algiers, where he sunk two more vessels, while a third which fought back with a heavier gun than the U-boat's was allowed to proceed. A hospital ship which stopped to pick up some survivors was stopped and searched before she too was allowed to go on her way. Working his way eastwards Valentiner sank four more ships on the 6th,

Kapitänleutnant *Max Valentiner, commanding officer of* U38 *and Germany's third ranking submarine 'ace'. Valentiner sank 141 ships totalling 299,326 tons.* (U-Boot Archiv)

while her bag on the next day consisted of the French *France III* and the Italian *Ancona*. The last victim was another Italian vessel which was sunk on the 9th east of Sicily. Then, despite the number of trawlers patrolling in groups, the *U38* passed safely through the Straits of Otranto and reached Cattaro on 11 November.

It was the sinking of the *Ancona* that caused the greatest outcry. This passenger liner of over 8,000 tons was met in misty conditions and ordered to stop after a round had been fired from the gun. The Italian at first tried to outrun the submarine but was unable to do so before she was stopped after being hit by several rounds and began to abandon ship. Before this was complete Valentiner fired one of his bow tubes which completed the destruction of the liner. Over 200 lives were lost some of whom were American. Flying the Austrian ensign during this attack it was the Austrians that had to pick up the diplomatic protests that ensued. Valentiner's excuse was that he thought the ship to be a troopship and that it was 45 minutes after the order to abandon had been given that he fired the torpedo. By that time there was smoke on the horizon which he took to be the possible approach of a patrol, summoned by radio from the *Ancona*. He also tried to put the blame on the Italian crew for failing to help the passengers in their eagerness to save themselves.

For the remainder of the year these large U-boats carried out a succession of patrols from Cattaro. Before the *U35* had returned the *U34* left on 3 November returning three weeks later, the *U33* sailed on 15 November, again for three weeks, and the *U39* on 26 November returning to Cattaro on 19 December. It was then the turn of Valentiner to take the *U38* out on 9 December not returning until after the New Year, while the *U34* sailed again just before Christmas. These U-boats between them had sunk 79 ships, excluding successes against warships, totalling 290,471 tons during the last three months of 1915. It is interesting to note that in the same period the total tonnage sunk in all theatres was 358,492 tons, so that the Mediterranean U-boats accounted for some 81% of this total, reflecting not only the vulnerability of shipping in the Mediterranean due to shortage of escorts and patrols but also the importance of the area to the Allies with their sea routes to the east and the need to supply the troops in both Gallipoli and Salonika.

Gansser's patrol in the *U33* led to what became a renowned incident when on 4 December he stopped the Greek steamer *Spetse*. The ship itself was released to continue its voyage but two British army officers onboard were detained in the U-boat, Lieutenant Colonel H D Napier the Military Attaché in Athens and Captain S Wilson who was not only a King's messenger but also a Member of Parliament. Both officers had attempted to throw overboard the papers they were carrying but most were recovered by the U-boat's crew to cause severe embarrassment because of the nature of the personal comments about prominent Greeks in some of the letters. More controversially, Gansser had been flying the Austrian flag when the *Spetse* had been stopped and both Napier and Wilson knew this. Although held in an Austrian prison it was knowledge that delayed their repatriation for many months.

It was during the *U38*'s patrol in December that Valentiner sank the P & O liner *Persia* (8,000 tons) with the loss of over 300 lives, including two Americans. The attack by torpedo had been carried out while still submerged, and without warning, so that there was at the time some doubt as the identity, and even nationality, of the attacker. Again, the Americans protested while blandly the Germans, Austrians and even the

Turks denied responsibility. For his part Valentiner claimed that the *Persia* had been armed, which she was, and was therefore a legitimate target.

While stressing the importance of the success achieved by the larger U-boats the work of the smaller types must not be overlooked. The German UB types had been sent to Admiral Souchon, while some of the UC boats had been sent to Asia Minor with supplies for the Turkish armies and essential stores for the German ships at Constantinople. For this task the bow section originally consisting of the mining chutes was rebuilt to take the cargo. By the end of 1915 following the collapse of Serbia the route to Turkey via the River Danube had been opened up and there was no longer a requirement for the boats to be used in this fashion.

The first of the submarines to be reconverted to the mining role was the *UC14* (*Leutnant* C Bauer), the work being undertaken in Pola during October. Between the end of November and the New Year the submarine carried out four minelaying operations, three off Valona and the other off Brindisi. By the end of the year the mines had accounted for an Italian transport and the destroyer Intrepido, both off Valona.

The *UC12* (*Kapitänleutnant* Palis) however was required to remain as a transport to continue to carry supplies to the Senussi, and left Cattaro

A rendezvous in the Mediterranean between U33 and an unidentified UB type submarine. Note the difference in size between the two craft. The British officer on the casing of U33 is Captain S Wilson, a King's Messenger captured together with his valuable papers. (IWM Q.54407)

U35 *sinking the steamer* Parkgate *by gunfire.* (Q.24072)

for this purpose on 9 December in company with the *U38* which was to tow the smaller boat whenever possible and to give any assistance possible. The larger submarine alone carrying personnel, rifles, ammunition and 6 tons of other stores plus a complete radio station and money. The presence of patrols in the Straits of Otranto caused the two boats to part company and as the *UC12* did not get to the rendezvous to the south in time Valentiner did not wait for his consort and headed on for Bardia which he reached on the 14th and landed his cargo without interference. He remained off the coast for four more days to render any support he could to the Senussi's campaign but without any chance of taking any action, so left to continue to harass shipping in the Western Mediterranean.

Meanwhile the *UC12*, unable to meet up with the *U38* continued south alone and on the 13th met with Forstmann in the *U39* who took her in tow. Again the cargo was safely unloaded in Bardia and the small submarine returned across the Mediterranean unaided reaching Cattaro on the 23 December. From there she went to Pola to be converted back to her minelaying role, although the demand for supplies to be sent to the Senussi was to continue through 1916 much to the concern of the newly promoted Kophamel.

CHAPTER SIX

The Sea of Marmara

Submarine operations in the Sea of Marmara during 1915 and the first few days of 1916 were, with minor exceptions, exclusive to the Entente, that is the British, Australians and French. The operations were originally conceived only as an attempt to carry the war passed the Dardanelles as had been planned for the surface fleet, but became part of the bigger campaign waged for control of the Gallipoli Peninsula, and as such were in later years described by Winston Churchill as the finest example of submarine warfare in the whole of the war. Covering eight months the operations involved eight British, one Australian and four French submarines during which seven boats were lost. From first to last there were few days when there was not at least one allied submarine roaming the Sea of Marmara.

The first to really believe that submarines could operate in the Sea of Marmara, as opposed to merely making a sortie up the Straits to attack any shipping that might be met, as Holbrook had done, was Lieutenant Commander Stoker who commanded the Australian *AE2*. He was convinced that his new submarine with its greatly enhanced battery capacity over that of Holbrook's *B11* could make a successful submerged passage up the Straits. Yet the idea was not new. As early as 1909 Russian plans in the event of war with Turkey envisaged that submarines would be used not only off the Bosporus but also in the Strait itself around the Golden Horn and in the Sea of Marmara, though it was not apparent just how the Russian boats were expected to reach their objective and return through the Bosporus which was even more treacherous to navigation than the Dardanelles, though shorter in distance. In the event they did not even attempt this. The Dardanelles is some 35 miles long. At its entrance between Cape Helles and the Asiatic town of Kum Kale it is some 2½ miles wide, broadens out to about 5 miles before narrowing again to less than a mile. Here, at what are known as the Narrows, the Dardanelles turn sharply till they are running almost due North being bordered on both sides by high ground and steep cliffs. The Narrows extend for some 4 miles to Nagara Point on the Asiatic shore, after which the Straits widen again to some two to three miles turning sharply till they run in a north-easterly direction once more towards the town of Gallipoli where they join the Sea of Marmara. In general the current in the Dardanelles runs from the Black Sea to the Aegean at a speed in excess of 1½ knots, though as

Holbrook found out there are in addition many fierce eddies. What was not generally known at the time was that there is also a sub-surface counter current which flows towards the Sea of Marmara.

Ever since his arrival from Australia Stoker had given great thought to the problem of taking his submarine through the Dardanelles to the Sea of Marmara and there making life uncomfortable for the Turks. Finally he wrote to the Admiral giving all the facts and proposing that the *AE2* be allowed to attempt the feat, adding that he was certain that this could be done provided 'the greatest care was taken in navigation'. Hardly was the ink dry when the *AE2* ran aground when entering Mudros harbour on a dark night when one of the navigation beacons had been extinguished. As a result the submarine was sent to Malta for repairs, and though Stoker himself was hardly popular with the Admiral as a result of this mishap his plan appealed to Commodore Roger Keyes who was then Chief of Staff. The more so as three more submarines, HMS *E11*, *E14* and *E15*, were at that time on their way out from Harwich, their commanding officers all veterans of the submarine war in the Heligoland Bight and well known to Keyes.

Lieutenant Commander T S Brodie was quite convinced that the passage of the Dardanelles was something that he could undertake successfully, and consequently his *E15* was selected for the first attempt to reach the Marmara. After a hurried period of maintenance she sailed on the night of 16 April. Sailing with the *E15* was newly commissioned Lieutenant C S Palmer, RNVR, who until the outbreak of war had been the Vice-Consul at Chanak, and now was aboard the submarine to give Brodie the help of his local knowledge. It was planned that after daylight seaplanes from the Royal Naval Air Service would overfly the Dardanelles and observe the submarine's progress. Because of this much of what subsequently happened was soon known by Keyes and the other submariners at Mudros.

Early next morning in the grip of a fierce eddy current the *E15* ran ashore on Kephez Point under the guns of Fort Dardanos and was hit several times by shore batteries before the crew surrendered. Mercifully casualties were light, though the luckless Brodie was killed by a shell as he was climbing out of the conning tower hatch. There the submarine remained like a stranded whale, but a worry to the fleet that the Turks might be able to salvage her and bring her into use against her former sisters. The *B6* was sent in to try and torpedo her, but fired only one torpedo before she too was nearly put ashore by the current, and this missed. The destroyers *Grampus* and *Scorpion* also failed in their attempt to torpedo the submarine, as did Holbrook in the *B11*, bombardment by battleships and from the air were equally ineffective. It was left to two picket boats, specially converted to carry two torpedoes each, to ensure that she would never fly the Turkish ensign, a fact confirmed when the *B6* once again entered Kephez Bay to inspect the wreck.

It was an inauspicious beginning, but not one to daunt Keyes and the remaining commanding officers. The *AE2* had by then returned from Malta and on 23 April when Stoker reported inboard the flagship

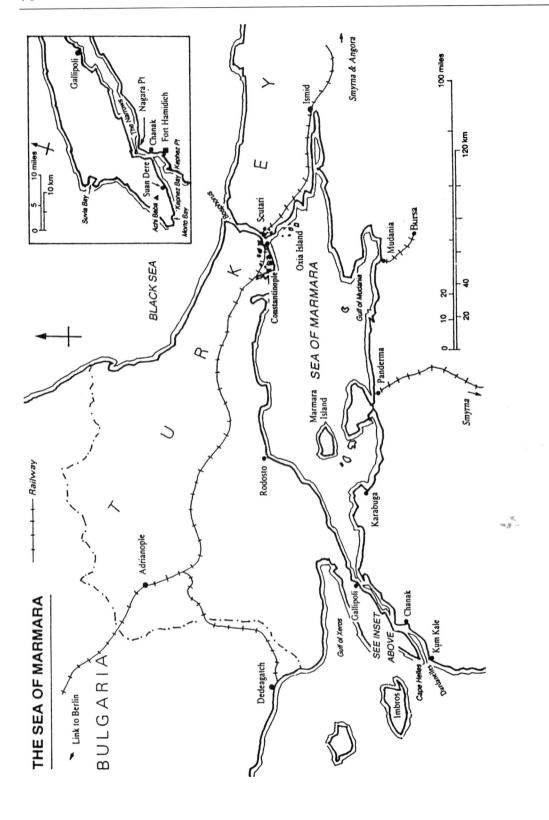

THE SEA OF MARMARA

he was told by Keyes that if he still believed that he could take his boat through to the Sea of Marmara then he would be permitted to try. At the first attempt the *AE2* reached the area of Kephez Bay when it was found that the drive shaft to the forward hydroplanes had broken, and unable to control her depth when dived, Stoker was forced to return. With repairs made Stoker was able to report that he was ready to try again. He left in the early hours of 25 April, a day that saw the landings on the Gallipoli Peninsula and also the day, as has been related, when Hersing left Germany in the *U21* for operations in the Mediterranean. At a depth of 70 feet the *AE2* passed through the Turkish minefields beyond Kephez, their mooring wires making an eerie scraping sound as the submarine's hull brushed passed. Coming shallow to check his position Stoker found that his periscope was all too easily seen in the calm sea and that the Turkish gunners were wide awake and not slow to open fire, though to his surprise Stoker found that he made faster progress than he had expected. He even took the opportunity of firing one of his precious torpedoes at a ship which he thought was laying mines and claimed a hit, then narrowly avoided being rammed by a destroyer on patrol before going aground, briefly, right under the guns of the fort guarding the Narrows. The remainder of the passage passed without incident and by evening the Australian submarine was lying on the surface in the Sea of Marmara recharging

Turkish officers inspect the shattered hull of E15 after she had gone aground and been abandoned in the Dardanelles on 17 April 1915.

the batteries. From there Stoker sent a short signal to de Robeck informing him of his success.

For the next five days Stoker roamed the Sea of Marmara causing a certain amount of confusion but without specific success. Then, he had a surprise meeting with another submarine. As soon as Stoker's signal was received announcing that he had successfully reached the Sea of Marmara Keyes made arrangements for him to be joined by a second submarine. HMS *E14* (Lieutenant Commander E C Boyle) was chosen and she sailed from Mudros in the early morning of 27 April.

Boyle's plan was to stay on the surface for as long as possible, but at 4 o'clock the submarine was illuminated by the searchlights by Suan Dere and the guns opened fire as Boyle took the submarine to 90 feet to pass under the minefields. Boyle's own report of events is typically laconic and makes the subsequent hours seem almost mundane.

> Rose to 22 feet [periscope depth] 1 mile south of Kilid Bahr [opposite Chanak] and at 5.15 am passed Chanak with all the forts firing at me. There was a lot of small ships and steamboats patrolling and I saw one torpedo boat of the *Berki Satvet* class [760 tons] at which I fired a torpedo and a range of about 1600 yards. I just had time to see a large column of water as high as the mast rise from her quarter where she was presumably hit, when I had to go deep again. Some men in small steam boat were leaning over trying to catch hold of the top of my periscope.

The latter incident says something for Boyle's periscope drill, but more importantly it demonstrates the almost total lack of any method of dealing with a submerged submarine at this time. It could be rammed or, if sufficient showed, then there was something to shoot at, but the depth charge was still in the future, though the Russians had been toying with such a device in the years before the war but even then they had none in service.

For Boyle and the *E14* the remainder of the passage was incident free and five hours later he was off the town of Gallipoli at the neck of the peninsula and was able to alter course to the eastwards into the wider spaces of the Sea of Marmara. There were several sailing ships and small steam boats in sight and Boyle decided it was more prudent to remain dived until late afternoon when the *E14* surfaced and the crew were able to get fresh air again while the batteries received a much needed charge. It was after they had surfaced that the *AE2* was spotted and Boyle closed to exchange news and arrange a meeting for the following evening.

Stoker had intended to move elsewhere in the Marmara but changed his plans so as to keep his appointment with Boyle, which was unfortunate. The Turkish torpedo boat *Sultan Hissar* was returning to Constantinople when she sighted a submarine on the surface, and altered course to close. At that moment the submarine dived, but something went wrong with the boat's trim for she porpoised with large bow

E14 at Mudros, about to sail on her first patrol in the Sea of Marmara, commanded by Lieutenant Commander E C Boyle, RN. E14 spent twenty-two days in the Marmara. (IWM Q.13394)

up or down angles. The *Sultan Hissar* rapidly closed the range firing accurately with her small gun and soon began to score hits. With water beginning to pour into the boat through the holes in the hull the *AE2* surfaced for the last time, just long enough for all her crew to swim clear before she sank to the bottom for the last time. After the war Stoker himself was to recall that sad moment as his command slowly sunk:

> The water was about two feet from the top of the conning tower, and only a small portion of the stern was out of water where there were half a dozen of the crew, the remainder being already in the water. Curious incidents impress one at such times and as those last six men took to the water the neat dive of one of the engine-room ratings will remain pictured in my mind for ever. Perhaps a minute passed, and then, slowly and gracefully, like the lady she was, without sound or sigh, without causing a ripple or eddy, the *AE2* slid away.

Among the survivors was Able Seaman Albert Knaggs, an ex Royal Navy man who had transferred to the Royal Australian Navy while the *AE2* was building. His diary of the events that followed survived the war though Knaggs himself was to die in a Turkish PoW camp in October 1916.

> Then the torpedo boat lowered a boat to take us off in which there was a German officer, but he could only take five hands so we had to swim for it. When we got aboard we saw that the torpedo tubes

were empty and a German sailor who could speak English told us that they had been fired at us, but missed. Aboard the torpedo boat the officers were kept in a dark cabin while we were forward in a mess deck. While our clothes were being dried on deck the torpedo boat proceeded to Gallipoli and made fast alongside a hospital ship, where we were interviewed by General Liman von Sanders who is in command on the Peninsula. At 8.00 pm the torpedo boat proceeded to Constantinople where we arrived next morning. Before we left the ship we were supplied with soldier suits, overcoats, slippers and red fezzes to march through the streets to prison. The officers rode in a carriage.

On the same day that the *AE2* was lost the French *Bernouilli* (*Lieutenant de Vaisseau* Defforges) was sailed to attack any Turkish shipping to found in the Dardanelles between the Narrows at Nagara and Chanak. However, the *Bernouilli* found the current too much to cope with and was forced to return to the Aegean without having seen any targets to attack, or indeed having been sighted by the Turks. The following day her sister submarine, the *Joule* (*Lieutenant de Vaisseau* A du Petit-Thouars) left to join Boyle in the Sea of Marmara. Within hours she had been lost having hit one of the mines off Kephez. There were no survivors, all that was left was part of one of her torpedoes which floated down on the current to be picked up by a patrolling destroyer.

Boyle remained in the Marmara until all his torpedoes were expended, returning to Mudros on 18 May after 22 days at sea. Even before meeting with Stoker and the Australian submarine Boyle had found that life in the Sea of Marmara was to be far from dull, for while there appeared to be many sailing and steam craft at sea, there was the constant worry of meeting a Turkish warship. With most of the possible targets only small in size and hardly worth one of the limited number of torpedoes, yet the *E14* suffered from a serious defect for this sort of patrol – she had no gun, and to stop and sink any of these small craft meant surfacing before putting a boarding party across to scuttle the victim.

On 29 April, before he was to meet the *AE2*, Boyle was off the port of Gallipoli where there seemed to be a good chance of meeting Turkish shipping using the port as a supply base for the front. Soon after midday four small torpedo boats were seen leaving harbour but Boyle was not in a position to attack them, then soon afterwards more smoke was seen which turned out to be three more torpedo boats escorting what Boyle took to be two transports. In glassy calm conditions it was perhaps inevitable that the submarine's periscope should have been sighted as Boyle manoeuvred to fire at one of the transports. The Turkish warships sped towards the submarine hoping either to ram or to hit with a shell fired from their forward guns. Boyle fired one torpedo at longish range just before going deep away from the rapidly approaching bow of one of the escorts. The submariners were rewarded by hearing a distant thud, and returning to periscope depth some 30 minutes later Boyle could see one transport and two torpedo boats heading away from the area, while the other transport with a torpedo boat in close company headed for the shore with a thick column of yellow smoke coming from her.

May Day proved to be a busy day with Boyle determined to get one of the patrolling craft which were frustrating him at every turn. During the morning he fired a torpedo at a small gunboat which he thought might be fitted out as a minelayer. It sank in less than a minute. Another torpedo fired at another gunboat failed to run straight and in consequence the *E14* in turn became the target for some while. A third torpedo was easily seen in the calm sea and as easily avoided. Later in the afternoon with no Turkish warships in the area a tramp steamer which was headed towards Gallipoli was turned round by firing rifle shots across the bows!

Another big success for Boyle was on 10 May when he torpedoed and claimed to have sunk one of two transports escorted by the torpedo boat *Gairet-i-Watanije*. The ship was the *Guj Djemal*, an ex-British White Star liner, carrying 6,000 troops and artillery to Gallipoli, though German accounts say that she was merely damaged forward and was towed back to Constantinople. After this he had only one torpedo left, and that was defective and could not be used. Yet such was the effect of merely the presence of a submarine in the Sea of Marmara he had to wait another week before receiving the signal recalling him to

Boyle and his ship's company on their return from the Marmara.

Mudros, as no other submarine was then available to attempt the passage through the Dardanelles. The crews of the small sailing vessels that abounded in the area were always reporting seeing periscopes, mostly the figments of their imaginations but just as effective as if they had been real. While on their way back down through the Dardanelles Boyle could only look at the Turkish battleship *Torgud Reis*, a mere 400 yards away, and nothing to fire at her.

It was a momentous patrol, marred only by the poor running of some of his torpedoes. Boyle's own report concludes with the remark 'a small gun would have been invaluable'. The Admiralty for their part acted with unusual swiftness and Boyle was gazetted with the immediate award of the Victoria Cross, while his officers both received the Distinguished Service Cross (DSC) and all the crew the Distinguished Service Medal (DSM).

The *E14* had only been given the order to return to Mudros when Nasmith and the *E11* were at last ready to relieve them. Nasmith had had no luck in the early months of the war during wearisome patrols in the Heligoland Bight, had been unable to force the passage of Kattegat and through The Sound into the Baltic, and then on passage to the Mediterranean had had trouble with a defective propeller shaft which had delayed the *E11* first in Malta, and then at Mudros while repairs were completed. Now he was told to 'go and run amuck in the Marmara'. After prayers the *E11* left Kephalo Bay early on 19 May and the passage of the Straits proved easier than Nasmith had expected. With Cape Helles just abaft the beam they had bade farewell to the escorting destroyer but Nasmith was able to remain on the surface for a while longer and only dived shortly before dawn. Before reaching Nagara Nasmith had seen the battleships *Torgud Reis* and *Heireddin Barbarossa*, but by chance they were then going up the Dardanelles and drawing away from the submarine. At this stage he found that every time the periscope broke surface it was promptly fired at by every gun that would bear, and to go deep was the only answer though it brought the other problem of navigating safely while blind. At 1.30 pm when Nasmith raised the periscope to check his position he found that they were well into the Sea of Marmara, the current at depth had been a great help and had carried them well beyond their navigational dead reckoning position. With the battery low and needing charging Nasmith recalled how the *E14* had been harried by patrolling gunboats, so he took the *E11* in towards the European shore where they could lie quietly on the bottom until after dark, after which they surfaced to charge.

The next problem was where to take the *E11* so as to create the maximum damage. Nasmith was determined that the *E11* should carry on from where the *E14* had left off and during the patrol the submarine was to operate throughout the length and breadth of the Sea of Marmara, her movements constrained only by the requirement to be periodically at the western end of the sea to be within range of the destroyer acting as a wireless link in the Gulf of Xeros. Off Gallipoli town a torpedo attack on two escorted transports left one of them dam-

aged and heading for the shore. Later a small sailing vessel was stopped and found to be carrying non-military supplies, she was released but not before the *E11* had spent some hours sailing along while secured alongside the Turkish vessel and hopefully hidden from prying eyes.

On 23 May while scuttling a small sailing vessel a Turkish gunboat was sighted and the *E11* was hurriedly dived as soon as the boarding party had returned onboard. Nasmith fired one of his precious torpedoes at the gunboat scoring a hit, but a lucky shot from the Turkish vessel, which was the *Pelengi Deria*, damaged the submarine's forward periscope which had been left up to observe the result of the attack. There was no chance of repairing this while in the Marmara and Nasmith had to rely on his other periscope for the rest of the patrol. It is interesting to note that at one time it is was considered that the RNAS might fly a spare one in to him, but there was found to be no spare readily available. It is more interesting to speculate just how the new periscope was to be transferred from aircraft to submarine and then fitted in enemy waters in the middle of the Sea of Marmara!

The following morning the *E11* surfaced by a small steamer and forced her to stop with a few rifle shots across the bow, – whereupon the crew began to abandon ship in some haste. What followed had the hallmark of comedy as Nasmith was hailed in English by a larger than life character who introduced himself as a reporter from the *Chicago Herald*. Seldom can a submarine commanding officer have been asked to give a press interview in more bizarre surroundings. But with a second ship by then seen to be approaching Nasmith had no time for such niceties, and the ship was prepared for scuttling. It was found that she was the *Nagara* bound for the port of Chanak with stores for the Turkish army, including a 15cm gun and its mounting, and with 250 rounds of ammunition.

On 25 May, the very day that Hersing was making a name for himself off Cape Helles, Nasmith took the *E11* into the heart of the Turkish Empire, the harbour of Constantinople itself where he hoped that he might find the *Goeben* or the *Breslau* at anchor. He was unlucky in that but on coming to periscope depth he saw a large supply ship lying at the jetty of the Topkhana Arsenal, while at anchor nearby was the USS *Scorpion*, an American warship acting as 'Stationnaire' for their Embassy, the Stars and Stripes at her stern proudly proclaiming her neutrality. Nasmith fired two torpedoes, one ran wild and to his horror circled round first towards the American and then on towards the *E11*. The other torpedo ran true and exploded against the supply ship, the *Stambul*, though by this time the submarine had gone deep to avoid her own rogue torpedo and Nasmith was unable to observe the damage. By this time the submarine had begun a battle against the currents which left Nasmith and his crew with little control over direction or depth, and when he returned to periscope depth some 20 minutes later they had been swept well clear of the harbour.

Where the rogue torpedo exploded is not known, but obviously caused no damage. As for the *Stambul* she was hit forward though not fatally. Even so the material effect of this hit on a ship lying so close to the city was great, all the troops being disembarked while in some quarters of the city panic reigned and shops were closed. Many citizens feared that this was merely heralding the long awaited arrival of the British fleet.

The incident only highlighted the need to conserve the small outfit of torpedoes, for with no gun the usefulness of the submarine was limited once they were expended. The answer was simple in theory, but both dangerous and hard work in practice. The torpedoes were set to float rather than sink at the end of their run so that the submarine could surface and look for any that failed to hit. They would then have to be re-embarked and prepared for another run. The first time this was practised Nasmith himself swam out to unscrew the firing pistol, an operation that might be likened to defusing a bomb while swimming. Then the torpedo had to be guided into the stern tube, and with the submarine trimmed down by the bow it could then be hauled back into the boat, another dangerous procedure since both inner and outer doors of the torpedo tube were open at the same time leaving the submarine unable to dive quickly should a Turkish patrol vessel come into sight. The problem did not end there since the torpedo then had to be broken down into its component parts, to be man handled through the boat, re-assembled and prepared for running before launching into one of the bow tubes. It was no easy task as any submariner will testify, yet it was done, and done again too.

Nasmith and the *E11* remained in the Sea of Marmara until once again a crack was found on the starboard intermediate shaft, the same defect that had delayed them during the passage out from Harwich, while in addition the port motor had developed an earth. The passage through the Dardanelles would be tricky enough at the best of times, now it presented a hazardous ordeal. After reporting their predicament Nasmith headed south in the early hours of 7 June. Despite the dangers of the situation Nasmith managed to torpedo one steamer off Nagara Point and then while going through the minefield off Kilid bahr they fouled a mine mooring. Unable to surface and clear it Nasmith had no choice but to carry on and hope that the mine would not be swung back on its mooring wire to explode against the submarine's hull. Wisely Nasmith kept this nightmare to himself during the last miles of the passage. With the submarine clear of the Dardanelles and with a destroyer waiting to escort him to Mudros he had the problem of surfacing safely. This was accomplished by coming up astern and with the

E11 (Lt Cdr M Dunbar Nasmith RN) returns to Mudros on 7 June 1915 being the second British submarine to penetrate the Dardanelles defences.

boat trimmed by the bow so that when the wire pulled free the mine drifted off to be dealt with by the minesweepers.

The *E11* returned to Mudros to receive the cheers of the Fleet. Like Boyle before him Nasmith was awarded an immediate Victoria Cross and his crew was also suitably decorated. It was a patrol that was both daring and successful; Nasmith claiming to have sunk a gunboat, two ammunition ships, two troop ships and two other steamers, while a third transport had been beached.

On 10 June, just three days after Nasmith's triumphant return, Boyle had once more taken the *E14* safely back into the Sea of Marmara. This time the submarine was additionally armed with a 6-pounder gun which had been fitted in Malta dockyard, it was to be a useful acquisition since there were by then few targets worthy of the expenditure of one of the limited number of torpedoes. He was to remain for another 23 days during which time he had a steady stream of successes against the small sailing craft and lighters towed by tugs which the Turks were using to carry their supplies.

Fresh out from England were two more submarines from the Harwich flotilla, veterans of months of fruitless patrols often in appalling weather in the Heligoland Bight where the enemy was rarely seen. On 19 June the first of these newcomers, the *E12* (Lieutenant Commander M K Bruce RN), left Mudros and successfully joined Boyle. Her patrol was short lived as she developed defects first on one motor and then the other. There were fears for her safety since if the defects worsened and prevented her diving then she would be cut off and unable to return, but she safely entered Mudros again on the 27th. The passage down the Dardanelles was accomplished using one motor only, and that at slow speeds, at one time the force of the eddies was greater than that of the motor and the submarine started turning round so that they thought they were caught in a net. Luckily they were untroubled by the enemy.

The *E12* had one particularly unpleasant experience during her short patrol. A steamer towing two sailing vessels was stopped and as the submarine approached to put her bow alongside so that a boarding party could be put aboard someone threw a grenade and a gun was uncovered. Luckily the grenade did not explode and the submarine's gun which was loaded and ready soon disposed of the other. After ten rounds from the submarine the steamer exploded when her cargo of ammunition was hit. The two sailing vessels had also opened fire with rifles and they too were sunk. On the submarine only one rating was lightly wounded.

The Turkish Navy had, in fact, taken into service about twenty small sailing craft which were then armed with a variety of weapons and given naval crews with the task of combating the allied submarines which all too freely roamed the Sea of Marmara. The crews were, however, not in uniform. It was a Turkish initiative taken without the knowledge of Souchon or his staff. It was not until mid June that Souchon became aware of these operations and ordered their halt for fear of British reprisals against any U-boat crew taken prisoner. By the end of the month all these Q-ships had left the Marmara and thereafter were only employed in the Black Sea.

With the return of the *E12* it was time for the *E7* to take her place. In command of the *E7* was Lieutenant Commander A D Cochrane, great grandson of the famous Lord Cochrane, 10th Earl of Dundonald. Cochrane took the *E7* through to the Sea of Marmara on 30 June though at the time he himself was far from fit.

Having met the *E14* and exchanged news the *E7* headed towards the small town of Rodosto where a number of sailing ships were sighted at anchor off the town. Going alongside the first one it was decided to destroy it by fire and the crew's quarters were dowsed in petrol. Unfortunately when this was lit both the First Lieutenant, Lieutenant O Hallifax, and one seaman were badly burned. Such was the extent of their burns that Cochrane resolved to send them back in the *E14* should they meet up again, for a submarine is no place for men with such wounds. But it was not to be and they had to remain onboard for the whole patrol while Cochrane was forced to conduct operations with only himself and one other officer. The sick list did not end there for during the patrol several of the crew had mild attacks of dysentery while towards the end Cochrane himself was suffering from eye strain and bad headaches.

It was to be another memorable patrol. Cochrane claimed to have accounted for one gunboat, five steamers including one of 3,000 tons, and 17 large sailing vessels besides a number of lighters and smaller craft. Although these claims do not match up with Turkish records which admit to 13 vessels sunk and a number damaged, it was nevertheless a patrol which emulated the deeds of Cochrane's famous ancestor. Like Nasmith before him Cochrane had entered the harbour of Constantinople and fired a torpedo at the jetty of the arsenal which was crowded with small craft, and like the *E11* so the *E7* was swept away by the current flowing down from the Bosporus, grounding on the Leander Shoal on her way out. Cochrane made good use of the submarine's gun shelling not only the powder mills at Zeitun just outside the city walls of Constantinople but also trains, railway viaducts and tunnels. One such action nearly had unfortunate consequences, for after the war it was discovered that one train attacked was carrying the survivors of the *AE2* – in this case the train was able to seek safety in a tunnel and no harm was done.

There was one interesting development. Off Marmara Island Cochrane sighted a Turkish destroyer towing a small submarine, it was in fact the *UB8*. The injured Lieutenant Hallifax kept a diary of this patrol and recorded the events that followed.

> Just before 1.0 pm when off Erekli Point, sighted heavy smoke on the port bow and found it came from a destroyer towing a submarine, so we dived and sped up to cut them off. They had seen us just before we dived and the tow had been slipped and the destroyer

started zigging about. We came to the surface again at 3.30 pm and saw them steaming passed Marmara Island so we went ahead on engines and dashed along the European coast close inshore in the hope of being able to get ahead of them unseen against the land, for they were only making about 6 knots. When off Meraphito the inhabitants opened a very accurate rifle fire which caused Cochrane to get inside the conning tower. There was one good shot who watched for C to shove his head up and every time a bullet whistled overhead or hit the bridge, which worried C as his coat was hanging on the fore periscope standard and he wanted to get it before diving! By 6.15 pm we were slightly ahead of the enemy who were only about 4,000 yards off and had evidently been steering more towards us than we had thought, so we dived and went full ahead for some time but just couldn't make it.

On 21 July Cochrane met with Boyle again, making his third patrol into the Marmara and by then promoted to Commander. Three days later the *E7* began her return to Mudros. He had to face a bigger and stronger net at Nagara and for a while remained caught but using the full power of the submarine's motors they broke free and reached the open sea with the battery completely exhausted. For this patrol Cochrane was awarded the Distinguished Service Order (DSO).

On 26 July it was time for the French to have another try when the *Mariotte* (*Lieutenant de Vaisseau* Fabre) was ordered to join Boyle in the Marmara. The *Mariotte* had been launched in 1911 and was larger than the other submarines being over 200 feet long and displacing 530/627 tons. The big advantage she had over the other French boats, and indeed the British E class, was her high submerged speed of over 11 knots and with a range of 100 miles at 5 knots. However, despite the high hopes of her crew she was not to be the first French boat into the Marmara for off Chanak she met an obstruction and in struggling to free herself she partly surfaced under the guns of the fort there. Damaged by gunfire and with a mine attached to her bows her captain had no choice but to scuttle and abandon ship. All her crew were taken prisoner.

The next submarine to go was the *E11*, Nasmith making his second patrol and arriving in the Marmara on 5 August ensuring that there were two submarines on patrol during the period of the August offensive on the peninsula and the Suvla landings. It was a crucial period for both sides in the land fighting and the Turkish army made a strong appeal for a battleship to be sent to give heavy artillery support. Admiral Souchon recognised the danger in sending a ship, and perhaps for this reason he did not send the *Goeben* but the *Heireddin Barbarossa* instead. The previous day the *E14* had torpedoed the torpedo boat *Peyk* which had then been beached with four other destroyers standing by her. Mistakenly they were not recalled and when the battleship sailed from the Bosporus after dark on 7 August her only escort, a small torpedo boat, had to turn back being unable to keep up. Next morning at dawn she began to zigzag but when off the town of Bulair she was struck by a torpedo, capsized and sank with the loss of over 250 of her crew. It was the work of Nasmith and the *E11*.

For this patrol the *E11* had also been fitted with a 6-pounder gun and with the *E14* both submarines made a determined effort to cut the road to Gallipoli where it was exposed to the sea by shelling passing troops and stores convoys. Their efforts however were inconclusive, serving only to harass the troops and delay rather than stop their progress.

The *E14* also managed to torpedo a 5,000 tons supply ship which beached herself. The sequel came a few days later when the same ship was hit by another torpedo this time dropped from an seaplane piloted by Flight Commander C H K Edmonds of the Royal Naval Air Service, the first such attack in naval history.

Before the *E14* left to return south Boyle met with Nasmith on 12 August and was able to give him two extra torpedoes. They were shot out of the *E14's* tubes, set so that their engines did not run, and then were guided onboard the *E11* through her stern tube. An unusual feature of this second patrol by the *E11* was the attack on the Ismid railway bridge which was carried out by the First Lieutenant, Lieutenant D'Oyly-Hughes, who swam ashore with demolition charges placed on a raft. After hearing a loud explosion from ashore the submarine crew were very relieved to see the figure of their First Lieutenant swimming out to them again. On 2 September the *E11* broke through the net bar-

Lt Cdr E de B Stocks standing by E2's collapsed 12pdr mounting on his submarine's return to Mudros on 14 September 1915. (IWM Q.13481)

rage at Nagara with little difficulty and so reached the open sea again.

Meanwhile another new arrival to the Mediterranean, HMS *E2* (Lieutenant Commander D deB Stocks) had reached the Sea of Marmara on 13 August. They were destined to remain over a month, until 14 September. Stocks expected to be joined in early September by Cochrane, bringing the *E7* into the Marmara again. But it was not to be. The submarine became caught in the net at Nagara, and despite desperate attempts she could not freed. The submarine's position was all to obvious to the Turks and under the guidance of von Heimburg of the *UB14* an explosive charge was lowered into the water and exploded near to the submarine. Cochrane realised that it was only a matter of time before such a charge fatally damaged the submarine and risked the lives of his crew. In the circumstances he had no alternative but to surface and allow his crew to escape before scuttling the boat. All were made PoWs.

It is interesting to speculate just what Cochrane had in mind for this patrol. Commodore Keyes in his own memoirs makes the statement: 'Before leaving Cochrane discussed with me a plan for inflicting damage in the Golden Horn which for ingenuity rivalled the most brilliant of his grandfather's (sic) exploits'. Unfortunately he does not elaborate, and Cochrane himself has left no clue, nor was any other Commanding Officer proceeding into the Marmara invited to undertake this venture. A photograph exists taken on the day before the submarine sailed for the Marmara which shows the *E7* alongside the aircraft carrier HMS *Ben-my-Chree* and with one of the carrier's seaplanes being lowered onto the submarine's casing. The RNAS had a good liaison with the submariners and always flew the commanding officers over the Dardanelles before going on patrol, and had even offered to try and fly a spare periscope in for Nasmith when he had one damaged – an attempt that was only abandoned when it was found that no spare periscopes existed. Now perhaps Cochrane saw a way to return favours and to take bombs and perhaps torpedoes into the Marmara for the airmen, and they could then land alongside the submarine to arm themselves, having initially taken off with no weapons but a full load of fuel. Perhaps he planned a joint raid on the Golden Horn. But, why did one else take up this unique tactic, if indeed that was what he planned?

A feature of the *E2*'s patrol was an attempt to blow up the railway line between Constantinople and Adrianople where it ran close to the shore west of the capital. Copying the tactics of the *E11* the First Lieutenant, Lieutenant L V Lyon, swam ashore with some demolition charges. Although a loud explosion was heard by those waiting onboard the submarine nothing was ever seen or heard of Lyon again, and nothing could be learnt from the Turks after the war.

The *E2* was followed by the *E12* making her second appearance in the area, by this time fitted with a 4 inch gun. Targets were becoming fewer and fewer and the patrol was largely routine until the return passage on 26 October. Then the net at Nagara nearly claimed another victim, but the submarine eventually broke clear.

A post-war photograph of Leon Ravenel, commanding officer of the French submarine Turquoise, *abandoned in the Sea of Marmara on 30 October 1916. Documents found on board by the Turks contributed to the subsequent loss of the British E20. Nevertheless Ravenel was cleared of any responsibility by a court martial.* (Service Historique de la Marine, Paris)

The new submarine *H1* (Lieutenant W B Pirie) joined the list of submarines that had successfully navigated the Dardanelles when she broke through on 2 October. The *H1* was one of ten submarines built to an American design in Montreal, Canada and then brought across the Atlantic where four went to the Mediterranean and the remainder to the North Sea. They were single hulled boats 150 feet long and displaced 364/434 tons and were armed with 4 x 18 inch bow torpedo tubes. Designed and built without a gun the submarine had been fitted with a 6-pounder in Malta as a matter of urgency before leaving for the Eastern Mediterranean and then the Sea of Marmara. The *H1* remained in the Marmara until the end of the month when with all her torpedoes expended and becoming low on ammunition she too successfully returned to Mudros.

The *Turquoise* (*Lieutenant de Vaisseau* Ravenel) became the first French submarine to reach the Marmara on 22 October, followed by the E20 (Lieutenant Commander C H Warren) the next day. The *Turquoise* was a sister of the ill-fated *Saphir*, while the *E20* differed from the other E class only in that she had been fitted with 6 inch howitzer. There were then, briefly, four submarines in the Sea of Marmara, though with so few targets available for them it does perhaps seem an extravagant use of assets. Be that as it may the *Turquoise*'s patrol was dogged with various mechanical defects, and after only eight days Ravenel decided that enough was enough, and that he would attempt the return passage while he still could. Before reaching Nagara the submarine grounded on a shoal, then shore batteries opened fire and damaged the periscope. Ravenel surfaced and surrendered. The *Turquoise* was captured intact and towed to Constantinople. Incredibly Ravenel had left all his secret papers onboard and these were found to contain a rendezvous with the *E20* giving both time and place. Also named were the *E12* and the *H1* though both had by then returned though the Dardanelles. The details of the rendezvous with the *E20* was given to von Heimburg who had the *UB14*, which had been under refit, ready for sea within 24 hours. The *E20* waited for his French colleague on the surface and failed to notice von Heimburg's stealthy approach, even in the mirror calm conditions. A single torpedo fired from just over 500 yards sealed the British boat's fate, whereupon the *UB14* surfaced and picked up nine survivors including Warren himself.

The *Turquoise* herself was taken into the Turkish Navy as their only submarine and named *Mustecip Ombashi*, but was not considered to be worth making operational and she remained in Constantinople as a charging station for German submarines. Indeed, the Germans were amazed that a submarine in such poor mechanical state could have been sent into the Marmara. She was restored to the French after the war. As for Ravenel, he survived the rest of the war in a PoW camp and was court martialled on his return to France.

The Court Martial took place in Toulon in the spring of 1919, Ravenel's judges consisting solely of submarine commanding officers. The main charges investigated concerned Ravenel's failure to destroy his secret papers and the fact that his First Lieutenant claimed that he was the first rather than the last to leave the submarine. During the hearing much was made of the many defects which plagued the *Turquoise*. The defence claimed that as the British had lost three of their E class – much superior boats to the *Turquoise* – trying to enter the Sea of Marmara it was feat for Ravenel to have reached the Marmara at all in view of the many material inadequacies of the French submarine. No mention was made of the loss of the *E20*. Whilst these factors may well appear as mitigating circumstances the subsequent acquittal is rather surprising to British eyes.

Little remains to be told of this gallant series of patrols for the army had failed to break the deadlock on the peninsula and already there was talk of a withdrawal. Nasmith and the *E11* arrived for their third patrol on 7 November, this time armed with a 4 inch gun which had been fitted in Malta. The first task was to land a secret service agent, after which Nasmith proceeded to look for the *E20*, being unaware of her loss or of the intelligence gained by the Germans from the captured *Turquoise*. Of the enemy's shipping there was little enough to be found. On 3 December he torpedoed the Turkish destroyer *Yarhissar* in the Gulf of Ismid, the ship breaking in half and sinking rapidly. The submarine surfaced to pick up survivors, 15 of whom were Germans, and then later the same day stopped a sailing vessel so that they could be transferred. On another visit to Constantinople a torpedo sank the steamer *Leros* alongside the quay at Haidar Pasha where it was waiting to be loaded. Although these were Nasmith's only successes with torpedoes on this patrol the gun records show that he fired 331 rounds at various targets, among them being the German steamer *Bosphorus* (5,000 tons) which was sunk in Panderma Bay. When Nasmith brought the *E11* down the Dardanelles for the last time on 23 December he had spent 47 days in the Sea of Marmara and a total of 97 days over the three patrols.

It was during December that the Germans sent first the *UB14*, temporarily under the command of *Leutnant* von Dewitz, and then the *UB8* to hunt the British submarines in the Marmara. On 9 December the former met up with the *E11*, Nasmith sighting the other's periscope but did not dare proceed with an attack in case it might be the *E2*. Just over a week later the *E11* was missed by a torpedo off Mudania Bay without sighting the *UB8*, though the German Official History does not mention this attack but states that von Voigt did not succeed in getting within range and the British boat disappeared in the growing darkness. The final episode belongs to the *E2*. Stocks arrived safely on 9 December. After the final decision to evacuate the peninsula had been taken he was told to return at his own convenience, this being done on 3 January 1916. With the land campaign over de Robeck saw 'no object in running such great risks' and no submarines were again ordered into the Marmara. A second patrol for the *H1* was cancelled while the submarine was on passage from Malta, and she was redeployed to the Adriatic.

As has been shown it had been a costly campaign. The submariners claimed to have sunk one battleship, one destroyer, five gunboats or torpedo boats, 11 transports, 44 steamers and 148 other vessels. German and Turkish sources put the figures at a lower level with 25 steamers sunk, ten others damaged and about 3,000 tons of smaller craft destroyed. Part of the discrepancy lies in the fact that some vessels were beached after damaged, repaired, refloated and then damaged again. Whatever the 'final score' it was undoubtedly a superb example of submarine warfare against an enemy's supply line, that they were unable to affect the land battle to an appreciable degree does not lessen the worth of the campaign. The official German Historian, in *Der Krieg zur See* writes:

The activity of hostile submarines was a constant and heavy anxiety. They dislocated very seriously the conveyance of reinforcements to the Dardanelles and caused many disagreeable losses. If communication by sea had been completely severed the Turkish Army would have been faced with defeat.

CHAPTER SEVEN

The British in the Northern Adriatic

On the face of it the northern Adriatic offered special scope for naval operations. The area was dominated by the main Austrian naval base at Pola, the shipbuilding and armament centre at Fiume, and the great industrial and commercial centre of Trieste once described as 'the lungs of the Austrian Empire'. Close by was the Italian naval base at Venice. Yet the geographical conditions favoured the Austrians for the waters on the Italian shore of the Adriatic are dark and muddy while on the Austrian side the water is crystal clear making submarines easier to spot, even under water. The Austrian defenders also had the advantage of being able to watch for the submarines from the high cliffs on the Istrian coast with the sun behind them, while the Italians had no such advantages.

Despite an imposing array of 12 submarines – *Jantina, Delfinot Atropo, Salpa, Argonauta, Zoea, Fisalia, Argo, Giacinto Pullino, Squalo, Trichero* and *Otario* – under the command of *Capitano di Vascello* Enrico Bonelli which were based at Venice, the Italian naval high command seemed to be effectively paralysed by the Austrian action taken in the opening hours of war. These operations were reinforced by the loss of the Italian submarine *Medusa*, a recent reinforcement to the Italian flotilla, torpedoed on the surface while returning to Venice on 1 June, and the cruiser *Amalfi* on 7 June while supporting a sweep by Italian destroyers off the Istrian coast. Both ships were sunk by German submarines: the *Medusa* by the *UB15*, and the *Amalfi* by the *UB14*. Both submarines were working up after being assembled at Pola, having been brought by rail from their building yard at Bremen, and, perhaps uniquely, both were commanded by the same officer, *Leutnant* Heino von Heimburg. Both had their German crews onboard, though the *UB15* had an Austrian second in command. The *UB14* was then to sail for the Aegean and the Dardanelles but to cover the fiction of Austrian nationality because of the neutral status of Germany and Italy she had the nominal Austrian designation of *U26*. On the other hand the *UB15* was handed over to the Austrians and became the *U11* when the boat was officially transferred on 18 June, over two weeks after the Italian submarine had been torpedoed.

However, the Austrians did not have things all their own way. Their first submarine loss of the war was the *U12* commanded by *Linienschiffsleutnant* Egon Lerch. She had sailed from Trieste on 7 August

for an operation off Venice. The next day Italian naval units dredging for a suspicious object which had been rammed by a destroyer two days earlier saw a large explosion take place in the minefield off Punta Sabbione. Divers were sent down to investigate and found the wreck of the *U12*. In January 1917 the submarine was raised and taken into Venice when Lerch and his crew were buried in the cemetery on the island of San Michele.

To support the Italians the Admiralty offered them the use of the six B class submarines which had until recently been employed on watch off the Dardanelles, but which were then unemployed. On 22 September Rear Admiral Cecil Thursby, RABAS (Rear Admiral Commanding the British Adriatic Squadron), was informed that the six submarines would be joining his command and would be based at Venice. The offer of assistance was not made unconditionally. The submarines would work in accordance with the wishes of the Italian staff at Venice but would receive their orders from a British officer with submarine experience who was being sent out from England since the Admiralty had 'some misgivings' about the Italians' capacity to direct properly the operations of the British boats.

Command of the British boats was given to Commander Wilfred Tomkinson who was not a submariner but who, under the patronage of Roger Keyes had held several appointments on the staff of the Royal Navy's growing submarine service. When Keyes was appointed in command of the 8th (Overseas) Submarine Flotilla at Harwich as Commodore (S) he arranged for Tomkinson to be appointed as the commanding officer of the destroyer *Lurcher* in which Keyes was to fly his broad pendant when at sea. When Keyes was sent to be Chief of Staff to Admiral Carden in the Aegean Tomkinson remained in the *Lurcher* until, on 24 September, he was ordered to turn over his command and report to the Admiralty forthwith. On hearing that he was being sent to Venice in command of what Keyes described as 'five (sic) broken down B boats' Tomkinson was not impressed:

> . . . to be candid I am very disgruntled with it and failed to see why I should be taken out of a good seagoing job and dumped in a shore job with absolutely no chance of going to sea.

Captain Sydney Hall, the Commodore (S), tried to mollify Tomkinson's disappointment by assuring him that he would be 'nearer to Pola than we are to Kiel', but to no avail. Tomkinson departed for Venice convinced that Hall had manoeuvred him out of the *Lurcher* at Harwich once his patron, Keyes, was no longer able to guarantee him favourable appointments.

Tomkinson arrived in Venice at the beginning of October having travelled overland from London. He was quickly followed by his submarines which arrived from Malta; the *B7*, *B8* and *B9* on 11 October, though the *B8* had to be docked immediately on arrival following a collision with the Italian tug *Luni*; the *B6* and *B11* arriving on 28 October, while the *B10* in dockyard hands at Malta was not destined to reach Venice until March 1916. The British were accommodated in the old cruiser *Marco Polo* (built 1892) which they shared with a number of other Italian units. Conditions onboard were far from ideal, one seaman

A mixed group of British, French and Italian submarines at Ancona in late 1915. In the foreground are the British B8 and B7 on their way north to Venice. In the centre are a mixed group of Italian and French boats. The Italian boats are unidentified but the French boats are Ampère and Papin, identified by the letters AM and PA on their rudders. (Dott. Achille Rastelli)

B / H
@ Venice
(Model)

damp and not worth sitting in'.
ning feature in that her armoured
the Austrian air raids which were
Venice in 1916. In May 1917 the
ructed quarters ashore when the
to a troopship.

repare the submarines for opera-
xercises in the lagoon. In this task
ion heads for the submarines' 18
sit from Malta in the Italian mer-
it hard to convince the Italians
acks against fast moving torpedo
commanding officers were woe-
activity. Tomkinson was to write
form of exercise seems to be

ctober, only one week after arriv-
ommand of Lieutenant Jermyn
ay patrol by a British submarine
nta Salvore on the Istrian coast.
others were to be. During the
mmed down in the water while
at night they went further out to
xcitement was the sighting of a
ull! They returned to Venice on
act that nothing had been sight-
ure: 'he [Rushbrooke] is a good
he'll make good use of it'.

five submarines carried out 13
rk was hampered by the large
and Austrian manufacture, and
vide any accurate information
ive minefields. The *B7* had to
uth of Venice) on 17 November
because of the large number of drifting mines. Despite this the main
enemy of these old submarines was the weather, the notorious *Bora* wind
off the Istrian coast which caused sudden storms characterised by short
steep seas and which made life extremely uncomfortable for the submariners. But the British withstood the weather better than the Italians.
Both Rushbrooke and Ouchterlony (*B7*) reported that the Italian submarines with which they had gone on patrol had returned early because
of storm damage. On 28 November Tomkinson was clearly showing
some exasperation with his Italian allies:

> Bonelli told me yesterday that they were not sending out any more
> of their submarines because they were so afraid of their hydroplanes.
> This is very bad as the weather today is quite fine and they can
> always come back if it gets too bad. They also say it is no good going

over to the Istrian coast because there is nothing there! The fact is they give any excuse for not going out.

The *B8* (Lieutenant Eric Tufnell) sighted an Austrian destroyer close inshore off Porto Quieto while on patrol on 8 November but was unable to close the range sufficiently to attack. It was to be the *B11*, now commanded by Lieutenant Samuel Gravener, which was the first British submarine to meet with the Austrians. On patrol off Punta Salvore on 11 December she was attacked by an Austrian flying boat which then suffered an engine failure and was forced to land about 500 yards from the submarine. Since the *B11* did not have a gun Gravener ordered the boat's maxim to be brought to the bridge, but this jammed as soon as they opened fire. Undaunted, Gravener tried to ram the aircraft but the Austrian crew managed to repair their engine and the aircraft took off before the submarine could reach them.

The New Year 1916 brought another confrontation, again involving a disabled aircraft. On 17 January eight Austrian aircraft raided the port of Ancona but on the return flight a flying boat was forced to land on the sea with engine failure. The Austrians at once mounted a major search and rescue operation, two destroyers and three torpedo boats put to sea to try and recover the aircraft while a cruiser and two other torpedo boats waited at Medolino for the order to sail. The *B11* was on patrol at this time with orders to undertake a dived reconnaissance of the anchorage at Unie Island. She had sighted the Austrian ships out looking for the flying boat but was unable to attack because of a damaged periscope so Gravener retired towards the Italian coast. Shortly after two o'clock in the afternoon the *B11* surfaced and an hour later an object was sighted in the water about 15 miles from Cape Promontore – it was the unfortunate flying boat, *L59*. The two crew, pilot *Seekadett* Alexander Ulmansky and his observer *Schiffsbauingenieur* Karl Kubasek, thought the approaching submarine to be one of their own, but on realising their mistake began destroying their charts and knocked holes in the floats so that it capsized. The two airmen were picked up by the *B11* and handed over to the Italians at Venice.

The wreck of the aircraft was later found by one of the Austrian torpedo boats but foundered while being towed to Pola. Minor though the incident was it gave a boost to British morale and did much to improve relations with the Italians. Tomkinson noted that 'the Austrians' behaviour and general bearing was very good and a great contrast with that of the German officers I have seen brought into Harwich'. Though Ulmansky was repatriated in 1917 Kubasek died in an influenza epidemic while in a PoW camp in Italy.

The *B8* was also at sea at this time with orders to patrol off Scoglio, and caught the backlash of the incident. She too sighted the ships looking for the flying boat but did not attack because the brightness of the moon rendered her too conspicuous, instead she was harried by the Austrians. By the time she surfaced her battery was nearly exhausted and since a complete charge could not be achieved before daylight Tufnell decided to abandon the patrol and return to Venice.

The remainder of January and February proved very disappointing. Only half of Tomkinson's submarines were available for patrol since the *B7* was ordered to Malta to refit, the *B6* was taken in hand by the local dockyard at Venice for the fitting of bow hydroplanes and the *B10* still had not arrived. An additional complication was an outbreak of influenza in the *Marco Polo* which counted among the casualties two of the commanding officers, Rushbrooke and Tufnell, who were laid low for some weeks. Nevertheless, ten patrols were made from Venice, eight in January and two in February, often in very bad weather. At the end of January Tomkinson had a visit from Commander Martin Nasmith who was keen to take the *E11* to Venice and saw great opportunities for a modern submarine to disrupt the coastal traffic in the Gulf of Fiume and among the Dalmatian islands. Nasmith stayed for a week and left to seek the approval of his superiors, but alas, de Robeck refused since he felt that the submarine could not be spared from the eastern Mediterranean.

Tomkinson was, no doubt, frustrated by the lack of activity around Venice and was aware that the limited capabilities of his submarines did not promise much for the future. In November 1915 he had already written to Thursby suggesting that two or three of the C class be sent to Venice to be manned by the submarine crews already there. In fact in Hong Kong there were three of the class lying idle in 'care and maintenance', requiring only to be towed to the Mediterranean, but no action was taken on the proposal. On 1 March he wrote again to Thursby requesting the replacement of the six B class submarines with more modern boats capable of greater offensive operations. His chief criticism of the class concerned their lack of battery capacity to enable them to remain submerged during daylight off the Istrian coast in waters constantly patrolled by both aircraft and surface ships. The approach of the long hours of summer daylight would only exacerbate the problem. The batteries could in fact produce some 2,000 ampère-hours, sufficient for eight hours dived at the submarines' most economical speed. By way of comparison the Italian submarines working from Venice had a battery capacity of some 8,000 ampère-hours, although some of Tomkinson's boats were gradually updated with a better performance battery, giving greater endurance, it was still far from satisfactory. Other failings of the class included a very slow diving time, up to three minutes when running on the petrol engine, and periscopes which were inadequate for use in attacks on fast moving targets. Tomkinson described the periscopes as the submarines' worst feature. The letter was received by Thursby on 4 March and curtly marked 'No action'.

Patrolling resumed at the end of February with Tufnell, fit again after his attack of 'flu, taking the *B8* out on the last day of the month for a patrol off the entrance to the Quarnero, the channel up the south east coast of the Istrian peninsula leading to the port of Fiume. It was the practice for British submarines going on patrol to proceed north east up the coast to Caorle and then pass through a safe channel in the mine-fields before altering course to their patrol area. When returning from patrol the reverse procedure was followed. Two hours after passing through the safe channel on 28 February a periscope was sighted abaft the *B8's* port beam and five minutes later a torpedo broke surface only 50 yards off the port bow. Tufnell increased speed and altered course but did not dive, claiming later that the periscope was only identified for certain when it was well abaft the beam. It seems he was lucky. The *B11* had a similar experience during the early morning of 17 March while returning from patrol when a torpedo came to the surface some 40 feet on the port beam. There was no sign of a periscope or the attacking submarine, but in his remarks on the patrol Tomkinson commented that there could be 'no doubt about the torpedo or its track', yet the Austrians make no claim for either of these attacks.

Lieutenant Rushbrooke left Venice with the *B9* on the morning of 29 March and that afternoon was lying trimmed down on the surface about 15 miles from one of the forts guarding Pola. There she was spotted by two Austrian aircraft, *L76* and *L67* on patrol from Pola. *L76* attacked first dropping eight bombs around the *B9* before straffing with machine guns but causing no damage, and then flew off, presumably to summon reinforcements. Meanwhile *L67* continued to circle the British boat occasionally firing her machine gun and then just as the *B9* dived roared overhead and dropped two bombs which fell on the starboard side alongside the conning tower.

Rushbrooke took the submarine to 60 feet but soon became aware that surface ships had arrived on the scene. He tried to come to periscope depth to see what was happening but was forced to go deep again on hearing more propeller noises. There he had great difficulty in keeping a steady trim due to changing water density, the submarine plunging to below 100 feet on three occasions in the space of 30 minutes. However, the Austrians had not prolonged the hunt and when he finally surfaced two hours later they were not in sight, while the *B9's* battery was all but exhausted causing Rushbrooke to abandon the patrol and return to Venice.

The *B10* finally arrived in Venice on 20 March after her long refit in Malta which followed the abandonment of her patrol from Brindisi. One benefit was a greatly enhanced battery capacity which gave much improved endurance. During her first patrol from 9 to 11 April she successfully entered the Quarnero and examined the anchorages of Porto Rabaz and Porto Lungo, remaining dived for 15½ hours. It was a remarkable feat for a boat of this class and Lieutenant K Michell, her commanding officer, wrote that 'the boat after 15½ hours continuous dive remained fairly fresh although breathing was rather difficult .. . frequent shifts on the steering wheel were necessary'. The submarine was out again later in the month examining anchorages in the Quarnero and Farasina Channel but without seeing any shipping apart from two torpedo boats which were not attacked because of rising seas. During this patrol Michell made another even longer dive of 16 hours.

B6 *lying trimmed down while on patrol off Pola during the summer of 1916. In an area where Austrian air patrols were frequent and vigilant, this practice proved almost fatal to two of* B6's *sister submarines:* B7 *and* B8. *(Royal Navy Submarine Museum)*

On 27 April while Michell was investigating the Quarnero the Italians asked Tomkinson to send two submarines to cover a minelaying operation off Cape Planka by the destroyer *Zeffiro* escorted by four more destroyers. Only the *B6* and *B11* were available and Tomkinson noted sourly that of the seven Italian submarines then at Venice none were ready for sea. The orders for the *B6* were that she should patrol on a line Pola/Ancona at a distance of 25 miles from Pola, while the *B11* would do the same between Pola and Porto Corsini. Both submarines were to attack any Austrian forces leaving Pola to cut off the *Zeffiro* and her escorts. The two submarines sailed that evening and the

B6 returned on the 29th having sighted nothing. For the *B11*, however, it was a different story.

The *B11*, now commanded by Lieutenant Frederick Kennedy, arrived on patrol in the early morning of 28 April and remained lying trimmed down on the surface. During the afternoon when the engines were started it was found that all the gear teeth on the rudder quadrant had stripped leaving the rudder hanging free. Kennedy ordered relieving tackles to be rigged and the submarine began to make very slow progress back to Venice. It was a remarkable feat of seamanship carried out in rising seas but after only 15 minutes the tackles carried away leaving the *B11* dead in the water again and drifting steadily towards an inhospitable and enemy coast.

Next morning, the sea having moderated, Kennedy found that he could keep the submarine going slowly astern into the north westerly wind at a speed of about 3 knots. At least it was not towards the enemy. At 10.30 five Italian destroyers were sighted to the west but they failed to see the small submarine despite distress rockets being fired. An hour later four more destroyers were seen and the *B11* was taken in tow by the *Giuseppe Missori* and arrived safely back in Venice during that evening. When the *B11* had failed to arrive back as planned Tomkinson asked the Italians to send forces out to search for her and a flotilla of destroyers left Venice immediately. Some destroyers from Ancona which were already at sea were also warned to look out for the missing submarine, and it was this force which eventually found her.

During May the British made eleven patrols, mostly off Pola; two each by the *B6*, *B7*, *B8* and *B11*, while the *B10* was out three times. The *B10's* three patrols included two more forays into the Quarnero where Michell was becoming an expert, the first supposedly in support of an operation by the Italian airship *M2* though the operation was cancelled by the Italians at the last moment in weather conditions which appeared to be ideal. The *B8*, having completed a minor refit since her previous patrol when she had been bombed, left Venice on 23 May for an area off Chioggia, to the south west of Venice. When she arrived in her billet, she being followed by the Austrian *U11* (the ex-German *UB15*) under the command of *LSL* Robert Teufl von Fernland. Fernland stalked his target believing her to be French, and at 7.49 am fired his port torpedo. This missed as the *B8* dived. Tufnell's account of the attack is that he sighted the *U11's* periscope on the starboard beam passing astern, whereupon he dived. He seems to have been unaware that he was fired at, though he made an immediate report of the other's presence by carrier pigeon.

The *B7* (Lieutenant Thomas Ouchterlony) was the next of the British submarines to meet the enemy, and again it was not to be a happy experience. On 4 June when about 15 miles south west of Pola she was attacked by two Austrian seaplanes while on the surface but lying trimmed down. Lieutenant Oliver North, the First Lieutenant, was on watch at the time with his head and shoulders out of the conning tower hatch. He dived the submarine as soon as he saw the aircraft but as the

B7 submerged the blast of the first bomb blew in the glass scuttles in the conning tower where the steel deadlights had not been secured. A considerable amount of water came in through the shattered ports and the boat plunged to 100 feet before being checked. The submarine was brought back to the surface and the water in the conning tower was drained into the bilges. However, the submarine was unable to dive again for the blast of the bomb had blown the actuating wheel off the port towing slip and this had jammed the hydroplanes in the 'hard to rise' position. Meanwhile a third aircraft had arrived on the scene and the smoke of four or five destroyers could be seen under the land, so it was with considerable relief that the hydroplanes were freed and the submarine dived again, though not before another five bombs were dropped, too near for comfort to the submarine without actually hitting. It was a close call for ten minutes after diving the noise of propellers overhead heralded the arrival of the destroyers who remained in the vicinity for nearly an hour.

Even then it was not plain sailing for the *B7*. While returning to Venice her engine broke down and Ouchterlony had to accept a tow from the tug *Genova* which took them back to Venice. The whole experience had undoubtedly shaken Ouchterlony for he was extremely distressed when reporting to Tomkinson. The next day he was no better and had to be confined to his cabin, and was later sent back to England and did not see service in submarines again.

Up to early June 1916 these obsolescent submarines had carried out nearly 50 patrols from Venice, yet not one torpedo attack had been carried out. It fell to Michell's *B10* to change that. The submarine sailed on 6 June in a joint operation with the Italian submarine *Giacinto Pullino* (built 1913, 345/405 tons, six 45 cm torpedo tubes, one 57 mm and one 37 mm gun). The plan was for the *Pullino* to penetrate the Gulf of Fiume to look for targets while the *B10* patrolled the Farasina Channel to catch any Austrian ships coming up from Pola. Without disagreeing with the aim of the operation, Tomkinson considered it the wrong time of year to carry it out with the long hours of daylight. The *Pullino* returned on the 10th having accomplished nothing, though while passing close to Cape Promontore, near Pola, in daylight she had been spotted by an Austrian flying boat and bombed.

Meanwhile Michell in the *B10* had sighted the Austrian coastal torpedo boat *TB3* escorting the steamer *Arsa* which was towing two lighters loaded with equipment for improving the defences on the island of Lussin. When 300 yards off the *Arsa's* port beam Michell gave the order to fire the starboard tube. In the event, both tubes fired, Michell later complaining that the concussion of one tube firing caused the other to do so too! Watching through the periscope Michell saw the track of one torpedo pass under the steamer and presumed that it had not had time to acquire its proper depth. But the attack had not gone unnoticed for the torpedo boat turned towards the submarine as Michell went to 90 feet, and there reloaded. By the time he had returned to periscope depth both the *Arsa* and the torpedo boat were no longer in sight.

B10 *in dry dock in Venice after being sunk in an Austrian air raid on the evening of 9 August 1916. Raised and placed in dry dock she was further damaged in a fire caused by negligent workmen.*

Michell then withdrew from the Quarnero and, as ordered, tried to attract attention off Zaglava and Galiola Island so as to distract from the *Pullino's* withdrawal.

By the end of June the British had been in Venice for nine months. Relations with the Italians were on the whole good, although there was some resentment on the part of junior Italian officers at the way the British had kept going out on patrol throughout the winter when the Italian boats could, or would, not leave harbour. British prestige in Venice was also damaged by the Royal Navy's apparent failure to win a decisive victory at Jutland, the finer points of the battle being lost on the armchair strategists in Venice (as indeed they were on many other armchair warriors). But, on the whole, Anglo-Italian relations were good and this was in no small part due to the conscious effort made in this direction by Tomkinson, as he acknowledged in a letter to Keyes in July.

> We have had a good many difficulties here one way and another but I think that we have done all that been asked of us with these boats and I pride myself that the Entente here is very much in evidence and we are very friendly with the Italians, and with the French, which is more than can be said for either of the other Italian naval bases.

It was again the *B10* that was to provide the excitement. At the beginning of July she patrolled into the Quarnerolo, the channel between the island of Cherso and the mainland, where no British submarine had gone before. She returned without sighting the Austrian navy, but while passing dived through a known mined area off Grucia Island on the afternoon of 4 July Michell observed through the periscope in the very clear water that a mine mooring wire had fouled the hydroplane, dragging the mine itself over the forehatch on a level with the top of the periscope. Michell wrote of the incident later.

> I turned over in mind what was the best thing to do as I was still going ahead slowly so could not attempt to come up as I might catch a horn or be observed by the forts in broad daylight. I let my Istrian pilot, Lieutenant Palese [Italian Navy] have a look as he was standing beside me at the time and he almost collapsed on the deck. I proceeded to go full speed and hard to dive and in about a couple of minutes I had the joy of seeing the mooring wire severed and the mine shoot up to the surface past the tip of my periscope.

Apart from this incident the patrol was test of endurance in very hot weather, the temperature in the boat while dived rising to 85°–90°F.

The remainder of July was peaceful, a further five patrols being carried out off Pola. During this period the *B8* broke down while returning on 11 July and the *B10* was harassed by seven Austrian torpedo boats on the 19th. But the end of the month was marked by the loss of a third Italian submarine in the area, for after the loss of the *Medusa* soon after the outbreak of war the *Jalea* had failed to return from a patrol in the Gulf of Trieste in August 1915 and was presumed to have been lost on a mine. Now there was to be another.

Tenente di Vascello *Ubaldo degli Umberti, commanding officer of the ill-fated* Giacinto Pullino. *The photograph was taken c.1912 when Umberti comanded* Fisalia. (Dott Achille Rastelli)

On 30 July the *Giacinto Pullino*, under the command of *Tenente di Vascello* Ubaldo degli Umberti, left for a patrol in the Gulf of Fiume. Again, Tomkinson considered the operation unwise, but commented 'it is a rather hazardous adventure when there is no known objective, but she has plenty of battery power and we are always saying that they never do anything offensive'. While en route to her billet the *Pullino* went aground on Galiola Island and was abandoned by her crew after they had wrecked the interior of the submarine. Among the crew subsequently picked up by the Austrians was one Nicolo Sambo whose identity was later established as Nazario Sauro. Sauro was a merchant seaman from Trieste and was therefore an Austrian subject liable for military service. He was employed by the Italians as a navigator where his intimate knowledge of the Istrian coast was invaluable. The Austrian account of the incident relates how Sauro was found drifting on his own away from the other members of the submarine's crew, and that he had head injuries which evidently were the result of physical assault. Under interrogation some of the *Pullino's* crew hinted that they felt that Sauro might have run the submarine aground deliberately. However, another account states that Sauro was well aware of his fate if identified by the Austrians and was found on his own as he had hoped to get ashore quietly and make his way to Trieste where he would have been hidden by pro-Italian elements in the city, his facial injuries being the result of a fall while abandoning the submarine.

Giancinto Pullino's ship's company marching into captivity at Pola in August 1916. (Dott Achille Rastelli)

The Italian submarine Giancinto Pullino *in the tow of Austrian salvage vessels. She subsequently sank while in tow and was not salved or broken up until 1931. (Dott Achille Tastelli)*

The whole affair is mystifying. Was the grounding of the *Pullino* the result of a simple navigation error, or did Sauro run her ashore in order to ingratiate himself with his former masters? Did the Italian crew hint this to try and save him? Whatever the truth, an Austrian court martial treated Sauro as a traitor and a deserter and he was hanged at Pola with little delay on 10 August. The Italians had their revenge on 31 July when the submarine *Salpa*, despatched to the Quarnero to destroy the *Pullino's* wrecked hull, torpedoed and blew the stern off the old Austrian destroyer *Magnet*, but failed to attack the submarine. The *Giacinto Pullino* was salvaged by the Austrians but sank on 1 August while under tow, raised again in 1929 she was broken up in Pola in 1932.

The beginning of August was marked by another loss, that of the *B10*. She returned from patrol on 9 August and secured alongside the *Marco Polo*. That evening 21 Austrian aircraft, led by the foremost Austrian air 'ace' *LSL* Gottfried *Freiherr* von Banfield, 'The Eagle of Trieste', raided the dockyard and military installations around Venice. During the raid at about 10.30 pm the *B10* was struck by a bomb forward on the port side near the towing slip which opened up the hull and did considerable damage. She sank almost immediately, without casualties as all the crew were in shelter onboard the Italian cruiser. The *B8*, lying alongside, was also damaged by the shock of the explosion which cracked some of the battery cells. Tomkinson was extremely chagrined by her loss, 'I would not have minded in the least if it had been the *B8* . . . the *B10* is our most valuable craft'. The Austrian communiqué announcing the raid claimed a considerable amount of damage done in the dockyard in Venice but were unaware of the real success of their raid. Historically the raid marks the first submarine to be sunk by aircraft, though the first submarine to be sunk at sea by aircraft was the French *Foucault*, an event then still a month in the future.

The *B10's* hull was raised on 23 August and was placed in dock where the full extent of the damage could be assessed. The hole in the hull was thought to be big enough to have been made by a torpedo, and though there was little real chance of her being fully operational in the short term the Italians set to work to make good the damage.

However, the good intentions faded in a fire which started with a workman drilling in the vicinity of one of the petrol tanks which had been left full despite warnings by Tomkinson and the British officers. With the fire there was the added danger from the live torpedoes which were still onboard and the dock had to be flooded, thus ruining the work already carried out, but convincing everyone that the submarine was damaged beyond repair. After any useful items had been salvaged she was sold to the Italian Government for scrap.

The rest of the story of the B class submarines in Venice is soon told. Between 12 August and 20 October 14 more fruitless patrols were carried out. By October it had been decided to replace the four remaining boats at Venice (the *B11* was at Malta refitting) with three modern submarines of the H class together with their own depot ship, HMS *Adamant*, which were then operating out of Brindisi. It had originally been intended that they would go to Venice only when the Italians had taken over the four submarines of the W class being built in Britain to an Italian design, but which were found to be unsuitable for operations in the North Sea. However, these were delayed and the loss of the *B10* finally convinced everyone that the B class could no longer be counted on as operational submarines. The last patrol, the eighty first, was appropriately enough carried out by the *B9* from 18 to 20 October off the Istrian coast, exactly a year after she had carried out the first of these patrols.

The arrangements for the departure of the submarines were protracted and Tomkinson's diary records his frustrations and fears that he would be stuck in Venice. He wrote to Commodore Hall in London pointing out that he had not wanted the Venice appointment in the first place, and repeatedly telegraphing the Admiral in Brindisi for information. But by 30 October all was arranged and the four submarines were cheered out of Venice by the Italians in the evening as they left for Malta, while Tomkinson himself left for London the next day. The 'spare crew' ratings and stores were all sent to La Spezia by rail from where they went on to Malta. Tomkinson's work was largely unappreciated by the Admiralty but his efforts were not forgotten by the Italians. Tomkinson received the Order of the Crown of Italy and became a *Chevalier* of the Order of St Maurice and St Lazarus. Eight of his officers, including Gravener, Tufnell, Rushbrooke, Kennedy, Michell and poor Ouchterlony became *Chevaliers* of the Order of St Maurice and St Lazarus.

It is worth recording that the active life of these old submarines was not then over. After lying at Malta for some time it seas decided that they should be converted to surface patrol craft with a raised wheelhouse and focsle and fitted with a 12-pounder gun. On recommissioning they were give S rather than B numbers and returned to Italy to take their place patrolling the Otranto anti-submarine barrage. But age began to tell and defects became increasingly frequent so once again they returned to Malta to pay off, being sold for scrap after the war.

The *Adamant* (Commander C G Brodie) with the submarines *H2* and *H4* left Brindisi for Venice on 27 October, the unarmed *Adamant* being given the 6-pounder gun from the *H3* for the passage north. The third submarine due to go to Venice was the *H1*, but had then only recently begun a refit at Malta, and would join later. However, it was decided that the submariners could use the same accommodation in Venice that the crews of the B class had used and that the *Adamant* would be of more use in the eastern Mediterranean, and she sailed for Mudros on 11 November leaving Lieutenant D W Fell, the commanding officer of the *H2*, as the Senior British Officer in Venice.

The first submarine did not go out on patrol until 9 December when Lieutenant H Smyth took the *H4* to the Istrian coast. From then until July 1917, when the boats were sent south again, a total of 31 largely uneventful patrols were undertaken, though with the onset of winter the bad weather affected operations, so much so that Rear Admiral Mark Kerr, who had taken over from Thursby in June 1916, received a sharp note from the Admiralty.

> . . . their attention has been called to the three H class submarines, attached to the Italian Fleet at Venice. It has been noticed from

Three British H class submarines at Venice in the spring of 1917. (Dott Achille Rastelli)

several recent reports from the Senior Officer that for a long period they have carried out no offensive operations, and although this was partly due to the weather, it is not understood how they should have been continuously prevented from movements to the extent reported. You are to arrange to pay a visit to Venice and take such steps as may be practicable to induce more active employment of the British submarines against the enemy.

Kerr's reply added to the Admiralty's information about the bad weather and added that after each gale the patrol areas were littered with large numbers of floating mines, and that in any case the whole area was limited by the large number of minefields, both Italian and Austrian.

It was left to the *H1* (Lieutenant John Owen) to make the first contact with the Austrians on 11 May 1917 when he attacked a torpedo boat off Pola. Owen stalked the torpedo boat from astern and fired two torpedoes, but as he did so an alert lookout on the Austrian ship sighted the feather from his periscope and gave the alarm. *LSL* Johann Rossel, commanding the *78T*, turned the torpedo boat to comb the tracks and saw one torpedo pass down either side of his ship while opening fire at the periscope. Owen took the *H1* deep to avoid being rammed and had to remain dived for the next seven hours while the *78T*, joined by the destroyer *Csikos* and two other two torpedo boats searched for him.

Two days later the *H4* sighted a small U-boat lying stopped on the surface off the Istrian coast. It was the Austrian *U10* under the command of *LSL* Hermann Rigele. Smyth fired two torpedoes, each angled 2½° outwards to give a spread, at a range of 400 yards. Both missed. Smyth later concluded that he had underestimated the size of the enemy and that one had passed astern while the other went ahead. Not unexpectedly the Austrian dived hurriedly denying Smyth the chance to fire his remaining two tubes. It was the last encounter between the two navies in the northern Adriatic.

By late 1917 the Adriatic was becoming an area in which submarine operations were seen to be impracticable and fruitless. The Austrian fleet remained safely behind its own minefields and could move in comparative safety to Cattaro if needs be, for since the loss of the *Pullino* the Italians had forbidden offensive patrols into the Quarnero. In the south the struggle to keep the U-boats from exiting into the Mediterranean was intensifying and submarines were urgently required to help in this task. In August 1917 the three British submarines were again sent south to Brindisi, though the Italians maintained a sizeable force of over 20 submarines in the north at Venice, Porto Corsini and Ancona.

CHAPTER EIGHT

The Southern Adriatic, 1916

Events on land at the end of 1915 altered the strategic situation for naval operations in the Adriatic in the following year. The combined German, Austrian and Bulgarian attack on Serbia and Montenegro had resulted in the occupation of those two countries. The valuable Montenegran observation posts overlooking the Austrian base at Cattaro were now no longer available giving the Austrian fleet more secrecy in its movements. Italian troops had to be ferried to Durazzo and Valona in Albania, and then supplied, while thousands of starving, poorly equipped Serbian soldiers had to be evacuated together with more thousands of refugees and Austrian PoWs. Later the Austrians even occupied Durazzo giving them another port on the coast opposite the Italian bases from which they could pose a threat to the many small ships on the Otranto barrage patrol.

The submarine war in the Adriatic in 1916 opened with the British consolidating their position at Brindisi. Lieutenant Commander Charles Brodie, the brother of T S Brodie who had been lost in the *E15*, commanding officer of the depot ship HMS *Adamant*, arrived in January to assess the facilities there for a British submarine base. The Italians offered the use of the old cruiser *Etruria* (built 1891) as a depot ship and although the offer was originally accepted in the end her services were not required as the *Adamant* herself was ordered to Brindisi, where she arrived on 22 February, when Brodie assumed the mantle of Senior British Submarine Officer. The Admiralty first allocated two of the new H class, the *H1* fresh from refit in Malta after her Marmara patrol and the *H4*, and two of the veteran E class, the *E12* and *E14*.

The British boats joined a French flotilla of ten submarines *Faraday*, *Franklin*, *Archimède*, *Foucault*, *Papin*, *Ampère*, *Arago*, *Coulomb*, *Messidor* and *Bernouilli* – which were already considerably experienced in operating in the Adriatic. The French submarines were under the command of *Capitaine de Vaisseau* Henri de Cacqueray, a forceful and determined officer who openly chafed at the restrictions imposed upon him by the defensive attitude of the Italians. Thursby wrote of him: 'he (de Cacqueray) dislikes Italians and they dislike him'. It was to become the cause of much friction between allies later on.

The Italians had between six and eight of their submarines operating from Brindisi, the number varying as the requirement arose to send boats to either Venice or Ancona for particular operations. The Italian

The French submarine Ampère, *one of the most successful French submarines in the Adriatic.* (Marius Bar)

boats were under the command of *Capitano di Fregata* G Giovannini, who was also responsible for issuing operational orders to the British and French submarines under the authority of the Duke of Abruzzi, although only after consultation with the appropriate senior officers. Thursby described Giovannini as 'a very good fellow and a good officer who works well with our people'.

Since submarines of the Entente were operating in the Adriatic from both Brindisi in the south and Venice in the north, it was important that demarcation lines were drawn to prevent incidents of 'Own Goals'. Thus the Brindisi submarines were not to operate north of a line running from San Benedetto del Tronto on the Italian coast to Cape Planka on the Dalmatian side. The aim of the submarines at Brindisi was to deny as much as possible the use of the port of Cattaro and the inter-island passages along the Dalmatian coast to the Austrians and their German allies. The prime targets were, of course, the U-boats operating out of Cattaro where the submarines operated in support of the many trawlers and drifters which patrolled the Otranto Barrage, which had begun to be set up in 1915. A secondary though no less important role was to deal with any units of the Austrian fleet tempted to make a raid on the barrage patrol. On hearing that that modern British submarines were to be sent to Brindisi an officer serving in HMS *Weymouth* wrote 'we should be able to show our allies how that part of the business should be run'. He was to be cruelly disappointed. The British submarines did not get off to a good start in the Adriatic, and the abortive patrol by the *E21* at the end of 1915 has already been recorded. It was to be no better in 1916. The first patrol by a British submarine in the new year was carried out by the old *B10*, which was diverted to patrol in the Gulf of Drin from 6 to 8 January while on passage to Venice. The patrol was not a success and the submarine was forced to return to Brindisi with defective main motors, and indeed had to return to Malta for repairs instead of going on to Venice. Then in late February and early March two British boats had encounters with surfaced U-boats but failed to make successful attacks, while on 11 February the *H4* returned to Brindisi with a flooded periscope and then had to remain in harbour while a spare one was brought from Malta.

On 28 February the *U15*, of the German UB type built in Bremen for the Austrians and commissioned by *LSL* Friedrich Fahrdrich on 12 September 1915, was lying stopped on the surface about 4 miles south west of Cape Durazzo when she was sighted by the *H1*. Lieutenant W Pirie, still in command after his Sea of Marmara exploits, fired only one torpedo which in Fahrdrich's words 'passed under the conning tower, grazed the keel, and ran on in a visible straight line on the other side of the boat'. The Austrian wasted no time in diving after such a lucky escape, and though Pirie's report claims that a torpedo was fired at the *H1* in return there is no mention of this in Fahrdrich's account of the action.

The second attack came on 15 March when the *H4* (Lieutenant Henry Smyth) fired two torpedoes at a surfaced U-boat off Cattaro. The identity of the submarine is not certain for the German account makes no mention of this attack, possibly because the U-boat was unaware of it. However, the *U39* (*Kapitänleutnant* Forstmann) was in the vicinity of Cattaro at the time just returning from a patrol in the Mediterranean. Again, both torpedoes ran deep and missed astern. Thursby commenting on both attacks in a letter to de Robeck wrote:

'Its too sickening, that is three torpedoes fired at two sitters and no hit. Certainly the big submarines you sent me have done me badly as they did you well. They are quite useless for this sort of work unless they have reliable torpedoes. I am too angry to say anything more.'

The larger E class had had no greater success. On 20 March the *E14* had to abandon a promising attack on a transport to avoid running aground due to a navigational error. Boyle, veteran of three successful patrols in the Sea of Marmara in the *E14*, did not like conditions in the Adriatic where in contrast to the eastern Mediterranean the water was clear and the enemy had excellent observation posts on high ground, and made no secret of the fact. He complained to Thursby that he could spend no more than two days on patrol since 'the strain on the captain was too great'. The first quarter of the year ended in another dismal failure when the *H4* attacked a 500 tons steamer on 30 March and missed due to firing while on the swing.

De Robeck was concerned that should the Austrian fleet break out of the Adriatic to attack Salonika itself or the transport routes between there and Alexandria – as the French and Russians thought – then he would have insufficient forces to deal with them, and used Thursby's report on the submarines' activities as the lever to have the *E12* and *E14* returned to his command. As a result the two E class were returned to the Aegean and replaced by the *H2* and *H3*, keeping the strength of the British flotilla at four boats.

In contrast the French submarines were doing rather well and evidently reaping the rewards of their experience in 1915 despite the inadequacies of their equipment. The steam driven boats of the *Pluviose* class had problems when diving quickly since expansion of the funnel when hot meant that it was difficult to secure the watertight shutter, while the accommodation, grim even by the standards in the Royal Navy boats, limited the amount of time on patrol. It is worth noting that the *Archimède* of this class was the only French submarine to carry out a patrol in the Heligoland Bight, and then had to withdraw on the surface since the appalling weather at the time distorted the funnel so as to prevent the submarine diving at all.

But the French had their failures as well as successes. The *Faraday* fired at a steamer off the Bojana river estuary on 8 February while the *Archimède* (despite her traumatic experience in the North Sea), destined to become one of the most successful French submarines, fired at the transport *Zagreb* on 28th of the month. Both attacks were unsuccessful. However, on 18 March the *Ampère*, on patrol off Cape Planka, torpedoes what her captain, *Lieutenant de Vaisseau* (*LV*) Leon Henri Devin, thought was a transport. Unfortunately the ship in question was the Austrian hospital ship *Elektra*, a 3200 tons liner owned by the Austrian Lloyd company of Trieste which had been chartered for use as a hospital ship in the first days of the war. Devin later claimed that he could not make out any of the distinctive red cross markings and therefore regarded the *Elektra* as a legitimate target.

Devin's torpedo struck the *Elektra* on the starboard quarter, making a large hole in the ship's side without disabling her. Captain Quarantotto, her Master, successfully drove the ship ashore where she was later salvaged and towed to Trieste for repairs, and was returned to her Owners. It was perhaps fortunate that the casualties were restricted to two killed: a sailor and a nurse.

April was a quiet month for the Brindisi based submarines though the *Archimède* claimed to have sunk a transport, the *Daniel Erno*, escorted by three torpedo boats. The Austrian was a lucky ship having been missed by the *Faraday* in February while now the French torpedo missed close astern and exploded on the shore. In May the success rate rose, but it was still the French that were showing the way.

On 4 May the *Bernouilli* (*LV* René Audry) on patrol off Cattaro sighted the Austrian destroyer *Csepel*. While Audry manoeuvred into an attacking position the Austrians sighted his periscope and opened a brisk fire. Undeterred Audry fired one torpedo which struck the *Csepel* on the starboard side aft, blowing off the stern. While the destroyer's crew dealt with the damage the commanding officer, *Fregattenkapitän*

Bauer, had the motor boat launched and went to the area where the *Bernouilli's* periscope had been seen and began dropping scuttling charges in the vain hope of sinking the submarine. The *Csepel* herself was later taken in tow by the *Balaton*, safely reached Cattaro, and was eventually repaired and returned to service.

Five days later the *Archimède* (*LV* Deville) sank the Austrian steamer *Dubrovnik* of only 480 tons in an attack which the Austrian Government described as 'an act of barbarism'. The *Dubrovnik* was steaming in the Narenta Channel between the island of Lesina and the Sabioncello peninsula on the Dalmatian coast, an area where the narrow and confined waters made it extremely hazardous to have taken a large submarine like the *Archimède*. There she was struck by one torpedo on the starboard side and began to settle as the crew lowered the boats and the passengers prepared to abandon ship. However, the *Dubrovnik* was not sinking fast enough for Deville for he fired a second torpedo which struck the ship on the starboard side under the bridge, shattering a lifeboat which was being lowered and killing those in it. The total loss of life on the *Dubrovnik* being fifteen men and three women. The *Archimède* struck again when she sank the transport *Albanien* on 12 May in the same area.

French activity in the Adriatic in early May 1916 was undoubtedly behind a Note issued by the Austrian Government on the 16th in which the sinking of the *Dubrovnik* was specifically referred to. Considering that her loss took place on the anniversary of the sinking of the very much larger *Lusitania*, and in view of the activities of the submarines of Austria's ally, Germany, the Note makes interesting reading:

The French submarine Bernouilli *which broke into Cattaro harbour on 4 April 1916 and blew the stern off the Austrian destroyer* Csepel. *French submarine commanders showed considerable gallantry in attempting to penetrate the defences of the heavily defended Austrian ports.* (Marius Bar)

. . . the torpedoing of a steamer is a truly brutal and inexcusable deed, committed in defiance of all the principles of humanity and rights of Nations.

The British response was to note with a certain amount of smugness that the 'brutal and inexcusable deeds' had not been committed by a British submarine. At the same time the Admiralty sought an assurance from Thursby that British submarines would avoid unnecessary loss of life when sinking enemy merchant ships.

The French flotilla received reinforcements at about this time in the shape of two newly constructed submarines, the *Artemis* and *Atalante*, the former being completed in 1914 and the latter in 1915. These submarines were of 414/609 tons displacement and were unusual in that they carried their armament of eight 45cm torpedoes outside the pressure hull. Two were housed in external launching cradles while the other six were carried in 'Drzewiecki' collars which allowed the torpedo to be angled out before firing. The submarines *Gay-Lussac* of the *Pluviose* class and the *Le Verrier* of the *Brumaire* class also arrived in Brindisi at this time.

What of the Italian submarines ? They, too, were out on patrol along the Dalmatian coast but met with no success. Captain Herbert Richmond, the British Naval Liaison Officer at Taranto wrote of their activities that:

'As to the Italian submarines they appear to be very badly handled. The Commander-in-Chief [the Duke of Abruzzi] told me that he thought that very few of the officers were good. They go to sea for a day or two and return to harbour for a week's repairs or rest.'

Thursby echoed Richmond's criticism when he wrote that the Italians 'lack initiative and avoid responsibility'. The British attitude may seem a little harsh but sums up the position fairly accurately. The Italians had a poor maintenance record and did spend a lot of time in Brindisi. Their submarines were lightly built and did not fare well in the often rough waters of the Adriatic particularly so when the notorious *Bora* wind was blowing off the Dalmatian coast.

Rear Admiral Mark Kerr relieved Thursby when the latter left to take over in the eastern Mediterranean from de Robeck, and promptly returned to the attack in a letter to Admiral Sir Henry Jackson, the First Sea Lord. It is strange too that he also immediately asks for the return to the Adriatic of some of the E class, only recently sent to the Aegean at de Robeck's request and with Thursby's agreement.

'Their submarines also want a shake up. If we could have two E class, or failing then four more of the H class, we could do a great deal more in patrolling and raiding. They [the Italians] want a lead and I feel the prospects are good, and Abruzzi is very keen.'

It was perhaps all the more embarrassing that the *H1* should have failed once again on 9 June when attacking what Lieutenant Pirie, her commanding officer, described as a UC type U-boat. He fired two torpedoes from a range of 1,000 yards but the enemy altered course when the torpedoes had covered about their run. The torpedoes were set to run 5° apart, one passed astern and the track of the other appeared to run alongside and pass a few feet ahead. German records do not mention this attack but it is possible that the submarine was the *UC12* returning from a minelay off Brindisi.

At the end of the month the Austrian armed auxiliary Slavija was attacked by the *Gay-Lussac*. The *Slavija* avoided the torpedo but the three torpedo boats escorting her subjected the French submarine to a severe depth charging. The Austrian *TB70* reported being attacked between Mazirina and Kremik on 6 June and three days later the minelayer *Dromedar* carrying 65 mines claimed to have been attacked while on passage from San Giovanni di Medua to Durazzo. There is no record of either a British or French submarine carrying out these attacks, so if they were not false alarms the attacks must be attributed to Italian submarines but the records are not specific.

July opened with another unsuccessful attack on a U-boat. This time it was the French *Atalante* (*LV* Le Neannec) which attacked a large submarine south of Traste but to no avail. On the other hand two of the Brindisi based submarines were lost within 24 hours of one another, the Italian *Balilla* and the British *H3*.

The *Balilla* was a large submarine of 728/825 tons displacement armed with 4 x 45 cm torpedo tubes and 2 x 30 mm guns. She had originally been ordered from the Fiat San Giorgio yard by the German Navy as the *U42*, the only U-boat ever to have been ordered outside Germany. However, in June 1915 she was seized by the Italians who incorporated her into their navy.

On the 14 July, under the command of *Tenente di Vascello* (*TV*) Farinati, the *Balilla* was on patrol off the island of Lissa when she was forced to surface because of a battery fire. While on the surface she was spotted by the Austrian signal station on the island which alerted the torpedo boats *65F* and *66F*, but by the time they reached the position the submarine had dived, though they reported that there was a strong smell of fuel in the air. Both torpedo boats then streamed their explosive sweeps and began a hunt for the submarine. Suddenly the *Balilla*'s conning tower appeared off their port bow and this sighting was followed by that of the tracks of two torpedoes heading straight for the *65F*. In evading the torpedoes the torpedo boat became entangled with her own explosive sweep which damaged her stern. It seems probable that the *Balilla* lost trim when firing, but whatever the cause the Austrians wasted no time in opening fire on the exposed conning tower scoring many hits and damaging the periscope, while the *65F* fired a torpedo for good measure which missed. The *Balilla* then managed to dive but broke surface again after a few minutes when she was finally sunk by a torpedo from the *66F*. There were no survivors. The dam-

The British submarine H3 at St John's, Newfoundland, in June 1915 before making the long passage across the Atlantic. She was mined off Cattaro with the Adriatic in July 1916.

aged torpedo boat was escorted back to Sebenico and after repairs was returned to service.

The next day the British *H3* (Lieutenant George Jenkinson) was on patrol off Cattaro when she was mined. Austrian observation posts on Point D'Ostro outside Cattaro had sighted the submarine early that morning and in the early afternoon a large explosion was seen in the outer defensive minefield. Small boats put out from Cattaro and a slick of diesel oil was found together with parts of a torpedo, and some wreckage. Admiral Kerr tells what is probably an apocryphal story in his memoirs that news of the submarine's loss was confirmed in a postcard sent to the Italian Ministry of Marine in Rome by Gabriel O'Byrne, the commanding officer of the unlucky *Curie* and then an Austrian prisoner of war. Apparently O'Byrne requested some books to be sent to him, though why he should be asking the Italians is a mystery, and one of the volumes he requested was 'Mineharsh 3 (vols)'. This request puzzled the Italians until, according to Kerr, 'a smart brain discovered it was a cipher which conveyed the valuable information "Mine *H3*"'. How O'Byrne in his prison camp is supposed to have discovered this is also not recorded.

The month ended as it had begun with an unsuccessful attack by a French submarine on a U-boat. The *Cugnot*, LV Hautefeuille, was on the surface when the enemy was seen at a distance of nearly two miles. The French boat was having to run on her motors since using her steam engines in the rough weather which was prevailing was impossible, Hautefeuille reporting that the waves were breaking over the funnels and extinguishing the boiler fires. Despite nearly exhausting his battery he was unable to close to a range at which he could fire his torpedoes and reluctantly had to break off the attack. In any case it is doubtful whether any of the Frenchman's external torpedoes fired from the surface in those sea conditions would have run satisfactorily, and the *Cugnot* was no longer fitted with the one conventional bow torpedo tube with which the boats of this class were completed.

During July there was an example of Anglo-French co-operation when the French decided to try in the Adriatic an experiment which had been so successful in the North Sea in 1915. The idea was that a trawler should tow a submarine on a line from Valona to Otranto, an area where enemy submarines could be expected. Should the enemy approach the trawler the submerged submarine would slip the tow and try to torpedo the other. By this means the submarine *C24* had sunk the *U40* having been towed by the trawler *Taranaki* off Aberdeen. The initial trials were carried out by the French *Gay-Lussac* (*LV* Cazalis) with the British drifters *Taits* and *Tea Rose*. Although no telephone was fitted at first between the drifter and submarine it was realised that this was imperative since flags or flashing lamps which had to be read through the periscope were liable to compromise the operation. Nevertheless, the first trial was a success and it was found that the *Taits* was able to tow the large submarine submerged at 4 knots, and that the submarine had no trouble either diving or surfacing. Beyond the fact that the Senior British Officer at Brindisi sought the return of the two drifters in September, and that the French were organising the necessary boiler cleaning and repairs in October there is no indication of how often the ruse was used. Perhaps one action at least can be inferred when the *Gay-Lussac* fired at the Austrian *U11* (*LSL* Robert Teufl von Fernland) west of Cape Linguetta in August. Cazalis had managed to get within 200 yards of the Austrian before his periscope was sighted while simultaneously his torpedo roared down the Austrian's starboard side. Von Fernland's claim that he had been chased earlier that day by the *Taits* may well have been a case of the drifter trying to get Cazalis closer to the enemy before slipping the tow. The fortunate Austrian was lucky to survive the next day too when he was bombed by an Italian seaplane.

This attack by Cazalis was just one of a string by the French submarines during August, none of which were successful. On the 5th the *Artemis* (*LV* Henri) missed the Austrian *U4* (*LSL* Rudolf Singule) with a single torpedo with the latter on the surface on passage to her patrol area in the Gulf of Taranto. However the *U4* dived so rapidly on sighting the torpedo track that a vent jammed on one of the ballast tanks and the submarine sank below her designed diving depth of 50 metres before Singule regained control. A direct result of this deep dive was that one of the petrol tanks began leaking into the boat and the fumes made the atmosphere untenable, so Singule had to surface, break off the patrol and head for Durazzo.

A week later the *Le Verrier* (*LV* McGrath) attacked a submarine south of Cattaro, but just as McGrath was about to fire the other dived, perhaps having sighted the Frenchman's periscope. The enemy boat is believed to have been the new *UB46* (*Kapitänleutnant* C Bauer) which was working up from Cattaro at the time. On the 14th the *Messidor* (*LV* Walser) sighted an unknown German submarine in the Otranto Straits but, again, a prompt dive meant the Frenchman was unsuccessful. Finally, on the 29th the *Faraday* (*LV* Bugard) on defensive patrol off Brindisi, sighted a periscope which was that of the Austrian *U17* (*LSL* Zdenko Hudecek) but could not attain a firing position. Hudecek remained blissfully unaware of the other submarine's presence and returned safely to Cattaro on the 30th.

In early August the Admiralty decided to transfer the British depot ship HMS *Adamant*, which had been based at Brindisi since January, to Mudros. The three remaining H class submarines would continue to operate from Brindisi but would have to rely on the Italians for support. Brodie expressed some concern at the ability of the Italians to maintain the submarines and asked Kerr if he would sanction the establishment of a shore based workshop 'since the Italians are incapable of carrying out repairs'. But the impending departure of the *Adamant* was the source of even more concern to the Senior British Naval Officer at Brindisi, Captain G W Vivian, the captain of the light cruiser HMS *Liverpool*. In a long letter to Kerr he wrote:

> As no doubt you are aware the feeling between the French and the Italians here is not exactly cordial: in fact it is very much the reverse. This feeling is particularly strong between Captain Giovannini of the *Lombardia*, the head of the Italian submarine service, and *Capitaine* de Cacqueray of the *Marceau* who is in charge of French submarines and who, as *Chef de Division*, is senior to Captain Giovannini. It is only necessary for Captain Giovannini to say a thing is white to make *Capitaine* de Cacqueray immediately to say it is black. I know and like both these officers but am bound to say that the aggressor is usually the Frenchman . . .
>
> I fear that if Commander Brodie leaves there well may be an open rupture between Giovannini and de Cacqueray and I do not think that Lieutenant Commander A C Horsley [the *Adamant*'s First Lieutenant who it was proposed to leave at Brindisi as senior British submarine officer] is likely to take Brodie's place as a peacemaker.
>
> As I understand that the *Adamant* is not really required at Mudros and unless her presence there is of real importance I cannot but think she would be better employed here.

Whether or not because of Vivian's appeal the *Adamant*'s move to Mudros was cancelled and she remained at Brindisi for the time being, leaving Brodie to mediate between his hot tempered colleagues.

Then the French lost another submarine. The *Foucault*, now commanded by *LV* Devin previously of the *Ampère*, on patrol off Punta d'Ostro (at the entrance to Cattaro) on 15 September when her outline was spotted underwater by the observer of an Austrian seaplane, *Fregattenleutnant* Maximilian Severa, which was returning to Cattaro from

Durazzo. The Austrian aircrew were uncertain of the identity of the submarine so flew on to Cattaro where they soon found that there were no friendly boats at sea in the area. The seaplane was then armed with two 50kg depth charges fused to explode at 30 feet, and four smaller bombs. The air station commander, *LSL* Dmitri Konjovics, decided that he would lead the attack personally, displacing the original pilot who can hardly have been well pleased at the move, but taking Severa as his observer. Another seaplane, similarly armed and piloted by *Frgtlt* Walter Zelezny with *Frgtlt* Otto Klimburg as his observer, accompanied Konjovics.

The two seaplanes headed back to where Severa had sighted the submarine. After searching for about half an hour Klimburg sighted the dived submarine's outline again in the exceptionally clear water. Zelezny brought his aircraft down low and dropped both depth charges which fell alongside the submarine's port side before exploding.

On board the *Foucault* the first indication that they were under attack was the explosion of the two depth charges. The officer of the watch had been using the periscope but had not seen the original approach of Severa's plane or the later arrival of the two seaplanes. The shock of the explosions damaged the motors and stern glands; the resulting leak causing a short circuit and electrical fire. Despite the damage Devin ordered the submarine to 250 feet where the fire was put out and efforts made to repair the motors. But the damage was too great and Devin reluctantly gave the order to surface.

The commanding officer and first lieutenant of the French submarine Foucault *with their Austrian captors.* (Kriegsarchiv, Vienna)

The French submarine Foucault *sunk by Austrian seaplanes on 15 September 1915 and the first submarine to be sunk by air attack.* (Marius Bar)

The Austrian aviators had observed the explosions and the submarine's disappearance. All that remained on the surface was a growing oil slick. They believed that the submarine was badly damaged at the very least and continued to circle the area, and were finally rewarded when the *Foucault* surfaced. Again it was Zelezny that was the first to attack, despite being engaged by the 37mm QF gun mounted on the submarine's after casing, dropping the four small bombs which fell around the conning tower but without hitting. At this stage Devin thought that further resistance was futile and made preparations to scuttle the submarine. The crew were ordered onto the casing, the carrier pigeons released (one of which reached Brindisi) while Devin remained below to make sure the main vents were open and that the submarine would not fall into enemy hands, only abandoning his submarine as she sank beneath him. The two seaplanes landed near the survivors and took Devin and his First Lieutenant prisoner and flew them to Cattaro. All the remainder of the *Foucault*'s crew, 27 officers and ratings, were picked up by the torpedo boat *100M* which had been ordered out from Cattaro. The prisoners were accommodated onboard the armoured cruiser *Sankt Georg* whose crew, according to the French official history, was composed mainly of seamen of Italian or Dalmatian origin and whose loyalty to the Habsburgs was often doubtful. In any case the French were given a 'cordial welcome'.

The attack by the two seaplanes on the *Foucault* had made history for it was the first occasion in which aircraft had sunk a submarine at sea in a deliberate attack. The loss of the British *B10*, only a month previously had occurred in harbour and was the incidental result of a general attack on Venice and the dockyard. This action demonstrated the potential of aircraft as an anti-submarine weapon.

After the loss of the *Foucault*, the patrol by the *H4* (Lieutenant Henry Smyth) on 27 and 28 September contained one of those incidents which can be read with some amusement afterwards, but which can have given Smyth little to laugh at. At 7.20 on the morning of 28 September the *H4* sighted an enemy submarine on the surface. To Smyth it appeared that the submarine was stopped and was trimmed so low in the water that only the top of the conning tower showed. He steered straight for the enemy to close the range and at 7.55 fired two torpedoes. Both ran straight and true but immediately on firing the target was seen to be merely the branches of a floating tree which had the appearance of a submarine's bridge! The British submarines completed another six uneventful patrols from Brindisi before they were ordered north with the *Adamant* to Venice to replace the obsolete B class submarines which had been operating there since October 1915. The move of the H boats to Venice was part of a complicated series of negotiations to provide the Italians with some efficient submarines. In 1915 the Italians had received the four S class submarines (265/324 tons, 2 x 45cm bow tubes) which had been built for the Royal Navy by Scotts on the Clyde to a design by Fiat-Laurenti, since at the time the Royal Navy had more submarines than crews available to man them. In 1916 there was another transfer of the four submarines of the W class (331/499 tons, 2 x 45cm bow tubes with four more torpedoes in drop collars, except that there were no drop collars in *W3* and *W4* but 4 x 45cm tubes). At the same time the Italians ordered eight H class submarines from Vickers at Montreal to be built to the same design as the ten boats serving with the Royal Navy. The Italians originally wanted to purchase two of the three boats already serving in the Adriatic and allow the British to take over two of those to be built in Montreal, but this idea was vetoed by the Admiralty. So, with the arrival of the four W class at Brindisi the *H2* and *H4* (*H1* was in refit at Malta) went north to Venice leaving the submarine war in the southern Adriatic to be carried on for the time being by the French and the Italians.

The year 1916 had not been a particularly satisfactory one for the Entente submarines operating in the lower Adriatic. They had not sunk a single U-boat and yet had lost three of their own: The British *H3* to a mine, the Italian *Balilla* to attack by surface vessels and the French *Foucault* to the latest form of anti-submarine warfare the aircraft. In contrast the Austrian submarines, reinforced by those of their German allies, operating from Cattaro were enjoying rich pickings of Entente shipping in the Mediterranean.

CHAPTER NINE

The U-boat Campaign, 1916

At the beginning of 1916 German U-boats were widely distributed throughout the Mediterranean and Adriatic. Hersing's *U21* was cruising in the Eastern Mediterranean off the Syrian coast; the *UB7*, *UB8*, *UB14* and *UC15* were in the Black Sea; the *UC14* was busy laying mines in the Adriatic while the *UC12* was being refitted for this work after her service as a transport submarine. Lastly the four ocean going boats, *U34*, *U35*, *U38* and *U39* were all based on Cattaro for commerce raiding in the Mediterranean. Six of the new UBII type submarines, *UB42* to *UB47*, were to arrive in 1916, as with the earlier UB boats they travelled overland from Germany for reassembly at Pola. The first, the *UB42* was commissioned on 23 March.

The first quarter of 1916 was quite successful for the Germans. Forstmann's *U39* was out in February working the approaches to Salonika where the 9542 ton transport *Norseman* was attacked on 22 January, the ship was beached but became a constructive total loss. Hersing's *U21* sank the French armoured cruiser *Amiral Charner* on 8 February. The old cruiser, built in 1893, went down off the Syrian coast south of Beirut while bound for Port Said. When she failed to arrive the signal station at Port Said tried to contact her by wireless but to no avail, the subsequent search being hampered by bad weather. It was not until 13 February that the patrol vessel Laborieux found a raft containing the only survivor of her crew of 335: a quartermaster named Cariou.

Hersing's attack on the *Amiral Charner* following the earlier activities of Valentiner in the *U38* at the turn of the year caused the Naval Staff to issue a mild reproof to both Commanding Officers for deviating from the prime aim of their patrol, namely the attack on merchant shipping. Instructions sent to the flotilla concluded that an all out attack on trade was the most important way of dealing with Germany's principle enemy. They added that however gratifying such successes were against warships they should not normally be attacked at the expense of merchant shipping. It was a significant letter.

Kapitänleutnant Lothar von Arnauld de la Perière, the new commanding officer of the *U35*, had earlier served as the torpedo officer in the cruiser *Emden* in the German East Asia Squadron and then as the ADC to the ageing but still very influential Grand Admiral von Tirpitz, while on the outbreak of the war he had been on the staff of Admiral von

Pohl. Seeking more active employment he declined an appointment in the High Seas Fleet and asked for training in the Zeppelin service. There were no vacancies in the air but he was sent instead to undergo the course for submarine commanding officers – this with no previous service in submarines. He was a reserved man not given to conversation but became very solicitous of his crew's welfare. He was destined to be the most successful submarine commander of the First World War with over half a million tons of Entente shipping to his credit: a figure that was achieved using tactics which earned him the respect of friend and foe alike. There was none of the brutality about de la Perière which characterised the actions of Valentiner and Gansser.

It was de la Perière's *U35* which had the first German encounter with a 'Q' Ship in the Mediterranean, during a short first patrol from Pola from 11 to 25 January. On 17 January 1916 the British ship *Sutherland* (3,542 tons) was stopped and sunk by gunfire about 170 miles east of Malta. Later that day the *Baron Napier* was similarly attacked but was able to return the U-boat's fire and report the incident by wireless. The Q Ship *Margit* under the command of Lt Cdr G L Hodgeson picked up the signals and, hoisting Dutch colours (a legitimate *ruse de guerre*), proceeded to the area to investigate. When the *Margit* was within two miles of the U-boat she was engaged by a few desultory shots from the submarine and ordered to stop and send a boat, at which the usual 'panic party' abandoned ship leaving Hodgeson and the gunners onboard. The submarine then submerged and circled the *Margit* observing her with about two feet of periscope exposed, de la Perière showing remarkable

U35 *at sunset in the Mediterranean, 1917.* (IWM Q.20380)

caution for a new commanding officer. The deception passed muster for the *U35* surfaced again and ordered the lifeboat alongside. At this moment the *Margit* abandoned the disguise, hoisted the White Ensign and opened fire on the submarine which dived hurriedly stern first. It was thought that the submarine was having troubles with the trim for the conning tower then broke surface only seventy yards away from the *Margit* which, despite the fact that many of her guns would not depress sufficiently, engaged her as best she could and one shot was seen to strike home before the submarine submerged. In fact the submarine had lost trim on firing a torpedo at the *Magrit* which not only missed but was unobserved. The *U35* was undamaged and returned to Cattaro, after sinking two more British ships and being thwarted in attacking four others by the increasing number of patrols in the area.

The *Margit* returned to Malta believing she had sunk the submarine for which action Hodgeson subsequently received the DS0.

Valentiner was also out in February, first taking six Turkish officers and men together with ten tons of arms to Bardia before acting against the Entente merchant shipping in the western Mediterranean. He too had a lucky escape when engaged by a Q ship and returned to Cattaro in early March having sunk a further nine ships, including an Italian.

De la Perière took the *U35* out again on 20 February and immediately began to establish his reputation by torpedoing the French liner *Provence II* (13,753 tons) off Cerigo Island on the 25th. The *Provence II* was carrying nearly 2000 French colonial troops to Salonika and there was heavy loss of life. Following this on 1 March he engaged the little British sloop HMS *Primula*. This little warship of 1250 tons and armed with two 4.7 in and two 3pdr AA guns sold herself very dearly. The *U35*'s first torpedo blew the *Primula*'s bows off yet the sloop turned and going full astern tried to ram the submarine. A second and third torpedo missed and it was de la Perière's fourth torpedo that finally sent the *Primula* to the bottom. 'Four torpedoes for that tiny wasp', commented de la Perière afterwards and he later claimed that the *Primula* was the toughest of all his adversaries. De la Perière's total for his first cruise came to 22,600 tons of Entente shipping: a remarkable achievement for a new submarine commanding officer. On his next cruise de la Perière torpedoed the large British transport *Minneapolis* (13,543 tons) in ballast on 23 March damaging her so greatly that she foundered two days later. It was his only success since the *U35* was by then badly in need of a refit.

Minelaying activities in the Adriatic were not neglected during this period and a determined effort was made to interfere with the evacuation of Serbian forces from Valona. On 4 January the *UC14* laid a field of 12 mines off Cape Linguetta which claimed the small 863 ton transport *Brindisi* two days later. The *Brindisi* was carrying food supplies for the relief of Serbian refugees together with 425 American volunteer soldiers of Italian descent, nearly half being drowned. Another victim of the *UC14*'s mines was the Italian armed merchant cruiser *Citta di Palermo* sunk on the 8th. The *UC12* was also active after her re-conversion to

minelaying work, laying two fields off Durazzo on 15 and 23 February
and a third field off Brindisi on 2 March. The first field laid off Durazzo
claimed the Italian hospital ship *Marechiaro* on 21 February. Under the
command of her new commanding officer, *Leutnant zur See* Frohner, she
prepared to lay a fourth field off Taranto and left Cattaro on 13 March.
Three days later she blew up as a result of the explosion of one of her
own mines. In April the hull was salved, and after repair was commissioned as the Italian X1. More importantly her salvage provided the
Italians which much useful evidence to confirm their worst suspicions
about German activities in the Adriatic. The submarine was plainly
German with a German crew onboard, although the body of an officer
in Austrian uniform was also found. Moreover both German and
Austrian ensigns were discovered. Here was irrefutable proof that
Germany was committing acts of war against Italy under cover of her
ally's flag.

Despite these successes 1916 opened with the Germans in a state of
indecision as to how far they could prosecute the '*Handelskrieg*' against
Entente shipping in the Mediterranean. The adverse reaction, particularly in the United States, to the sinking of the *Ancona* in November
1915 and the *Persia* the following month led to new instructions being
sent to Kophamel at Cattaro in early January to the effect that passenger steamers were in principle to be left unmolested even when they
were armed, with the exception of those in the Aegean or under escort
in the approaches to the Aegean.

Admiral Henning von Holtzendorf at the *Admiralstab* had already
complained to the Chancellor, von Bethmann-Hollweg, about these
restrictions but it was Kophamel who was most vociferous in protesting,
arguing that the only way to bring Britain to her knees was to engage
in a ruthless campaign of sinking anything flying the British ensign. He
went on to point out that since the British were now arming all their
merchant ships it was becoming more dangerous for a U-boat to
remained stopped on the surface while ascertaining the identity of the
ship and the nature of her cargo. Kophamel's complaints seemed to be
vindicated by the figures of Entente shipping losses for the first two
months of 1916 which represented a considerable decrease on the figures for the last two months of 1915: only 17 ships totalling 72,389 tons
were sunk by torpedo or gunfire while a further eight ships totalling
7,423 tons were lost to submarine laid mines.

Kophamel was initially successful in his complaints, for the *Admiralstab*
issued revised instructions which amounted to the introduction of unrestricted submarine warfare in the Mediterranean. British and French
merchant ships could now be attacked without warning only so long as
the U-boat commander had confirmed that the ship in question was
armed. Moreover von Holtzendorf now ordered, and the Austrians
issued similar orders, that if an attack were to be made submerged then
the U-boat should not surface but should depart from the scene submerged thus avoiding repetitions of the disagreements of the previous
year about the use of the Austrian flag. The order was issued on 11

February, and was due to take effect from 29 February so that the warning could be issued to the neutrals. At this stage the German Foreign Office, which was still possessed of influence in these matters, succeeded in having these orders revoked on 24 February. The new orders issued by the *Admiralstab* specified that passenger liners were not to be attacked even if armed. This stricture had a crippling effect on operations in the Mediterranean where it was exceedingly difficult to distinguish between an innocent passenger liner, an armed troopship and armed merchant cruiser – usually a former liner!

The bitter debate in Germany over just how far to go went on and came to a climax at a meeting attended by the Kaiser at Charleville on 4 March in which the opponents of unrestricted submarine warfare, led by the Chancellor, won the day though only just, and for a limited period of one month only. The casualty of the conflict was Grand Admiral von Tirpitz who resigned on 10 March, not willing to remain in office with no clearly defined policy for submarine warfare in effect. However, the victory of the moderates at Charleville was clearly upset with the sinking of the steamer *Sussex* in the English Channel by one of the Flanders based submarines on 24 March, more American lives being lost. An American ultimatum arrived on 20 April and the German Government gave way. The unrestricted campaign in the north was called off and Bethmann-Hollweg promised that merchant ships would not be attacked without warning.

The German submariners in the Mediterranean had some justification for resenting these restrictions placed on their operations. Entente submarines had, after all been carrying out unrestricted warfare against Austrian ships using the vital supply line down the Dalmatian coast. The attacks on the *Daniel Erno*, *Zagreb* and *Dubrovnik* (see chapter 8) were all carried out without warning. Moreover the Ampère's attack on the hospital ship *Elektra* had raised not the slightest comment from the United States.

Minelaying continued in April with the *UC14* laying more mines off Corfu and Bari. The minelaying activities of the UC boats were to be enhanced by the arrival in May of a large minelayer, the *U73*, joined later in the year by her sister the *U72*. Of 755/832 tons displacement they were armed with one bow and one stern 50cm torpedo tubes (four torpedoes being carried), one 88mm gun and 34 mines. The carriage of mines was the boat's main function and submarines of this type had already proved themselves in northern waters. The mines were all carried dry in racks in a large mine room at the after end of the boat and expelled by cog drive through two horizontal 100 cm tubes, each tube carrying three mines at a time. The large amount of space taken up by the mines and their associated trimming and compensating tanks meant that the engine room had to be moved forward to the centre of the boat in turn moving the control room, conning tower and batteries further forward. Since there was no space for internal tubes the two torpedo tubes were sited on the upper deck: the bow tube to port and the stern tube to starboard. The 88mm gun was fitted aft of the conning tower.

Despite, or perhaps because of the novel nature of the design the UE boats, as they were known, had their problems. Their diesel engines were undersized for the displacement and in order to achieve the desired range of 8000 nautical miles at 7 knots saddle tanks with fuel bunkers were fitted on both sides. In rough seas they dipped deeply into the waves which slowed them down even more.

Nevertheless the *U73* under the command of *Kapitänleutnant* Gustav Siess lost no time in making her mark in the Mediterranean. She sailed from Cuxhaven on 1 April and after laying 12 mines off Lisbon, laid the remaining 22 mines off Malta before heading for Cattaro where he arrived four days later on 30 April. By then the minefield off Malta had claimed its first victims: the pre-dreadnought HMS *Russell*, flagship of Vice-Admiral Sir Sydney Freemantle, and the sloop HMS *Nasturtium*, both on 27 April, followed by the armed yacht *Aegusa* two days later.

May and June 1916 saw a rise in the number of vessels lost to U-boat attack. From 16 May to 1 June Forstmann's *U39*, operating off the Algerian coast, sank 21 (9 British, 10 Italian, 1 Norwegian and 1 Spanish) ships and bombarded the port of Portoferraio on the island of Elba. In achieving this total Forstmann expended five torpedoes, five explosive charges and 365 rounds of 88mm ammunition; the high consumption of ammunition was undoubtedly due to a bombardment of Portoferraio. Forstmann's Austrian liaison officer, *LSL* Gaston Vio, commented that Forstmann preferred to sink ships by gunfire during the day but use explosive charges at night so that the flash of gunfire would not attract the patrols.

De la Perière's *U35* left Cattaro on 9 June for a cruise in the western Mediterranean and during the following three weeks sank seven British steamers. On 21 June he brazenly put into Cartagena and delivered a personal letter from the Kaiser to King Alphonso of Spain and departed within the 24 hours allowed to a belligerent warship visiting a neutral port. During this cruise de la Perière sank forty ships totalling 56,818 tons. However this cruise was notable in that *U35* was carrying an observer from the *Admiralstab* in Berlin whose duty it was to observe the effect on the restrictions placed on U-boat commanders regarding the sinking of merchant ships. Armed with his liaison officer's report Holtzendorf met with Bethmann-Hollweg on 12 July and demanded the right to sink without warning merchant ships along the transport routes from Malta to the Aegean. Holtzendorf argued that since the British were disguising the guns on their transports it was practically impossible to tell whether or not a ship was armed and there were a number of other features which indicated that ship was on military service, such as extra W/T aerials or the distinctive numbers painted on the hull, other than the presence of armament. To counter the Chancellor's worries about neutral ships, especially American ships, Holtzendorf produced the ingenious argument that neutral ships were easily recognised because of the distinctive markings they carried! Bethmann-Hollweg reluctantly agreed and the new orders were issued on 15 July but with the rider that a U-boat commander who exceeded the orders would be held responsible.

The success of the German campaign against shipping in the Mediterranean was constantly being threatened by demands for U-boats to engage in supply running operations to the Senussi in North Africa. Despite the defeat of the Senussi revolt in March there were continual demands from Enver Pasha, with the strong support of the German general staff, for more supplies to be sent to North Africa. A plan to use an Austrian registered steamer the *Graf Wurmbrand* collapsed when it was realised that the ship lacked the endurance to reach the north African coast from the Adriatic. So very reluctantly Kophamel was forced to order Hersing's *U21* to take *Oberleutnant* Freiherr von Todenwarth together with four Turkish officers and NCOs together with arms, ammunition and a wireless set onboard for transport to North Africa. Hersing sailed from Cattaro on 10 April but failed to land Todenwarth and his party, partly because of the surf over the beaches and partly because they failed to reach an understanding with the local Arab chiefs in the area. After four days Hersing gave up the attempt and left to begin his campaign against shipping. In this too he was hardly successful and sank only one ship, the *City of Lucknow* (3,677 tons), before returning to Cattaro on 4 May. Todenwarth and his party were eventually landed by the *U39* in July but there was an understandable reluctance by both the *Admiralstab* and *Kophamel* to engage in operations of this sort.

The quarter, July–September 1916, saw a total of 317,230 tons of shipping, 149 ships, being sunk by torpedo and gun together with a further 6 ships of 4,312 tons falling victim to submarine laid mines. Of this total 90,150 tons belongs to de la Perière's record patrol from 26 July to 20 August in which he sank 54 steamers and sailing craft (11 British, 32 Italian, 2 French, 1 Japanese and 8 neutrals though no Americans): the most successful cruise of any submarine commander during the war. Having acquired the services of a crack gunlayer from the High Seas Fleet, de la Perière preferred to use his 88mm gun and expended over 900 rounds of ammunition. In all accounts the problems of stowing such a large amount of ammunition have been glossed over; certainly *U35*'s practice cannot have been in accordance with any magazine safety regulations!

What were the Entente powers doing to combat these fearsome losses? A conference held at Malta from 2–9 March which reduced the number of patrol zones, established in 1915, to eleven and adopted the principle of fixed patrolled routes for maritime traffic. The French Commander in Chief would establish the routes but each nation would be responsible for its own zones. The system did not work. There were too few escorts and the Italians and French did not patrol their zones properly. More seriously the Germans soon learned of the prescribed routes which would be patrolled, from log books and documents recovered from merchant ships before they were sunk and it is alleged that an Indian seaman in New York sold the Germans a copy of the sailing directions for vessels going from Algiers to Mudros. As a measure against the U-boat the Otranto Barrage was not justifying the resources spent on it. *LSL* Gaston Vio commented that the *U39* had a fairly easy passage through the Straits in May 1916 despite sighting over ten patrol vessels. However, Forstmann noted ominously that if the Entente forces extended their patrol areas north and south of the existing drifter line it could make entering and leaving the Adriatic difficult for U-boats since they would have to make the passage submerged thereby draining their batteries and making them more vulnerable to nets and deep minefields. Indeed, for many years it was thought that the Otranto Barrage was responsible for the loss of the *UB44* (*Oberleutnant zur See* Wager) which was lost with all hands while on passage to Constantinople. At the end of July two drifters depth charged an object caught in the nets and observed a considerable underwater explosion. The two drifters attempted to tow the submarine, still enmeshed in the net, into shallow water but the net broke away and sank. Alas, the *UB44* did not sail from Cattaro until some days after this incident.

What of the Austrian U-boats during this period? The Austrians were making strenuous efforts acquire more submarines capable of more adventurous patrols, the five boats building in Germany on the outbreak of war were now sorely missed. The Austrian government first turned to the Whitehead yard at Fiume for replacements. The yard had built three *Havmanden* class submarines for Denmark before the war, and in March 1915 the Austrian Government had ordered four boats to be built to these plans, the order being split between Pola Dockyard (*U20* and *U21*) and the Hungarian UBAG yard at Fiume (*U22* and *U23*). The boats were of 173/210 tons displacement and were armed with two 45cm bow torpedo tubes and a 8mm gun. Their construction was a protracted affair, none of the boats being available in 1916.

The failure of the Austrian shipbuilding industry to supply the needs of the Navy meant the Austrians having to turn to Germany for submarines and interest centred on the *UB1* type. The *U10* class (*U10, U11, U15, U16,* and *U17*) were ordered in April 1915. The first two boats *U10* and *U11* were the German *UB1* and *UB15* respectively and, as already related, until their Austrian crews became available in June/July 1915 operated under the German ensign. The other three boats were ordered under their Austrian numbers and never saw service with a German crew. Continued Austrian interest in the UB design meant that a further eight boats, the *U27* class being ordered and built in Austrian yards at the end of 1915 but none would be ready before the beginning of 1917. Thus the Austrians had to make do with their pre-war submarine fleet, less *U3* and *U12*, plus the five *U10* class submarines. There was also the *U14*, the former French *Curie*, which had been raised in February 1915 and refitted. The Austrians were not impressed with the French design and she was withdrawn from service in February 1916 and was under refit until November. She emerged a much better boat with new engines and a proper conning tower instead of the low French platform.

The small size of the Austrian U-boats prevented them for joining their German allies in the Mediterranean and they confined their activities to the Adriatic and the Gulf of Taranto. On 20 January 1916 Teufl von Fernland's *U11* was patrolling in the Gulf of Drin when a hospital ship was sighted. In marked contrast to the behaviour of his German allies Fernland surfaced his submarine and exercising his right of search under international law ordered the ship, the Italian *König Albert* (ironically a German ship owned by Norddeutscher Lloyd and requisitioned by the Italian government) to proceed to Cattaro where she was examined by an Austrian commission. When all was found to be in order except for an unfortunate Czech, a deserter from the Austrian Army, who was taken ashore, the ship was released and allowed to proceed on her way. It was an example of civilised behaviour by a U-boat commander in a war that was becoming characterised by propaganda which held that German and Austrian U-boat men were cowardly and bad, but Entente submariners were heroic and good.

Between March and June 1916 Austrian submarines made 24 patrols. On 18 March 1916 *LSL* Hugo von Falkenhausen's *U6* sank the French destroyer *Renaudin* off Durazzo. The destroyer broke in half having been struck on the starboard side by the bridge and sank in less than a minute. However the *U6* herself was sunk on 13 May while trying to break through the Otranto Straits to patrol along a line between Santa Maria di Leuca and Valona. Caught in the nets she was forced to the surface and sunk by gunfire by the drifters *Calistoga* and *Dulcie Doris*, all her crew becoming prisoners of war. However the First Lieutenant, *Fregattenleutnant* Egon Wachner, still had a rôle to play. He was able to smuggle – by means unknown – the information that the White Star liner *Britannic*, then serving as a hospital ship had been seen at Naples embarking ammunition, an act which if true was incompatible with the ship's status as a declared hospital ship. The Austrians made a furious protest which was swiftly and emphatically denied by the Admiralty. It merely emphasises the suspicion with which hospital ships were regarded by both sides in the Mediterranean at this time.

In June Fähndrich in *U15* sank the 3,495 ton Italian armed merchant cruiser *Citta di Messina* together with her French escort the destroyer *Fourche*. He had sailed from Cattaro on 21 June for a patrol off the Albanian coast when two mornings later he sighted the *Citta di Messina* eighteen miles east of Cape Otranto with her destroyer escort. At 08.38 her fired his port tube and was rewarded by hearing a large explosion followed by the noises of exploding boilers. Fähndrich went deep to about 150 feet and heard seven depth charges dropped though none were near enough to cause any damage. Rising to periscope depth about an hour later he saw no sign of his victim but the destroyer was still in the area. Fähndrich was another that must have been careless using his periscope for the *Fourche* was seen to alter course toward him. So Fähndrich fired a second torpedo and was rewarded with another hit. It was a remarkable attack for a small submarine and showed that the Austrians were every bit as competent as their German allies.

Other Austrian successes in 1916 included the armed merchant cruiser *Principe Umberto* sunk on 8 June by Schlosser in the *U5* and the Italian destroyers *Impetuoso*, sunk by Hudacek in the *U17* on 10 July, and the *Nembo* sunk on 17 October by Zopa's *U16*. However Zopa's attack on the *Nembo*, though successful, led to the loss of his submarine for while observing his handiwork through the periscope Zopa failed to notice the approach of the merchant ship *Bermida*. The *Bermida* rammed the submarine which began to take in water. By blowing everything Zopa brought the *U16* to the surface where Zopa gave the crew a lecture about their future conduct as prisoners of war followed by a last cheer for the Emperor before they abandoned the submarine which sank. The survivors, all but two of the submarine's crew, found themselves swimming in the water along with the survivors of the *Nembo*, and became prisoners of war. The *Bermida* seems to have been unaware of ramming the submarine for official Italian accounts attribute the *U16*'s loss to the explosion of the *Nembo*'s depth charges which were not set to 'safe' before she sank. It was not until Zopa was released from captivity in 1918 that the true cause of the submarine's loss became known.

Together with these successes against warships, Austrian submarines accounted for sixteen merchant ships the largest of which was the 4,309 British *Inverbervie* sunk on 14 September by Singule in the *U4*. Yet despite these modest totals Austrian submarines exercised a tremendous influence on the movement of Entente, especially Italian, warships in the Adriatic, although Austrian officers were ever conscious that they were the junior partner in their alliance with Germany.

The success of the German boats in the Mediterranean had not passed unnoticed in Berlin. Kophamel had been requesting reinforcements for months but the track record of the boats under his command gave strength to his arguments. On 22 August he requested the despatch of another three large submarines to enable to keep two submarines on patrol at any one time. By the time his request reached Berlin Holtzendorf had already secured the Kaiser's approval for the despatch of the *U32*, *U63*, *U64* and *U65* to the Mediterranean which was two more than Kophamel asked for. Moreover the August tonnage figures showed that Kophamel's flotilla had disposed of over a million tons of Entente shipping and after some prompting the Kaiser sent him a personal telegram of congratulations.

August 1916 saw the Italian declaration of war against Germany. In theory there was no longer any need for German submarines to operate under the Austrian ensign but the lie once told, was not so easily forgotten. The deception had been faithfully carried out right up to Italy's entry into the war though it is doubtful whether it was ever really successful. If the 'Austrian' flag suddenly disappeared from the Mediterranean, and after all no Austrian submarines had actually operated in the Mediterranean to date, then there would be undesirable comment in the neutral press. Holtzendorf was keen to see the fiction maintained on the grounds that it would deceive the Entente powers as to the real number of German submarines operating in the

Mediterranean but Admiral Karl Kailer von Karltenfels, Haus' representative at the *Marinesektion* at Vienna, was reluctant to countenance the continued use of the Austrian ensign by the Germans. Haus and Kopllamel reached agreement on this matter at Pola on 10 September. The six large submarines which had conducted operations against Italy (*U21*, *U33*, *U34*, *U35*, *U38* and *U39*) were retrospectively taken into the Austrian Navy as of the date they passed through the Straits of Gibraltar. At the end of September 1916 three of these boats would leave the Austrian Navy list while the other three (*U35*, *U38* and *U39*) would nominally remain as Austrian submarines and the Austrian Government would represent them at prize court hearings or at any other negotiations arising out their actions (which given Valentiner's record in the *U38* must have been an unpleasant prospect) although this would in no way alter the *Admiralstab*'s operational control of them.

The campaign against Entente merchant shipping continued unabated. Sinkings continued to remain at a high level with 123 ships totalling 349,018 tons being sunk in the last quarter of 1916 by gun and torpedo, one of which was the French troopship *Gallia* torpedoed on 4 October by the *U35* south of Sardinia. The *Gallia*, struck by one torpedo, sank stern first with the loss of 600 of the French and Serbian troops onboard. De la Perière himself described it as a 'frightful affair . . . the sea became a terrible litter of overturned, overcrowded and swamped lifeboats and struggling men'. A further seven ships totalling 78,981 tons being lost to submarine laid mines. The high mine casualties are partly accounted for by a minefield laid in the Zea Channel on 28 October by *Kapitänleutnant* Siess in the *U73*. This field claimed its first victim, the 12,009 ton French liner *Burdigala*, on 14 November and the huge 48,158 ton liner *Britannic* on 21 November: the largest single merchant casualty of the war. The *Britannic* was still serving as a hospital ship but was mercifully empty at the time of her loss and casualties were light. One of her survivors was a nurse, Violet Jessop, who had been a stewardess on the *Britannic*'s ill fated half-sister ship *Titanic*; a remarkable double escape. Many years later Violet Jessop was able to return to survey the *Britannic*'s wreck, courtesy of Jaques Cousteau and his deep diving ship *Calypso*. Other mine casualties at this time were the hospital ship *Braemar Castle*, beached and later salvaged having been hit while off the ordered route and the liner *Minnewaska* which hit one of the mines laid in Suda Bay (Crete) by the *UC23* (*Leutnant* Kirchner, previously in command of the *UC13*).

In November there was an incident which demonstrated the differing relationships between the Germans and their Austrian allies, at various levels of command. Haus had asked Kophamel to provide a German submarine to rescue ten Austrian officer prisoners from a PoW camp on Sardinia. The officers would escape on a given night and would be picked up by the submarine. Kophamel was anxious to support this request because of the co-operation given him by the Austrians at Pola and Cattaro, but his superiors in Berlin thought otherwise. The request was refused on the grounds that the objective was not worth the

risk. Given that the Admiralstab had previously agreed to Valentiner's *U38* attempting to rescue PoWs from Llandudoed on the north coast of Wales in August 1915 it is perhaps cynical to wonder at the *Admiralstab's* reaction had German PoWs been involved.

December 1916 brought no abatement in shipping losses, de la Perière and the newly arrived UCII type submarine, *UC22 (Leutnant Heino von Heimburg, previously in command of the UB14)*, which had arrived at Cattaro on 12 October were particularly active. The UCII type submarine minelayer was a scaled up version of the successful UCI type but carried two bow tubes and a stern tube as well as an 88mm gun. More importantly they could reach the Mediterranean by sea thus avoiding the vexatious problem of dismantling the submarine and bringing the sections to Pola by rail. *Oberleutnant zur See* Wolfgang Steinbauer with the *UB47* showed that the UBII types were effective units too despite their low speed. Having torpedoed 18,150 ton Cunard liner *Franconta* off Malta on 4 October, he brought 1916 to a memorable close (for the Germans) by sinking the old French battleship *Gaulois* on 27 December. The *Gaulois*, which had done such sterling work at the Dardanelles, was en route for Corfu from Salonika and was torpedoed 30 miles east of Cerigo while under the escort of a destroyer and two trawlers, who picked up the survivors.

1916 had been a very successful year for Kophamel and the boats of his flotilla and those of his Austrian allies. With new boats en route and the Entente powers apparently unable to stem the tide of sinkings the prospects for 1917, from Kophamel's view, looked extremely good.

The White Star liner Britannic, wearing the livery of a hospital ship, at Mudros with the ambulance ship Galeka *alongside.*

CHAPTER TEN

1917–18: The U-boat Crisis

At the beginning of 1917 the Germans finally introduced unrestricted submarine warfare in an effort to force an end to the war by starving Britain into surrender. Although the actual decision was taken on 9 January 1917 at a conference at Supreme Headquarters at Schloss Pless the Germans had considered intensifying the campaign in the Mediterranean for some time, the specific question of the Mediterranean being deferred by Holtzendorf until a general decision had been reached. In the operational orders issued to Kophamel most of the Mediterranean was declared a prohibited area where all ships, with the exception of hospital ships, could be attacked without warning. Certain 'sanctuaries' for neutral shipping had been established notably around the Spanish coast and a twenty mile wide corridor running eastwards through the Mediterranean to Greek territorial waters off Cape Matapan.

The Germans also planned to strengthen their Mediterranean Flotilla. Holtzendorf planned that another nine UCII class submarines would be sent to the Mediterranean, one of which would be converted to a transport submarine for conveying supplies of war material to North Africa. He also intended that ten more of the UBII class submarines should be sent since the short distance between base and patrol areas, especially on the Malta-Cerigo route, made them particularly suitable for operations in this theatre.

In taking the decision to introduce unrestricted submarine warfare the Austrians had not been consulted by the Germans, nevertheless the Austrians had to be persuaded that unrestricted submarine warfare was in their interests also. On 20 January 1917 Holtzendorf went to Vienna to attend a conference at the Marinesektion bringing Zimmerman, the German Foreign Secretary, with him. The leading Austrian authorities including the new Emperor Karl (Franz Joseph had died in November 1916), Foreign Minister Czernin and Hungarian premier Tisza were not in favour but Haus, in an interesting reversal of the 'strong German-weak Austrian' stereotype, was very much in favour and already taken measures to provide for the increased number of German submarines which he anticipated would soon be operating from Austrian bases.

The result of the meeting in Vienna was almost a foregone conclusion. Haus and General Conrad von Hotzendorf, the army Chief of

Staff, were the only Austrians who supported the Germans, the objections of Czernin and Tisza being ignored. Haus brought up the, often overlooked, point that submarines of the Entente powers had, in effect, been practising unrestricted submarine warfare for some time and cited the examples of the *Elektra* and *Dubrovnik* referred to earlier. In the end at a Crown Council on 22 January, the Austrians gave their consent although as Czernin noted,

'. . . it was one of those instances that prove when a strong and weak nation concert in war, the weak one cannot desist unless it changes sides entirely . . . with a heavy heart we gave our consent'.

The actual details of the Austrian agreement would be worked out at a conference at Pless and the statement was duly issued on 1 February. The Austrians also announced that their submarines would henceforth operate outside the Adriatic on the Malta-Cerigo route and the Germans promised to assist in the provision of codes and intelligence.

The Pless conference was, literally, the death of Admiral Haus. He caught a chill in the unheated railway carriage used for the meeting which developed into pneumonia and died at Pola onboard his flagship on 8 February 1917. He was succeeded by Admiral Maximilian Njegovan who had been in command of the 1st Battle Squadron and as he shared many of Haus' views it was unlikely to change Austrian strategy.

One consequence of Njegovan's appointment as Austrian *Flottenkommandant* was that greater priority was given to submarine construction in Austrian shipyards, the Austrian U-boat arm being considerably expanded in 1917. First, the four submarines of the *Havmanden* type, the *U20*, *U21*, *U22* and *U23*, eventually joined the fleet toward the end of the year. Then on 21 July 1917 the Germans transferred the *UB43* and *UB47* to the Austrians who renumbered them *U43* and *U47*. This was not the generous gesture it appeared to be, for the boats were in such a worn out condition that the Germans were simply saving themselves the trouble of refitting them. A more hopeful development was the commissioning between 14 February 1917 and 19 February 1918 of the ten submarines of the U27 class, the *U27* herself, *U28*, *U29*, *U30*, *U31*, *U32*, *U40*, *U41*, *U43* and *U47*, all of which were UBII type boats ordered in October 1915 to be built at Pola and Fiume. The Austrians had ambitious plans for a force of 63 ocean going submarines, in order to keep a force of 21 at sea, of which six – were actually ordered (*U50*, *U51*, *U56* and *U57* of the U50 class and *U52* and *U53* of the U52 class), and although some were laid down none was ever completed.

The Germans did not choose a particularly auspicious moment to begin the new campaign in the Mediterranean for after the efforts of the previous year the greater part of the Mediterranean flotilla was in refit or under repair and it would not be until April 1917 that the flotilla was up to strength. Even so, Kophamel was in command of a considerable number of submarines. The ten large submarines, all veterans of the Mediterranean campaigns of 1915 and 1916 had been joined by the *U47* and *U63* at the end of 1916. The two UE type mine-layers, *U72* and *U73*, were still operational as were the UB type boats *UB14*, *UB42*, *UB43* and *UB47*. Of the UC types, the *UC14* was still in service, although soon to be dismantled and sent to Flanders where she was mined off Zeebrugge in October. She had been joined by the *UC20*, *UC22*, *UC23*, *UC24*, *UC25*, *UC34* and *UC35* which had sailed from Germany at the end of 1916. They were to be followed by the nine boats promised by Holtzendorf in January: the *UC27*, *UC37*, *UC38*, *UC52*, *UC53*, *UC54*, *UC67*, *UC73* and *UC74*. To this number would be added the *UB48*, *UB49*, *UB50*, *UB52*, *UB53*, *UB68*, *UB69*, *UB70*, *UB71*, *UB105* and *UB129* of the UBIII type as they became available during 1917. The increasing size of the German flotilla caused the *Admiralstab* to consider some changes in command. This was no reflection on Kophamel's ability, on the contrary for in June he returned to Germany to take up command of a new large submarine, the *U151*. In all navies submarine operations were, and are, often characterised by junior officers holding comparatively senior appointments, at that time the Germans undoubtedly felt that Kophamel's relatively junior rank, he was only a *Korvettenkapitän*, may have made it difficult for him to deal with the hierarchical and protocol conscious Austrian naval authorities. On 9 June *Kapitän zur See* Pullen assumed command of the flotilla with the title of *Führer der Unterseeboote im Mittelmeer* (commonly abbreviated to *FdU*) with the rank of Commodore, a move which reflected the growing importance of the Mediterranean flotilla to the *Admiralstab*.

The first six months of 1917 were outstandingly successful for the boats of the Mediterranean flotilla. A total of 799,350 tons of merchant shipping were sunk by gun or torpedo with another 33,614 tons lost to submarine laid mines. To these figures must be added the 39,481 tons sunk by Austrian submarines which began to operate outside the Adriatic from April. It was Steinbauer in the *UB47* who began the year, literally, by sinking the 14,229 tons troopship *Ivernia* on 1 January off Cape Matapan. Then on the 9th Hartwig's *U32* sank the British battleship *Cornwallis* off Malta with three torpedoes, the old ship stayed afloat long enough for all but fifteen of her complement to be taken off but it was a serious loss none the less. One exasperated British officer wrote, 'Do you realise we have lost seven battleships since the show started . . . I'd give anything to push a submarine's face'. Then, Forstmann's *U39* was responsible for the loss of the French troopship *Amiral Magon* of 5,666 tons while a mine laid from Siess' *U73* off Port Said claimed the old Russian battleship *Peresviet* en route from the Far East to the Arctic on 4 January.

The system of sending merchant shipping along fixed patrolled routes which had been agreed among the allied powers in 1916 was not working, primarily because all a U-boat commander had to do was find the route and then roll up the shipping as it came along. But there were more serious inadequacies. Liaison between the allies was never satisfactory and the loss of the Italian troopship *Minas* on 15 February illustrates the point perfectly. The *Minas* was bound for Salonika with Serbian troops onboard and was under escort by Italian destroyers. On reaching the demarcation line between the British and Italian zones the Italian escort turned back, leaving the troopship to proceed unescorted. There was no British escort to meet her since the authorities at Malta had not been informed of the ship's movements, and while proceeding unescorted, the *Minas* became an easy victim for Forstmann's *U39* sinking with a loss of 870 lives.

Two days after the loss of the *Minas* another troopship, the French *Athos* carrying Senegalese troops and coolies, was torpedoed by von Fischel's *U65* with a loss of over 1,000 lives. Merchant ships were not the only casualties: *U64* (Moraht) torpedoed the French pre dreadnought battleship *Danton*, built in 1909, on 19 March off Sardinia with the loss of 806 lives, one of the biggest death rolls for a single warship loss in the Mediterranean. Moraht had a lucky escape for after firing *U64* lost trim and broached in full view of the *Danton's* escort, the French destroyer *Massue*, which made a determined attack with depth charges, an attack which Moraht avoided by going deep. By the time he returned to periscope depth the *Massue* had returned to the work of rescuing the *Danton's* crew. Another warship loss was the French minelayer *Cassini* sunk on the night of 28 February off Cape Bonifacio. Her loss was the source of lurid stories that the submarine had fired on the survivors in the water, yet in all probability the *Cassini* had fallen victim to a mine laid by the *UC35* a few days earlier.

March also saw the loss of the Austrian *U30*, one of the UBII type U-boats built by the Austrians in Fiume. On 31 March she sailed from Cattaro under the command of *LSL* Friedrich Fähndrich, who previously had commanded the *U15*, and was never seen again, although it was 11 May before the *Flottenkommando* announced that she must be presumed lost. Her loss has been credited to an attack carried out by the British drifters *Plough Boy* and *Sarah Maria* on 29 April in the Otranto Straits. However, the *U30* was only due to stay out for three weeks at the most and she should have passed the Otranto Barrage northward bound some eight or nine days previously. No allied submarine attacked an enemy submarine in this period, nor was any attack by a German U-boat reported, thus ruling out the possibility of an 'Own Goal'. In the absence of any firm evidence *U30's* loss must be ascribed to either a mine or an accident.

The number of sinkings achieved during April 1917 were the best of the entire war. No less than thirteen German and Austrian boats were out on patrol, between them sinking 51 steamers and 43 sailing ships: 25% of the total for the first 6 months of 1917. A particularly bad day for the allies with the loss of three valuable troopships was 15 April: the Austrian *U29* (*LSL* Leo Prasil) sank the British India liner *Mashobra* off Cape Matapan; the *Arcadian*, en route for Egypt from Salonika with 1000 troops onboard, sank in only six minutes after being torpedoed by the *UC74* (*Kapitänleutnant* W Marschall) 26 miles NE of Milo, with the loss of 242 troops and 35 of the crew; while at the same time the 10,963 tons *Cameronia* was sunk east of Malta by the *U33*, now commanded by *Kapitänleutnant* Siess (earlier in command of *U73*), with 140 casualties. The following day Siess sank the French troopship *Sontay* (7,247 grt) even though the ship was part of a convoy of three ships escorted by a destroyer and an armed yacht. But these were only the major losses, though the steady attrition of merchant shipping with their valuable cargoes was of serious concern and threatened to bring the Allies to their knees.

A new feature of the campaign waged by the Mediterranean U-boats was the occasional foray made into the Atlantic. De la Perière's *U35* was the first to pass westward through the Straits of Gibraltar on the 12 April followed the next night by *Kapitänleutnant* Walther Hans in *U52*, who had already sank the large passenger ships *Ravenna* and *Missourian* off the west coast of Italy. Between them these two U-boats caused havoc in the eastern Atlantic, Hans sinking six and de la Perière seventeen ships before both submarines returned to Cattaro.

This period represented the very nadir of allied efforts to combat the U-boat, with one staff officer describing the system of allied control in the Mediterranean as anarchy. Predictably, the allied response to the German campaign was yet another conference, this time at Corfu between 28 April and 1 May and held onboard the *Provence*, flagship of the French commander in chief, Vice-Admiral Gauchet, 'a dour Norman'. Early in January 1917 the British had unilaterally abandoned the system of fixed routes for their shipping, although the London Conference later confirmed the decision. Instead, merchant ships were ordered to scurry between defended anchorages making full use of neutral waters where possible. Although the system of 'dispersing' shipping did result in a small drop in losses there was no avoiding the fact that there were certain choke points through which shipping had to pass, such as the waters around Malta or the approaches to Salonika, and these were well known to the U-boat commanders.

The Corfu Conference failed to produce a coherent strategy for dealing with the U-boats. There was little argument in deciding that the system of fixed patrol routes was not working. Coastal navigation was recommended as was the routing of east of Aden traffic around the Cape together with a rudimentary convoy system. Perhaps the most important decision of the conference was that control of the anti submarine war should be vested in a British flag officer with his headquarters at Malta, thereby leaving Gauchet to concentrate on the threat posed by the Austrian battlefleet at Pola and the *Goeben* at Constantinople. The French had tried to claim the appointment for a French admiral but this had been rejected by the Admiralty on the grounds that it was the Royal Navy which was bearing the brunt of the anti submarine campaign. The French did not press the matter and were satisfied by a British promise that the theoretical supremacy of the French Commander-in-Chief at Corfu would be recognised. The Admiralty had wanted to appoint Admiral Sir Rosslyn Wemyss to the post but on his return to London in July their choice fell upon Vice-Admiral Sir Somerset Gough-Calthorpe who took up his appointment at Malta on 6 August.

The Otranto Barrage was another subject discussed by the Corfu Conference. Kerr, the flag officer commanding British naval forces in the Adriatic, had suggested that the barrage, which then consisted of a mobile barrage of indicator nets and drifters running for 44 miles from the Italian coast to Fano Island and supported by British motor launches and French and Italian submarines, was not working and that the 120 drifters would be better employed on patrol work. His proposal was not accepted. Instead the conference went for an increase in the barrage defences with a net running all the way across the Adriatic fitted with mines which would be constantly patrolled. The Otranto Barrage was undoubtedly a nuisance to U-boats transiting the straits in that the drifters and patrols could keep a submarine down, thereby exhausting the battery, but it was no more than that. Max Valentiner summed up the situation perfectly: 'the attempt to block completely a piece of water 40 miles across is condemned to failure at the outset'.

The Barrage was also vulnerable to attacks by Austrian light forces operating out of Cattaro. The Austrians had already demonstrated their willingness to use cruisers and destroyers to disrupt the drifter line but the most celebrated raid took place on 15 May when the light cruisers *Novarra*, *Saida* and *Helgoland* raided the barrage sinking fourteen of the forty seven drifters on patrol and damaging a further four. A further result of the raid was that the drifters were withdrawn at night. The Austrian *U4* (Singule) and *U27* (Fernland) were deployed off Valona and Brindisi respectively in support of the operation while the German *UC25*, *Kapitänleutnant* Feldkirchner, laid a minefield off Brindisi. The story of the raid and of the Austrians' escape from superior allied forces is well known but the day really belongs to *UC25*.

After Feldkirchner had laid his mines he sighted the British cruiser HMS *Dartmouth* returning to Brindisi. From a position off the cruiser's port side Feldkirchner fired two torpedoes one of which struck on the port bow and did tremendous damage, Captain Addison reporting that it was only the armoured deck that was holding the ship together. The cruiser was abandoned but as it became clear that she was not in immediate danger of sinking she was boarded by a skeleton crew and, with the assistance of tugs, was taken in to Brindisi, where it was found that the torpedo had blown a hole which measured some 30 feet by 22 feet. This valuable ship was to be out of action for some time while repairs were made. But the Dartmouth was not the only victim of *UC25* that day. The French destroyer *Boutefeu* had been unable to join the rest of the allied forces earlier in the day due to boiler trouble, but had left Brindisi in the evening to help screen the stricken *Dartmouth*. As she passed through the safe channel she was working up to a speed of 22 knots when she struck one of the mines laid by *UC25* and sank with the loss of 12 of her crew.

May saw a decline in the tonnage of merchant shipping sunk possibly as a result of the counter measures adopted a Corfu. A limited convoy system had begun to operate from Malta to Alexandria on 22 May with some success for only two ships were lost between 22 May and 16 July. Nevertheless losses were still serious and represented a steady toll being taken of allied shipping: 38 steamers and 43 sailing vessels being sunk during the month. The most serious loss was the troopship *Transylvania*, torpedoed by *U63* on 4 May. One of her two escorts was the Japanese destroyer *Matsu*, one of eight Japanese ships of the 10th and 11th Destroyer Flotillas under the command of Rear Admiral Kozo Sato who flew his flag in the cruiser *Akashi* which were then Japan's contribution to the Mediterranean campaign. The *Matsu* went alongside at great risk and rescued nearly all of the 3,000 troops onboard. A week later another of the Japanese destroyers, the *Sakaki*, had her bows blown off by a torpedo from the Austrian *U27* (*LSL* Robert Teufl von Fernland) south of Crete, killing 68 of the crew. The *U27's* attack resulted in her becoming the object of a determined six hour depth charge attack by *Sakaki's* consorts, an attack vividly described by the submarine's First Officer, *Fregattenleutnant* Kalman Hardy,

> . . . we went, as usual, down to 25, then 50, even 75 metres as a series of bombs exploded over and around us. First the lights went out, then the gyro compass stopped working, soon afterwards the packing rings started to leak. At times I observed our men. They quietly and silently carried out the skipper's orders given by a few gestures of his head and hands only. The enlarged shadows of the crew appeared on the wet bulkheads of the boat like enormous ghosts.

The month of May also saw the only deliberate torpedoing of a hospital ship in the Mediterranean. On 26 May 1917 the *UC67* (*Oberleutnant zur See* Karl Neumann) torpedoed the hospital ship *Dover Castle* in broad daylight off the Algerian coast. The *Dover Castle* sank but not before her wounded were safely transferred to an escorting destroyer. Neumann was tried for war crimes after the war but was acquitted after he claimed he was obeying orders. In his defence he also stated that the *Dover Castle* was escorted and zigzagging in contravention of the Hague Convention and was therefore a permissible target. It was true, for since mid-April the British had decided to escort their Hospital Ships as part of the war of words, with charge and counter-charge of attacks on these ships and their misuse by one side or another.

The island of Crete came within the area of British responsibility, and a system of patrols by small craft was instituted, including many requisitioned local *caiques*. In view of the state of Greek politics at the time with some elements being pro-German whilst others were pro-British, there were fears that the U-boats might be using the island to re-provision or to gain information about the movement of merchant shipping. For a while the local patrols were augmented by the presence of the submarine HMS *E21*, though no contact was ever made with the U-boats. Using the submarine to pretend to be German to test the reliability of local informants ended in farce and the submarine returned to Mudros.

May also saw the loss of two U-boats: the Austrian *U5* (Schlosser) which hit an Austrian mine on 16 May while on trials off Pola (she was later raised and refitted but never saw service again) and the *UC24* (Willich) which was torpedoed on 24 May by the French *Circé* off Cattaro.

In June de la Perière returned to the Atlantic area west of Gibraltar sinking eleven ships totalling 31,000 tons before returning to Cattaro. While de la Perière was raiding the western Atlantic, the new *UC52* (*KL* Ludwig Sahl) on passage to Cattaro from Germany, had to put into Barcelona to undertake repairs on 11 June. The Spanish authorities granted the submarine asylum on condition that she then refrained from attacking ships while bound for Cattaro. Meanwhile the Royal Navy threw a ring round the approaches to Barcelona, including the submarine *E38*, four torpedo boats and four motor launches, to catch the *UC52*. On the night of 29 June Sahl slipped out, evaded the British patrols and reached Cattaro safely, having honoured the assurances he gave the Spanish authorities. However, the Spanish had decided that they would not continue to have their neutrality used, or abused, and announced that henceforth any submarine entering their waters would be interned.

Another submarine with a lucky escape in August 1917 was Forstmann's *U39*. Having left Pola on 19 July Forstmann had sunk 19,000 tons of shipping by 3 August. On 5 August he attacked a convoy off Malta. The sea was a flat calm, so Forstmann was sparing in his use of the periscope. Nevertheless the distinctive 'feather' was spotted and when Forstmann next raised the periscope he found a merchant ship practically on top of him. There was a fearful crash and the boat was rolled over and downwards and the crew heard the sound of the merchant ship's keel grating over the casing. But the pressure hull held and when *U39* surfaced Forstmann found that that the 88mm gun had been knocked off while the compass and the periscopes had been rendered useless. His troubles were not over, four days later while proceeding on the surface with many of the crew taking a 'make and mend' on the casing, two aircraft were spotted. There was mad rush for the hatches and *U39* submerged, but as Forstmann was tightening the clips on the conning hatch, he heard desperate banging on the hatch. Shouting to the control room to blow the forward tanks he opened the hatch and in fell a very wet and badly scared stoker, who had been left on the casing. Forstmann could see the two planes almost on top of him before he closed the hatch a second time and dived the submarine.

In the second half of 1917 although there was a decline in merchant shipping losses, the situation gave no cause for congratulation on the allied side with 751,008 tons of merchant shipping sunk as a result of actions by German and Austrian submarines: 723,846 tons by gun and torpedo and 27,162 tons by submarine laid mines. Victims included the liners *Mongara* and *Mooltan* sunk on 3 and 26 July respectively. The

Mongara was torpedoed just off the breakwater at Messina and the next day a minefield laid by the same submarine claimed the sloops *Aster* and *Azalea*. The two ships were proceeding together when the *Aster* was seen to stop and begin blowing off steam. The *Azalea* stopped and sent over her boats to take off *Aster's* 9 crew but while the rescue work was going on *Azalea* begin to drift into the minefield. Captain C V Usborne, commanding officer of the minelayer *Latona*, was taking passage in the *Azalea* and recorded how he and other officers watched mesmerised from the bridge as the sloop drifted down onto a mine which could be clearly seen bobbing below the surface. When the mine was about six feet away from stem, reality dawned and full speed astern was ordered but too late, the blast nearly took the sloop's bows off but she was towed to Malta and beached. Minelaying claimed another casualty in October, the hospital ship *Goorkha* off Malta, loaded with 400 wounded from Salonika, fortunately the patients were transferred to the *Braemar Castle* and the *Goorkha* was able to make port.

The introduction of convoy to the Mediterranean in October was of considerable importance in defeating the U-boats. Out of 653 ship sailings in the UK-Port Said convoys, only 13 were lost, while in local convoys the results were equally satisfactory. Life was becoming a lot harder too for the Mediterranean U-boats. But allied countermeasures were not the only cause for the decline in sinkings, since many of the German submarines were simply worn out, like de la Perière's *U35* which was in dockyard hands for four months Despite the arrival of new UBIII and UC type submarines the Germans were plagued with mechanical problems. The new *UB52* and six others were out of action for the last quarter of the year. Another of the new boats, von Mellenthin's *UB49* had suffered from a brush with an escort in September while bound for Cattaro and had been forced to take refuge in Cadiz where she was promptly interned by the Spanish. Von Mellenthin was nothing if not resourceful and the following month he broke out of Cadiz and successfully brought his submarine to Cattaro.

Politically, the situation changed when the Greeks were finally brought into the war on the side of the Entente. There was now no need for the U-boats to observe any rules which restricted their operations in Greek waters or might have antagonised the Greeks. For the Allies the changed situation brought little in the way of benefits; some units of the Greek fleet became operational for escort duties but their submarines *Delfin* and *Xifias* were not required for service. With Greece actively in the war, the farce whereby the allies had used Greek island bases, with or without Greek consent, was over.

A further complication for Pullen was the continued interference of the Army in the planning of his operations. The cargo supply runs to North Africa continued with the *UC20* and *UC73* employed exclusively on these operations during the summer. In August 1918 *Oberleutnant* H Rohne and the crew of the *UC20* brought back to Pola what must be the strangest cargo carried by a submarine during the war, not forgetting the goat presented to the crew of HMS *B10*. A Senussi sheikh had decided to send the Kaiser presents in the form of a camel, a goat and a sheep. How the animals were embarked into the tiny hull of the submarine is not recorded, though it must be presumed that the camel was only a baby. The contribution to the atmosphere in the small submarine made by three animals during the return journey is better imagined than described. Understandably, on arrival at Pola, the camel was found to be too sick for transport to Berlin and it lived out its days at a zoo on the island of Brioni. The fate of the goat and sheep has not been recorded but given the shortage of fresh meat in the Dual Monarchy their fate can be imagined. Yet, it is worth recording that the case of the *UC20* is not unique. In 1942 both the *U339* and *U274* were presented with similar problems, though both tactfully got rid of their gifts when out of sight of the donor. HMS *Trident* had the more difficult task of taking a reindeer from North Russia back to Blyth in 1941!

Pullen was also required to occasionally deploy his submarines off the Palestine coast where Turko-German forces around Gaza were under pressure from General Allenby's army which was being supplied by sea and relying on naval gunfire support. The *Admiralstab* had countered early demands made in March 1917 but in October the Turks made a further request. As a result three submarines, the *UC34*, *UC38* and *UC37* were diverted from patrol, although the last named continued to work off Crete having failed, perhaps, to receive the order. They were joined by a fourth, the *UC51*, which was sailed from Pola. The *UC34* and *UC51* found few targets but *Oberleutnant zur See* Hans Wendlandt in the *UC38* did very well, sinking the monitor HMS *M15* and destroyer HMS *Staunch* off Gaza on 11 December, The German Army were suitably impressed and General von Falkenhayn claimed the intervention of the U-boats had saved his army, yet the U-boats had failed to influence the campaign for Gaza fell on 7 November, and while engaged in supporting the army the U-boats could not take part in *Handelskrieg* against allied shipping.

Wendlandt's *UC38* was the second German submarine to be lost in the Mediterranean in 1917. After his successes off Gaza he returned to Cattaro and then set out for a patrol in the Ionian sea. On 14 December he sank the French cruiser *Chateaurenault*, carrying 985 troops, near the entrance to the Gulf of Corinth. The cruiser's escorts, the destroyers *Mameluke* and *Lansquenet*, launched an effective depth charge attack. The *UC38* was blown to the surface and sunk by gunfire, although Wendlandt and a good proportion of his crew were able to abandon the submarine. On 30 December the Germans ended the year with another striking success when the *UC34* sank the troopship *Aragon* off Alexandria and while rescuing survivors the destroyer Attack was either torpedoed or ran onto one of the mines laid earlier by the same submarine. The next day the fleet auxiliary *Osmanieh* was lost in the same minefield bringing 1917 to a dismal end. Yet however improbable it seemed at that time to the allies, the corner had been turned.

The beginning of 1918 saw the Mediterranean flotilla both reinforced and reorganised. The last six of the UBIII type boats sailed from

Germany, *UB68*, *UB69*, *UB70*, *UB71*, *UB105* and *UB129*, though only four arrived at Cattaro. The *UB71* (Schapler) was sunk by *ML.413* off Gibraltar on 17 April and *UB70* (Remy) simply disappeared. The reorganisation of the flotilla was testament to the fact that Pullen could not manage to co-ordinate the operations of all the submarines under his command so the flotilla was divided in half: the 1st Flotilla at Pola under *Kapitänleutnant* Otto Schultze and the 2nd Flotilla at Cattaro under *Kapitänleutnant* Rudolph Ackermann. However *Kapitän zur See* Pullen retained his title as *FdU* and his responsibility for the overall direction of operations.

Two more submarines were lost in January when the *UB69* (*Oblt* Klatt) fouled an explosive sweep towed by HMS *Cyclamen* on the 9th and on the 18th *UB66* (*Oblt* Wernicke) was depth charged by the sloop *Campanula* after attempting to attack a convoy off Cape Bon. In the space of few days the Germans had lost as many submarines as they had in 1917. Then on 21 February the Austrians lost their first submarine of 1918, the *U23* (*Linienschiffsleutnant* Klemens von Bezard). When attacking the Italian transport Menfi, en route to Valona, from Brindisi von Bezard fired both bow tubes and lost trim causing the *U23's* conning tower to break surface. The Italian destroyer *Airone* dropped a pattern of depth charges on the spot, then streamed her explosive sweep and was rewarded with an enormous explosion followed by a large oil slick rising to the surface.

The convoy system which had finally reached the Mediterranean in October the previous year was finally beginning to affect sinkings. The convoys followed no set routes and after a U-boat had made its presence known in an area it was noted that allied traffic was routed away from the submarine forcing the U-boat commanders to spend more time, and fuel, in searching for targets which were harder to find and better protected. The tonnage figures for the first six months of 1918 were an indication of the problems beginning to face the U-boat commanders and the success of the allies' countermeasures, 615,992 tons of allied shipping fell victim to the U-boats in the period, though the figures were no grounds for complacency.

The mechanical and material problems which had dogged them in the latter part of 1917 carried over into the new year. The Austrian dockyard at Pola could not keep pace with the work required to keep the submarines at sea, and at one stage seventeen boats were there awaiting refit. The situation was no better at Cattaro where the staff of the depot ship *Gaa* won an unenviable reputation for sloppy work. The commercial yards at Trieste and Fiume were able to ease the pressure somewhat but the Germans soon realised that they had to stand on their own feet as far as repair work went. Then in February the Germans at Cattaro were spectators as the Austrian Navy mutinied. Trouble broke out in the cruiser *Sankt Georg* and the depot ship *Gaa* on the 1st, but was over by the 3rd. Nevertheless, uncertainty about the reliability of the Austrians cannot have eased the minds of German U-boat commanders going out on patrol. The 'marriage' of the Germans and the Austrians had never been particularly successful – the Germans were a homogeneous ethnic group with harsh discipline but better pay and equipment while the Austrians were a multi national navy suffering from a lack of cohesive identity and insufficient material resources. A further consequence of the mutiny was the replacement of Admiral Njegovan as Austrian Commander in Chief by the younger *Linienschiffskapitän* Nikolas Horthy who was specially promoted to flag rank by the Emperor.

May proved a disastrous month for the U-boats with four of their number being lost. The old *U32* (Albrecht) was lost while attacking a Gibraltar-Alexandria convoy on 8 May between Sicily and Malta, falling to an attack by the sloop HMS *Wallflower*. Then on the 17th the *UC35* (Korsch) mistook the French patrol vessel *Ailly* on convoy duty off Sardinia for a small steamer and surfaced to sink her with gunfire. The *Ailly* fired back holing a ballast tank aft and damaging the conning tower. Korsch gave the order to abandon the submarine and although half the crew got out of the submarine only five, together with a captured Spanish seaman, were picked up. Forstmann's *U39* was the next to go. *Oberleutnant zur See* Metzger had taken over the boat when Forstmann had returned to Germany. On the afternoon of 18 May he had been bombed by French seaplanes off Cartagena and badly damaged. Return to Cattaro was impossible so Metzger opted for internment in Spain and took the veteran boat into Cartagena that evening. The last boat to be sunk in May was the *UB52* (Launburg) torpedoed by the British submarine *H4* (see chapter 11) on 23rd while homeward through the Otranto Barrage.

In June only one submarine was lost but that was *U64* and her veteran commander *Kapitänleutnant* Robert Moraht. In rough seas on 17 June he torpedoed a transport bound for Malta from Marseilles but his periscope was spotted by the escorts. The sloop *Lychnis* dropped depth charges which forced the *U64* to the surface where she was struck a glancing blow as the sloop tried to ram. Moraht took the submarine down again but the boat was making water aft and the steering gear was smashed, and he had little option but to surface and try and fight his way out. As the *U64* surfaced the gun crew scrambled out and vainly tried to engage the escorts but to no avail. The submarine succumbed under a hail of shellfire. Five survivors, including Moraht, were picked up. Moraht was an honourable man who had conducted his operations with more than due regard for international law. Yet such was the efficiency of British propaganda about U-boat atrocities that his British captors could not see the true man for he was described, by no less a person than Captain Edward Evans, 'Evans of the Broke', as 'a very nasty piece of work, arrogant and insolent and a well known murderer with a very bad reputation'. Thus did the decent German naval officer pay for the actions of Valentiner, Gansser and Neumann.

Yet the U-boats were by no means a spent force. Merchant ship losses from 1 July until the end of the war totalled another 237,098 tons to be added to the 616,262 tons of the first six months of the year. Among the losses were the 13,528 ton *Minnetonka* torpedoed by Moraht's *U64* on 30 January and the P&O liner *Omrah* torpedoed on 12 May. Moreover, even though the experienced U-boat 'aces', like de la Perière and Hersing, who had made their names in the Mediterranean had all returned to take up bigger commands in Germany, the younger less experienced U-boat commanders of the *Mittelmeer* division proved that they were no less capable than their predecessors. On 18 March *UC25*, acting on intelligence that the British repair ship *Cyclops* was at Port Augusta, penetrated the harbour defences and torpedoed and sunk a ship which her commanding officer, *Oberleutnant* Karl Dönitz, believed to be the *Cyclops*. Alas, German intelligence was at fault for the target was an old coaling hulk which bore a striking resemblance to the British vessel. Nevertheless it was a bold operation, skilfully executed, and one that earned Dönitz, who had learned his trade under Forstmann in *U39*, a decoration by personal order of the Kaiser. Warships were not immune either: the British destroyer *Phoenix* was torpedoed on 14 May by the Austrian *U27* (*LSL* Josef Holub); the only allied warship to be torpedoed while on duty on the Otranto Barrage. In general the Austrian submarines were still concentrating on the areas around the entrances to the Adriatic and seldom going further afield. The patrol by Holub's *U27*, Austria's most successful submarine, which was out from 29 June to 26 September is all the more worthy of mention. Holub nearly ran out of fuel and had to call in at Beirut to replenish, besides sinking two steamers and 22 sailing vessels. The last major Austrian success of the war came on 2 October when the veteran *LSL* Hermann Rigele, now in command of the *U31*, blew the stern of the cruiser HMS *Weymouth* while she was engaged in a bombardment of Durazzo: four men were killed by the explosion. The Austrian *U29* (*LSL* Robert Dürrigl) was also in this area but was persistently harried by aircraft and American motor launches. At one stage Dürrigl recorded thirty six depth charge explosions in little more than an hour.

But the general trend was going against the U-boats. On 4 July the Austrian *U20* (*LSL* Ludwig Müller) was torpedoed by the Italian submarine *F12* in the northern Adriatic (see chapter 11), while on 9 July the *U10* (*LSL* Friedrich Stertz) went aground off the Tagliamento estuary, again in the northern Adriatic, after striking a mine. She was refloated but did not see action again. On 3 August the *UB53* (*Oblt* Sprenger) was outward bound from Pola and had dived deep to avoid the nets and minefields of the Otranto Barrage. When he judged himself to be clear of the barrage Sprenger gave the order to surface. Almost immediately the boat was shaken by a large explosion for the Austrians were unaware the minefield had been extended and the submarine had been mined. By blowing everything Sprenger managed to surface the submarine. After a vain attempt to proceed on the surface Sprenger gave the order to abandon the submarine and the crew were picked up by the destroyer HMS *Martin* and drifter *Whitby Abbey*. The last U-boat to be sunk in the Mediterranean was *UB68* commanded by *Oblt* Karl Dönitz who had taken over the submarine after leaving the

UC25 in August. On his first patrol in his new command Dönitz encountered a convoy off Malta on 4 October. Dönitz attacked from outside the screen and succeeded in sinking of the 3,883 ton *Oopack*. He then proceeded parallel to the convoy but while attempting an submerged attack lost the trim and the submarine broached in full view of the escorts where she was sunk by gunfire from the sloop *Snapdragon* and trawler *Cradosin*. Dönitz and the majority of his crew were taken prisoner, but his engineer officer, *Oberingeneur* Jeschen, deliberately remained in the boat to ensure that the vents were open and that *UB69* did not fall into enemy hands.

It must be emphasised that despite these losses the U-boats were by no means beaten. New tactics were under consideration to beat the escorts. *Kapitän zur See* Kurt Grasshoff, who had taken over from Pullen in August 1918, was making some of the first experiments in using more than one boat to attack a convoy simultaneously. Von Mellenthin in the *UB49* is believed to originated these tactics early in 1918 and worked with a number of boats, including Steinbauer in the *UB48* and Dönitz's *UC25*. But the experiment was not successful due to poor communications, poor weather and the evasive routing of the convoys around areas in which U-boats were known to be operating. However the seed of an idea had been sown, and under Dönitz's direction would bear fruit in the next World War.

By this time no amount of determination would enable the U-boats to prevail against the allies. At the end of September 1918 the general outlook for the Central Powers was bleak, the final German offensive on the Western Front of March 1918 had finally run out of steam by July and the German High Command began serious consideration of an armistice. On 12 October the German premier, Prince Max of Baden, announced German acceptance of President Wilson's 'Fourteen Points'. But mere acceptance was not enough, the allies wanted concrete proof that the Germans were sincere in their desire for peace and on the 16 October the Germans were informed that they must cease unrestricted submarine warfare forthwith. The following day the Germans agreed and issued orders to their U-boat commanders to cease attacks on merchant ships. Yet in their final effort the Germans nearly achieved a spectacular success when Steinbauer penetrated a screen of four destroyers and torpedoed the French battleship *Voltaire* off Cerigotto on the night of 10/11 October. Despite two torpedo hits, good damage control and a well worked up crew enabled her to avoid the fate of her sister, the *Danton*, and to reach Milo under her own power.

The Austrians too were ready to accept the inevitable and *AOK* ordered all Austrian U-boats to cease *Handelskrieg* on 17 October and concentrate on the defence of the ports along the Dalmatian coast. Grasshoff had contracted typhus and relinquished his command to Pullen who returned in October. With the allied 'Army of the Orient' finally advancing northwards from Salonika Pullen realised that the future of Austrian-Hungarian Empire, and therefore the future of the

German bases in the Adriatic, was in doubt and the main priority for the Germans became one of saving whatever they could. The campaign against merchant shipping was over.

CHAPTER ELEVEN

The Adriatic, 1917–18

The focus of Entente submarine activity in the Mediterranean during the last two years of war was the Adriatic although British and French submarines continued to patrol in the Aegean, where the French submarine *Floreal* was lost in collision with the British armed boarding steamer *Hazel* on 2 August 1918. In the western Mediterranean some submarines were also based on Gibraltar and Bizerta.

The Adriatic, with the important Austrian bases of Pola and Cattaro, remained the crucible though it must have been a very frustrating place for those operating there. Targets were few as the Dalmatian coastal trade had practically died out, largely as a result of their successes in 1916. When Austrian merchant ships did move they did so in convoy under heavy escort and behind protective minefields. The U-boats were equally elusive. The French official history records that in 1917 Entente submarines spent 500 days on patrol. During this period there were 367 German or Austrian submarine movements from Cattaro, yet only 26 of these were sighted, 12 attacks made and one U-boat sunk. The figures for 1918 are very similar. In contrast, the Entente powers themselves lost ten submarines in the Mediterranean in 1917–18 of which six were sunk in the Adriatic: two – the Italian *Zoea* and *Ferraris* – as a result of bad weather, the Italian *H5* became the victim of an 'own goal' incident, while the French *Bernouilli* and *Circé* and Italian *W4* because of enemy action.

Throughout 1917 the French and Italians bore the brunt of the work in the southern Adriatic since until August the British H class were still working from Venice and the larger E class submarines were required for the Aegean although some patrols were carried out from Malta. The composition of the French force would remain very much the same with the submarines of the *Pluvoise* and *Brumaire* classes which had done such good work in 1915–16 providing the backbone of their force together with the *Archimède, Gustave Zede, Circé,* and *Amazone* and four boats of the *Ampitrite* class: *Artemis, Ariane, Atalante* and *Arethuse*. The *Archimède* and the other steam driven boats had done sterling work but were not suited to the Adriatic where the Austrians were very vigilant and where, therefore, a submarine needed to be able to dive quickly, something the steam driven boats with their many hull openings were not able to do. The *Pluvoise* class were all to be withdrawn in 1917 and the *Archimède* in April. Their replacements were two submarines of the *Bellone* class, the *Gorgone* and *Hermione*.

The Italian submarine forces underwent considerable expansion during 1917-18 as a result of new construction by Italian shipyards and in Canada and by transfer of submarines from the British. As regards new construction there were two submarines of the *Pacinotti* class which were basically upgraded versions of the *Balilla* and armed with three 45cm bow tubes. A far more substantial programme was the 21 boats of the F class based on a design for the Brazilian Navy built by Fiat San Giorgio before the war. These submarines were of 262/319 tons displacement and armed with two 45cm bow tubs and a 3 inch AA gun. Sadly, the *F8* was lost in an accident while on trials on 14 February 1917 off La Spezia, although she was later raised and commissioned in September. The Italians also purchased eight H class submarines from Canadian Vickers at Montreal. Built to an American design they were identical to the British H class then serving in the northern Adriatic, the only important difference being that the Italian boats were built with a standard for the wireless aerial at the after end of the conning tower. The transfer of the seven submarines of the S and W classes from the Royal Navy has already been mentioned.

Another serious accident befell the *Gugliemotti*, one of the two *Pacinotti* class. The submarine was making her way south from La Spezia and crossed the north-south convoy route east of Corsica on the night of 10 March 1917. Also in the area was a convoy escorted by the sloop HMS *Cyclamen* which had been warned of German submarines in the area but not of the *Gugliemotti*'s likely presence. Since one of the ships in convoy was a troopship the *Cyclamen* was taking no chances when she sighted the low shape of the submarine, and promptly rammed her. On picking up the few survivors the *Cyclamen*'s signal – one of the war's classics – demonstrated a certain black humour: 'Have rammed and sunk enemy submarine. Survivors appear to speak Italian.' The *Cyclamen* thus achieved the dubious distinction of being the only warship to sink a submarine of both sides during the First World War*, but there is no denying that the event was a tragedy in which 14 Italian seamen lost their lives.

It was the French who showed the most drive in the Adriatic during 1917, a fact which did not go unnoticed by Vice-Admiral Sir Somerset Gough-Calthorpe, the British Commander-in-Chief, who when writing to the Admiralty at the end of November commented that 'the Italian submarines at Brindisi have done little serious work'. On 14 January the old steam driven *Archimède* torpedoed the Austrian transport Zagreb off Cape Planka in a difficult attack skilfully executed in shallow water and within sight of several Austrian coast watching stations. It was the fourth transport to be sunk by the Archimède during the war in a theatre where targets were few and far between, and her success made her the most successful Entente submarine outside the Marmara. Unfortunately her commanding officer, *Lieutenant de Vaisseau* [*LV*] Paty de Clam, described by the French Commander-in-Chief as an officer of consu-

---

* See Chapter 10 for the sinking by HMS *Cyclamen* of the *UB69* on 8 January 1918.

mate skill, was killed in an accident soon after his return to Brindisi.

The French submarines were often in the right place at the right time but were consistently unlucky. Undoubtedly one reason for their lack of success must have been their continued reliance on the Drzewiecki external drop collars as the means of delivering their torpedoes. During the raid on the Otranto Barrage by the Austrian light cruisers on 15 May 1917 the *Bernouilli* (*LV* Audry) was on patrol off Durazzo and fired at the Austrian destroyer *Balaton*, but missed. The other submarine on patrol that night was the Italian *F12* off Cattaro and she failed to sight the Austrian forces either leaving or returning to the port.

But it was the U-boats that were the main targets and these proved remarkably elusive. On 31 March 1917 *LV* de Cambourg's *Circé* attacked de la Perière's *U35* without success, while on 2 April *LV* Cazalis in the Archimède missed the Austrian *U27* (*LSL* Robert Teufl von Fernland) setting out from Cattaro on her first war patrol. Fernland saw the torpedoes coming in plenty of time to outmanoeuvre them, noting that the *Archimède* broached after firing the second torpedo. On 5 April de la Perière had another escape when the *U35* was again unsuccessfully attacked, this time by the *Faraday* (*LV* Bougard). However, in May the French were finally rewarded with a success when de Cambourg in the *Circé* sank the *UC24* with two torpedoes. Only two of the German submarine's crew survived to be picked up by her Austrian escort.

One result of the sinking of the *UC24* was that the mine defences around Cattaro were considerably improved with several new fields being laid. Anti-submarine patrols by torpedo boats and aircraft were also increased making the area decidedly unhealthy for any Entente submariner. The first casualty of the new defences was the Italian *W4*. She had sailed from Brindisi for a patrol off Cattaro on 3 August and was never seen again. While accepting that she may have foundered as a result of an accident it is, however, most likely that she became a victim of one of the new minefields.

The French *Ariane* was the next to be lost, torpedoed off Bizerta by the *UC22*. The *Ariane* (*LV* Viort) had joined the French submarines operating in the Adriatic in November 1916 after commissioning at La Rochelle. After a work-up at Bizerta she was ordered to Malta and thence to Brindisi. Before leaving Viort called on Vice-Admiral Guepratte and asked to be kept at Bizerta in the event of a U-boat appearing in the area when he could then proceed with the *Ariane* to locate and destroy the enemy. Although touched by the young officer's spirit Guepratte could do nothing but refuse since 'orders were orders'. Accordingly Viort and his submarine left for the Adriatic. In March the *Ariane* returned to Bizerta for repairs and again Viort sought to remain in the area to have the chance of sinking a U-boat. Again Guepratte had to refuse since Viort was not under his command. After another period in Bizerta in May 1917 the *Ariane* began post refit trials in the Gulf of Sirte in June. At the same time two U-boats made their presence felt in the area and Guepratte, mindful of Viort's enthusiasm, ordered the *Ariane* to patrol off Cape Bon. But, the submarine was delayed in reaching her patrol area because of a breakdown of one of the diesels, and was struck by two torpedoes fired by the *UC22* while lying on the surface effecting repairs.

The Italians concluded what had been a bad year with two more losses, both as a result of bad weather. The *Zoea*, one of the 250/305 tons *Medusa* class built in 1913 and armed with two bow torpedo tubes, went aground near Rimini during a storm on 26 November. She was towed off by the tug *Ciclope* and taken to Venice for repairs but after a survey had to be written off as a total loss. The next day the *Galieo Ferraris*, sister of the ill fated *Giacinto Pullino*, went aground near Porto Garibaldi. She too was refloated but again was considered as beyond repair.

What of the British submarines? They had been based on Malta and operating in the central and Eastern Mediterranean. Their operations had not been without incident although in general they reflected the same disappointing lack of success as the French and Italian boats. On 29 April the *E2*, then commanded by Lieutenant Commander Samuel Gravener, found the *UC67* in the act of sinking an Italian sailing vessel off Marsala in Sicily. The Germans were too busy watching the Italian crew rowing hard for the shore to notice the *Gravener*'s stealthy approach. He fired one torpedo – the *E2* in common with the first eight boats of the class had only one bow tube – which struck the German on the port side, but did not explode. The Germans wasted no more time, the boarding party was hastily recalled and the U-boat dived to safety. In a letter written to Gravener after the war one of the *UC67*'s officers, Fritz Boie, wrote: '. . . after diving the helmsman, he was an old and good seaman, with a look at the clock said to me 'Today is Sunday and at 10 o'clock my bride is sitting in church and praying for me."

Her prayers were evidently successful for the *UC67* survived the war. A more likely cause for her deliverance on this occasion was that either Gravener had fired at too short range and the torpedo had not sufficient run to arm itself, or that he had used too great an impulse pressure to fire the torpedo, a common error among British submariners at that time, with the result that the torpedo had run deep striking the U-boat on her curved underside and been deflected without activating the firing pistol.

The British were destined to play a more active role in the Adriatic as a result of the need to strengthen the Otranto Barrage forces. On 20 October Admiral Gough-Calthorpe informed Commodore Howard Kelly who commanded the British naval forces in the Adriatic, that HMS *Adamant* (Commander K M Bruce) with the submarines *E11*, *E14*, *E21* and *E25* would proceed to Corfu where a base was to be established. The submarines would then operate a dived patrol south of the drifter line between Cape Santa Maria di Leuca and Fano Island, thus increasing the size of the area which would be dangerous to submarines entering or leaving Cattaro. They were to be joined in due course by two French submarines. The little port of Govino on the west coast of the island was used by the *Adamant* and the submarines, and since the depot ship was unsuitable as an accommodation ship a tented camp was set up near the old Venetian battery, about 1½ miles from the pier, a nearer site having to be abandoned as too near a swamp. Even so, though pleasant in winter months, the camp would have proved almost uninhabitable in summer unless drainage work had been carried out.

Also joining the British forces were the three H class submarines which returned from Venice in August. The condition of these submarines left a lot of be desired since all were in need of refit. Kelly reported that:

> . . . the peace time life of the batteries of the *H2* and *H4* has almost expired and they have already completed the number of charges authorised. Also the deterioration of their batteries is considerably greater in hot weather and these boats have now completed three summers in the Mediterranean.

The problem lay in where the refits were to be carried out. Initially it was proposed that the hull and machinery work should be carried out in an Italian dockyard and the submarines going to Malta for battery work, since that dockyard was congested with damaged ships. However, as Lieutenant Commander David Fell, the commanding officer of the *H2* and senior officer of the three submarines, pointed out that this arrangement would take considerably longer as the batteries would have to be removed twice, once for the inspection of the battery tanks and again for the battery change. In the event the matters was deferred and the three boats began patrols from Brindisi at the end of August 1917, the first patrol being carried out by the *H4* between 24 and 27th off Cattaro. From then until the end of 1917 the three boats carried out 21 largely uneventful patrols off Cattaro. Attacks were made on U-boats on 4 September by the *H1*, on 17 October by the *H4* and 30 October by the *H2*. None were successful.

By 15 November the battery of the *H2* was in such poor condition that it could no longer be relied upon and it was essential to start on the refits of the three submarines. Taranto could not accept the British boats before the end of the year because of work on the Italian submarines *H6*, *H7* and *H8* and it was therefore decided to send the *H2* to Malta, with the *H4* to follow, where work would start on 1 December. It was expected that dealing only with essential defects and the battery the task would take five or six weeks. Meanwhile the *H1*, in better condition than the other two was docked at Brindisi in mid-December.

It was not until early 1918 that the E class submarines became available for the Adriatic. All four were badly in need of refit and the *E21* and *E25* were required for operations off the Azores, based on Gibraltar. By then the Corfu base had been abandoned and the decision taken to base the submarines at Brindisi under the operational direction of the Italian Commander-in-Chief. Their patrol area was also changed and moved to north of the main barrage forces to an area between Cattaro and Durazzo on the Dalmatian coast.

The command structure at Brindisi was unsatisfactory to say the least. All Entente submarines were nominally responsible to their own national Commanders-in-Chief but worked under the operational control of the Italian authorities. Thus the British boats under Commander Charles Benning, were part of Commodore Kelly's British Adriatic Force but their orders were issued by the Italian senior submarine officer, *Capitano de Fregata* Mollana. The French submariners under *Capitaine de Corvette* Magnier were in a similar position. Fortunately Howard Kelly, an officer whose indiscriminate sarcasm to all around him was notorious, enjoyed excellent relations with both the Italians and the French.

HMS *Adamant* arrived at Brindisi on 28 March 1918 and was followed two days later by both the *E21* and *E25*, to be joined later by the *E2*, *E11* and *E12*. In April they were joined by the minelayer *E46*: a standard E class submarine with the two beam tubes removed and carrying 20 mines, ten a side, in five vertical chutes in the saddle tanks. In May the *E48* joined the flotilla. The *H7* and *H8* were also under orders to join the Adriatic flotilla but did not partake in any offensive patrols before the end of the war. Finally, the monster *M1*, armed with a 12 inch gun, arrived in the Mediterranean*. All British submarines came under the command of Commander Charles Benning, a veteran of the early days of the submarine war in the Heligoland Bight and whose last command had been the steam driven fleet submarine *K1*, which had been lost in collision in November 1917. In the subsequent Court Martial Benning had been reprimanded for hazarding his ship but a note in his record adds that there was 'no evidence regarding his want of capability and certainly none of any lack of zeal'.

The new year opened with the loss of another submarine, the *Bernouilli* and her experienced commanding officer *LV* Audry. She was mined off Cattaro in the middle of February. Worse was to follow. In an effort to demonstrate the 'international' nature of the Entente submarine operations it was the practice for one British, one French and an Italian boat to proceed on patrol together, occupying adjoining patrol areas. This practice was not viewed with universal enthusiasm by the British, at least, who were not confident of the navigational abilities of their allies. On the evening of 16 April the *H1* (Lieutenant John Owen) sighted a submarine lying stopped on the surface about 1 miles away. When the range came down to 1200 yards Owen fired two torpedoes and observed one hit. On surfacing to rescue any survivors Owen was horrified to find that his target had been the Italian *H5* (*Tenente di Vascello* [*TV*] Quentin). Owen picked up only two officers, including Quentin, and three ratings.

The Italian boat had surfaced at 7.35 pm to charge the batteries

---

* See Chapter 13.

while it was still light, an argument which Commodore Kelly described as 'looking for trouble'. Quentin was unaware that he had drifted into the *H2*'s operating area. It was at 7.45 when Owen had sighted the other and asked his navigator, Lieutenant Hayes, to confirm his assessment that the target was a U-boat. Hayes agreed and said he thought it was a UB type submarine. Accordingly Owen began his attack and fired eight minutes later. The torpedo struck the *H5* on the port side near the galley, probably killing instantly most of the crew who were assembled there for their evening meal.

The Court of Enquiry which met to determine what had happened had an exceedingly difficult task. National rivalries at Brindisi were never far below the surface, and any report which laid too much blame on either party could have far reaching and damaging effects on inter-allied relations. The report managed an accurate assessment of what had happened, yet without laying the responsibility at any one doorstep. That good relations were maintained is largely due to Captain W Hope, of the cruiser HMS *Dartmouth*, who was extremely adept at dealing with the Italians. The only positive thing to come of the sad affair was that mixed patrols were abandoned. Henceforth submarines of the three navies would take turns going on patrol, the British going out for five or six days at a time, the French and Italians for less. By the spring of 1918 the Otranto Barrage forces had grown considerably in numbers with ships, submarines and aircraft of five nations, Britain, France, Italy, Japan and the USA, operating in a very restricted area. In June 1918 a flotilla of 36 US submarine chasers joined the Barrage forces, crewed largely by reservists and Ivy League undergraduates. What they lacked in professional skill – was more than compensated for by their enthusiasm, they seldom returned to harbour without having expended all their depth charges and with tales of successes that would annihilated the Austro-German submarine fleet several times over. In the circumstances it was inevitable that there would be more cases of 'mistaken identity'.

On 28 May the French submarine *Le Merrier* attacked two British destroyers who were passing through her patrol area. She had not been warned of their movements but fortunately *LV* Landriau, the submarine commanding officer, recognised the two ships as friendly and broke off his attack in time. Another French submarine, the *Volta*, was shelled by some destroyers before they too realised their error. But it was the French *Artemis* which had the thinnest time at the hands of her allies. On 23 July she was attacked and bombed by two RNAS aircraft and forced to go deep to escape. Then, in what must have been the ultimate indignity for a French submarine, the *Artemis* spent Bastille Day evading the attentions of British destroyers which first shelled her and then dropped depth charges around the submarine.

The offensive against the U-boats remained the main priority. Between May 1918 and the end of the war British submarines were in contact with U-boats on six occasions, yet only one of the attacks was successful. On 23 May the *H4* (Lieutenant Oliver North) sighted a U-boat three points [33¾°] on her port bow, silhouetted in the light of the moon and seen to be on a northerly course. In a snap attack North fired two torpedoes at a range of only 250 yards and scored two hits. The U-boat was the *UB52* homeward bound for Cattaro. The commanding officer, *Leutnant* Otto Launburg and a signalman alone survived to be picked up by the *H4*. The rest were a series of frustrating unsuccessful attacks, one by the *E2* and two each by the *E12* and *E21*. On each occasion the British boat was either unable to gain a firing position or the torpedoes missed. Two of these attacks are worthy of mention.

On 5 August the *E12* (Lieutenant F Williams-Freeman) fired two torpedoes at a U-boat. Both torpedoes were set to run at a depth of 8 feet, yet the port torpedo ran under the enemy while the starboard one missed ahead. The U-boat then turned towards the *E12* in an attempt to ram the British boat, but Williams-Freeman turned to port under full helm and fired her starboard beam torpedo which also missed, and the U-boat was not seen again. On 19 August the *E21* (Lieutenant H C Carlyon Britton) fired two torpedoes in a shot from abaft the beam at a U-boat at a range of 2000 yards, both missed. The *E21* remained in the area and two days later was rewarded by sighting the conning tower of a U-boat lying trimmed down on the surface. The *E21* closed the range and when the target was 600 yards away Carlyon-Britton fired the starboard tube. Again the torpedo missed, passing just ahead of the conning tower. In desperation Carlyon-Britton tried to ram the enemy but the U-boat was diving fast at a very steep angle and the *E21* passed over her. In fact both the attacks by the *E21* were on the same submarine, *LSL* Otto Kasseroller's *U32*, on patrol along the Brindisi-Valona route and having an unhappy time. In between the two attacks by the *E21* she had been bombed by aircraft.

The British were equally unsuccessful in their attacks on the few Austrian warships and transports which were sighted. The only success belongs to the *E21* which torpedoed a small transport on 30 June. After firing Carlyon-Britton went to 50 feet and put the helm hard over, for he was less than 1200 yards from the shore. Those stationed in the submarine's fore ends heard an explosion followed by the sound of wreckage falling on the water. Five minutes later when Carlyon-Britton raised the periscope he saw the escorting torpedo boat with her boats lowered and rescuing survivors. Undeterred by the humanitarian work in which the torpedo boat was engaged Carlyon-Britton fired his stern tube at a range of about a mile, but the torpedo was avoided. The *E21* then proceeded dived out of the area and made her way northward being chased by another torpedo boat and bombed by aircraft. The transport was the 405 tons *Vila* which sank in three minutes, 16 of her crew being rescued by the *TB35*. In the event this was the only Austrian merchant ship to be sunk by a British submarine between 1915 and the end of the war!

Carlyon-Britton was evidently a determined officer whose attack on the *TB35* might be considered by some to be rather unnecessary. On 6

August his activities involved the British Government in a diplomatic row with the Austrians over the vexed question of hospital ships. The *E21* had sailed from Brindisi for a patrol off the Dalmatian coast when at 5.30 am on 6 August he sighted a ship off Cape Rodoni which he definitely identified as a hospital ship, and did not attack. At 1.20 that afternoon he sighted what he later described as 'the same or ship of similar class to the one sighted in the morning' but evidently not a hospital ship. Accordingly he fired two torpedoes on the targets quarter, but both missed. In fact one struck the ship on the port bow but did not explode. This was perhaps the luckiest of the many British torpedo failures of the war for the target was the Austrian hospital ship *Baron Call* carrying 855 wounded from Durazzo. The Austrians delivered a justified protest about the attack to which the British Government replied, rather lamely, that although a British submarine was responsible the attack was justified since the *Baron Call* had not been correctly marked in accordance with the Hague Convention.

By this stage in the war the Austrians were very aware of the threat to their shipping from submarines and their anti-submarine patrols were very vigilant and backed by aircraft. The *Suchflotilla* (Hunting Flotilla) under the command of *Fregattenkapitän* Viktor Pohl consisted of small steamers fitted with hydrophones and armed with depth charges, backed up by torpedo boats and aircraft. The *H1* was just one submarine to have suffered the attentions of the *Suchflotilla*.

The British E21 *alongside the Italian depot ship* Lombardia *at Brindisi in 1918. Note the 4-inch gun forward of the conning tower.* E21 *was the most successful British submarine in the Adriatic.* (RNSM)

On 26 September while on patrol off Menders Point the *H1*, now commanded by Lieutenant Hugh Heaton, sighted a convoy of two steamers escorted by three torpedo boats. While manoeuvring for an attack at periscope depth Heaton heard what sounded like hail. It was in fact a seaplane using machine gun fire to indicate the submarine's position to the escort. The three torpedo boats closed and began to drop depth charges on the submarine. Despite the distraction Heaton pressed home his attack but as the bow caps were being swung open prior to firing the starboard torpedo ran hot in the tube and it was found that the side stops in all four tubes had been jerked out by the force of the depth charge explosions. Heaton was forced to break off the attack.

Three days later Heaton attacked another merchant ship firing one torpedo at a range of 2000 yards. He kept the periscope raised and observed an explosion but was unable to judge the effect on his target as two torpedo boats closed in and began dropping depth charges, the effects of which he described as 'extremely upsetting'. The side stops on the remaining three torpedoes were again forced in, the Sperry compass began to wander and it was found later that the warhead of one the remaining torpedoes was crushed despite the bow cap having been closed. The *H1* had to break off the patrol and return to harbour. It is interesting to note that in a post war analysis of this attack Heaton remarked that the short length of the torpedo tubes of the H class meant that the torpedo began to arm itself as soon as the bow cap was opened since the flow of water passed the end of the tube operated the arming fan.

The Austrian merchant ship Baron Call. *On 10 October 1918, while serving as a hosptial ship and carrying 855 wounded (and wearing the correct recognition marks), she was attacked by the British E21. The torpedo struck but failed to explode.*
(Kriegsarchiv, Vienna)

The passage of the *E46* (Lieutenant H G Higgins) to the Adriatic demonstrated that the submarine was nobody's friend in the Mediterranean, as indeed elsewhere. On 25 March she was shelled by a French trawler – one of her own escorts – and suffered the same experience in early April when she was shelled by a convoy's escort despite having made the correct recognition signal. This submarine laid only three minefields in the Adriatic, although she had already carried out a further nine operations in the Heligoland Bight. The first was in the Gulf of Drin on 8 July, the second north of Hvar on 4 August and the third north of Korcula on 31 August, 20 mines being laid on each occasion. No results are recorded of any ships being sunk or damaged by the *E46*'s mines. It is most likely that because the mines supplied could not be laid in depths greater than 50 fathoms [300 feet] they had not been laid in the optimum positions.

In his Patrols off the Dalmatian coast Higgins showed himself to be a bold and determined commanding officer, often penetrating through the Austrian minefields while dived in order to investigate coastal traffic. He may regard himself as unfortunate that his efforts were not better rewarded. On 22 July the *E46* was on the receiving end of the most serious Austrian air attack on a British submarine. The previous day the submarine had been off Cape Plasma when she was attacked and six bombs were dropped. Then on the 22nd when the submarine was dived at 25 feet the navigator noticed that were aircraft on patrol and that it did not look healthy. He was proved to be right. The first attack was at 6.30 am and carried on intermittently until 11.15. In total 22 bombs were dropped and the *E46* was forced below 140 feet with one battery cell on fire. The fire was quickly extinguished but Higgins did not deem it safe to surface until 9.30 that evening.

On 7 August the submarine was off Lissa, having laid her second minefield, when she sighted the 237 tons *Jadro*. Two torpedoes were fired which ran under the shallow draft steamer and exploded on the beach. Lissa seems to have been a fateful area for the *E46* for she was back again on 5 September when Higgins followed a torpedo boat which entered the harbour. Unfortunately there was a 36 feet rock shoal between the submarine and her target, and the *E46* struck with such force that she was thrown to the surface. As he had not been observed Higgins carried on intending to fire his stern tube from periscope depth as the bow tubes were unusable – later when the submarine docked at Brindisi a 500 pound piece of rock was found wedged in one of the openings! However, the compass had not recovered from the collision and was wandering badly and thwarted Higgins' plans. The submarine's First Lieutenant, Lieutenant T I Bell, later described what happened:

There was another crash and lurch as we ran up the beach under Polpat point. The depth gauge showed 8 feet and our conning tower, gun and ensign were all clear of the water. We went full astern and after a short time began to move. Through the periscopes we witnessed a remarkable scene. We had suddenly appeared like sea mon-

ster in the middle of a fishing fleet of small boats. The men in them were in a state of terror, cutting their nets and pulling for dear life, some jumping overboard and some praying. They were Albanians and probably never heard of a submarine before.

The Austrian *U47* (*LSL* Hugo Freiherr von Seyfferlitz) had two encounters with Entente submarines. Off Cape Rodoni on 26 July the *U47* sighted a submarine lying stopped on the surface in the light of the moon. The submarine was the *Le Verrier* (*LV* Landriau) charging her batteries. But, in making his attack von Seyfferlitz gravely overestimated the range on firing and he was much too close, the torpedo passing harmlessly by before it had time to arm. The bridge watch on the *Le Verrier* were appalled to see the enemy periscope approaching them and strike the hull. They quickly broke the charge, dived and even fired a torpedo in return, but without result.

The *U47* was luckier in September. On the 20th von Seyfferlitz again sighted an enemy submarine, later identified as the *Circé* (*LV* Viaud), lying stopped on the surface off Cape Rodoni and charging her batteries. One torpedo was fired which missed because the range was too great. After surfacing he could not see the other submarines but she reappeared about ten minutes later. Again the Austrian dived and manoeuvred to bring the other submarine into the light of the moon. An hour later he fired his second torpedo and was rewarded by the sound of an explosion. He surfaced and was able to pick up only one survivor, *LV* Eugene Lapayrère who had been thrown clear of the bridge by the explosion.

The loss of the *Circé* was the last significant event for the Entente submarines operating in the Adriatic although patrols continued until hostilities were concluded. Their campaign had been an unsuccessful one carried out in a theatre in which the Austrians held many of the cards. The Austrians could lurk behind their minefields, they were operating in waters of which they had intimate knowledge. The clear waters off the Dalmatian coast were no help to Entente submariners and the high coastline gave the Austrian coastwatchers a considerable advantage when looking for submarines. But the fact remains that the dived patrols off Cattaro did not significantly interfere with U-boat operations – only two U-boats were sunk during 1917–18 – nor did they interfere very much with coastal traffic. When visiting Pola after the war Commodore Howard Kelly was mortified to be told by an Austrian officer that the Austrians had been sending a loaded merchant ship to Durazzo every night and yet not one interception of this traffic had been made by the submarines.

The other side of the coin was equally depressing. Britain, France and Italy lost 12 submarines as a result of enemy action in the Adriatic. To this number must be added the Italian *H5* lost by accident, and the two Italian boats lost as a result of bad weather.

CHAPTER TWELVE

The Black Sea

When the Turks first closed the Dardanelles and then announced that they were laying minefields in the area they effectively cut the easiest and shortest route for supplies to the Russians from their western allies. Movement of stores from England to the northern port of Archangel took 10 to 14 days, often in appalling weather conditions and with the port blocked by ice in winter, while to Vladivostok from the west coast of the USA took nearly three weeks with similar limitations. Once in Russia supplies sent by these routes still had long journeys by an inadequate railway system before reaching the area in which they were needed. The closure of the Dardanelles also meant that with the outbreak of war the Russian navy in the Black Sea was left to fight the war without reinforcement, on paper a not too difficult task even with the addition of the *Goeben* and *Breslau* to the Turkish fleet. Initially the only submarines in the Black Sea were Russian, though obsolescent and of limited value, while later the German U-boats at Constantinople could be sent either north through the Bosporus to the Black Sea or through the Dardanelles into the Aegean and Mediterranean.

The focus of operations was the Bosporus, under 300 nautical miles from the main Russian base at Sevastopol. Here was the area that was the centre of Turkish industry, while in Constantinople, the capital, there was the Turkish naval base with its repair facilities and docks. Some 120 nautical miles to the east lay the port of Zonguldak which was the centre of the Turkish coal mining area so vital for keeping the fleet at sea, while even further away to the east lay the Caucasus with the front line between the Russian and Turkish armies. The absence of a railway system between Constantinople and the areas behind the front line left the Turkish army dependent either on the poor coast roads of Anatolia along the southern shore of the Black Sea, or on the use of coastal shipping for their supplies.

Prior to the outbreak of war with Turkey the Russians, like their French and British allies, were anxious not to give any offence to the Turks that would hasten the start of hostilities. For Vice-Admiral Eberhard, the Russian Commander-in-Chief in the Black Sea, there was the problem of what to do should the *Goeben* and *Breslau* be met on one of their increasingly frequent exercises in the Black Sea. Russia was at war with Germany, though these German ships were nominally part of the Turkish fleet. Should they be attacked or not? In fact Eberhard

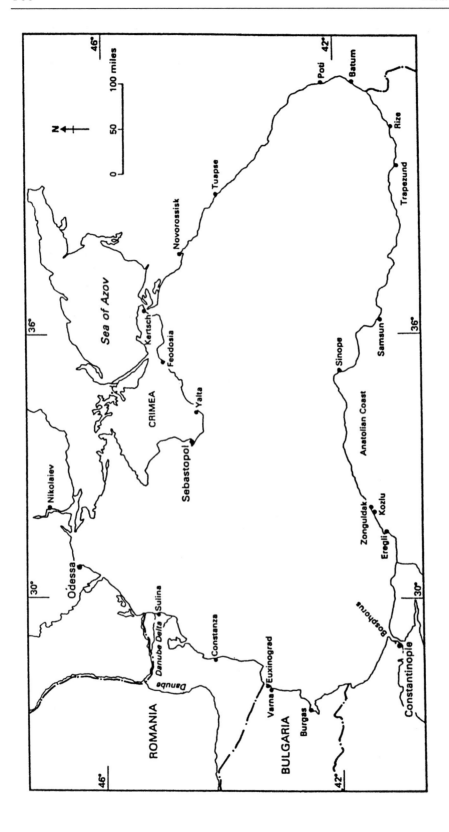

OPPOSITE *Map 5. The*
Black Sea.

was aware that the two ships were at sea with some units of the Turkish navy on 27 October and took the Black Sea fleet out from Sevastopol. He then received orders from the Tsar's headquarters to avoid any confrontation except in dire necessity and consequently returned to harbour, there to be caught with his ships secured alongside and coaling when the *Goeben** arrived and carried out the bombardment that led to war.

Despite this setback Eberhard was soon at sea, and flying his flag in the battleship *Evstafi*, he led a strong force towards the Bosporus where the destroyers were to lay some 240 mines. Regrettably many were laid in the wrong place and became as much a hindrance to the Russians in future operations as they were meant to be to the Turks, while others exploded prematurely. It was not a happy beginning. As well as these minefields the Russians laid many defensive fields off their own coast, as well as preparing to support the army to defeat a landing which the General Staff feared was imminent in the Odessa region.

On the 17 November the Russians were at sea again, this time at the eastern end of the Black Sea bombarding the port of Trebizond, the forward base for the Turkish army in the Caucasus. The following day while returning to Sevastopol they met briefly with the two German ships off Cape Sarych, the southernmost point of the Crimea, each side suffering damage and casualties in a brief action at short range before the mist hid them from each other. A second major operation by the Black Sea Fleet was carried out at the end of December when more mines were laid off the Bosporus and the port of Zonguldak was bombarded.

In none of these operations in 1914 by the Black Sea were the Russian submarines involved. Not surprisingly, there were only four in commission at the outbreak of war and they were old and hardly suitable for distant operations. The *Losos* and *Sudak* were Holland type only 65½ feet long with a displacement of 105/122 tons, armed with one 380mm torpedo tube and with insufficient endurance to reach the Bosporus and return. They were of a class ordered in 1904 to meet the challenge of the war with Japan in the Far East, though with that war then over these two boats had been sent overland direct to the Black Sea after completion in 1907. The role of the *Sudak* in rescuing the crew of the minelayer *Prut* on the opening day of the war has already been recorded.

The other two submarines available to Eberhard were slightly more modern, the *Karp* and *Karas*, having been built in Germany for the Russians. They were 130 feet overall and displaced 207/235 tons, with

* The Germans had technically handed over both the *Goeben* and *Breslau* to the Turkish navy where they had become the *Yavuz Sultan Semli* (or *Yavuz* for short) and the *Medilli* retaining their German crews who were seconded to the Turkish navy. However, both ships were regarded by their enemies throughout the war as remaining part of the German fleet and were always referred to by their German names. Whilst perhaps not technically correct this practice is continued in this story as being less likely to cause confusion among the majority of readers.

an armament of two 450mm torpedo tubes and two more torpedoes carried in Drzewiecki drop collars. With two Korting paraffin engines they had a theoretical range of over a thousand miles, but the engines were old and unreliable. The three boats of this class (the third had been sunk in an accident in 1909) were the forerunners of the German *U1*, which even in 1914 was considered unsuitable for operational use.

Other submarines were building. Three boats of the *Morzh* class were laid down at Nikolaev under the 1911 Programme to a Bubnov design, and were launched in 1913. At 220 feet overall they displaced 630/760 tons, were armed with two guns and fitted with four torpedo tubes – two forward and two aft – while eight more torpedoes were carried in drop collars. They had ample range for the Black Sea but their completion was delayed since their diesel engines had been ordered from Germany preventing delivery, and they had to be fitted with less powerful engines taken from the Amur River gunboats, reducing their surface speed to under 11 knots from the planned 16 knots. The *Nerpa* of this class did commission in 1914 but was not ready for operations until the following year. Also ordered to be built at Nikolaev under the 1911 Programme were three boats of the *Narval* class, with similar dimensions to the other boats but to a Holland design. The *Narval* herself and the *Kit* completed in 1915 while the other, the *Kashalot*, was not ready until 1916.

There was one other boat still under construction in Nikolaev in 1914 when war started, the *Krab*. She was begun in 1908 and intended to be the first specially designed minelaying submarine, and was the idea of Naletov, a railway engineer, who had never previously attempted the construction of a ship let alone a submarine. It is hardly surprising that the construction of this 512/752 tons submarine had dragged on and she was not ready until the summer of 1915. On trials her temperamental behaviour inspired her nickname of 'The Box of Surprises', not the least of her troubles being the fact that it took up to 20 minutes to dive the boat. After completion of building it was left to her crew who used considerable initiative to overcome the many design and construction faults before it was even thought advisable to use the boat operationally. By then the German UC type minelayers had even stolen the honours of being the first in action, though the *Krab* was, in theory at least, a better proposition being able to carry 60 mines compared to the Germans' 12, and also having an armament of a 75mm gun and two torpedoes in drop collars while the Germans were unarmed. The mines were carried in two horizontal tubes inside the submarine's casing and were laid over the stern by means of a chain conveyor belt, not dissimilar in principle to the system used in the 1930s by HMS *Porpoise*.

In early January 1915 four more Russian submarines reached the Black Sea, they were the *Shchuka* and the *Som* of the same class as the *Losos*, and the *Skat* and *Nalim* of a slightly larger design but also built in 1904. All these four had arrived overland from Vladivostok, though their obsolescence precluded any significant operational reinforcement.

The Russian navy's tasks for 1915 were largely defensive in nature but included the commitment to hinder the shipment of supplies along the Anatolian coast, either eastwards for the army or coal from Zonguldak to Constantinople. A later directive to the Commander-in-Chief in February ordered the Black Sea to be ready to co-operate with Anglo-French operations against the Dardanelles with diversionary attacks near the Bosporus and, depending on the outcome of the Dardanelles operation, by landing Russian troops in the area. Despite these fine words General Headquarters considered that operations by the fleet too near to the Bosporus to be risky, the presence of the single powerful battlecruiser *Goeben* creating an air of over-caution. Submarines became involved in these operations only on 5 March when the *Nerpa* left Sevastopol to carry out her first wartime patrol, spending three days off the Bosporus. By the middle of the month the *Tyulen* was also ready for operations and the two boats then patrolled the area between the Bosporus and Kefken Island, about 50 miles to the west, during a sweep and bombardment by the fleet, after which they were sent out alternately. In this way chance gave the *Nerpa* the first opportunity of attacking the Germans, on the 4 April the submarine saw the *Goeben* and a number of other fleet units approaching the Bosporus but the range was too great for an attack.

So the pattern of patrols continued with the submarines sent to patrol in the approaches to the Bosporus while the Russian destroyers from Sevastopol and torpedo boats operating out of Batum were sent to attempt a blockade of the Turkish supply route along the coast. Though the surface ships carried out some very notable sweeps along the coast, no great successes were achieved by the submarines. Gradually the submarine areas were extended to include positions off the coal port of Zonguldak. Both the *Goeben* and *Breslau* were sighted at different times by the *Tyulen* during May, but again the range was too great for any attack.

A third submarine, the *Morzh*, became operational in June and joined the other two in the patrol cycle. The *Tyulen* scored the first success at the end of that month when she destroyed the sailing barque *Tahiv* and some other smaller sailing craft, though it was August before the same submarine sank the first sizeable ship. On 10 August the steamer *Zonguldak* (1,545 tons) was sunk by gunfire while in company with four other steamers and escorted by a Turkish torpedo boat. The following day both the *Tyulen* and the *Morzh* attempted to torpedo the *Goeben* but their torpedoes were seen and evaded. On the 13th the *Tyulen* was again in action with her gun against a schooner near Eregli, to the west of Zonguldak. On this occasion the submarine's aggression nearly led to her undoing as the schooner turned out to be more heavily armed than the submarine. It was the Q-ship *Dere*, recently redeployed from the Marmara, with both guns and crew taken from the cruiser *Hamidieh*.

It is difficult to try and explain the lack of enterprise or success of the Russian submariners at this time. During the four months to the end of September these three submarines carried out 16 patrols off the Turkish coast, spending 69 days at sea. Yet, with the sole example of the one patrol by the *Tyulen* quoted they showed little enterprise, failed to get close enough to attack either of the German ships in May and missed the *Goeben* in August in their only torpedo attack. It was not as if there were no targets, for the Turks were sending their ships along the coast as the Russian destroyers found during their sweeps. The Russian submarines in the Baltic fared little better, though there they were not so modern. Submarines demand good professional understanding between all members of the crew but at this time there was a great gulf separating the ratings and the officers of the Tsarist navy, a gulf that was in no way diminished by submarine service. A harsh discipline, poor education leading to reduced standards of training, and an unwillingness on the part of the officers to accept that they too had to be capable of taking part in all activities must certainly be partly to blame for the lack of success. Lieutenant Norman Archer, one of a British naval mission in Sevastopol, perhaps sums up the difficulties in an entry in his diary in early 1916:

> . . . would guarantee now how to teach a child in arms how to run one [Mk.VIII torpedo] in words of one syllable including also a preliminary course as to which is the arse and which is the elbow of the torpedo. It is rather frenzied trying to teach a man with no intellect, who can't write, read or reason – parrot wise is the only way and thus they do very well because they are very conscientious and will carry out orders to the letter.

The *Krab* also started operations at this time, first with a defensive minelay off the Crimea at the beginning of July, and then a week later off the Bosporus as part of a much larger fleet operation designed to cover the move of the new battleship *Imperatritsa Mariya* from the builders yard at Nikolaev to Sevastopol. The *Krab* was commanded by Senior Lieutenant L K Fanshaw, but also onboard for the patrol were the commander of the submarine flotilla, Captain 1st Grade V R Klochkovsky, the flotilla navigating officer, Lieutenant M V Parutsky, and the officer who had been responsible for overseeing the building of the submarine, Engineer Lieutenant V S Lukyanov. It was to be no straightforward operation as the *Krab* began her career of unreliability.

During the first dive it was discovered that the boat became very heavy by the stern, with the after trimming tank being topped up through a leaking valve. Then they found it was impossible to pump water from one trimming tank to another at periscope depth because the pump was insufficiently powerful, and the *Krab* was eventually surfaced to pump out the offending tank with a fire hose! Having completed a battery charge the *Krab* dived to begin the final approach to the Bosporus, but even this led to problems as Fanshaw wrote afterwards in his report:

> Because of the lack of time which remained before submerging into the Bosporus, it was not possible to cool the engines as we should

have and we dived with them hot. Because of the high temperature from the engines and the heat given off by the electric motors during a prolonged [sic] period of six hours underwater there were a lot of kerosene and oil fumes which were so severe that in the stern section the majority of the crew were overcome by them, but which also affected those in the control room where our eyes were streaming and breathing was difficult. After surfacing part of the crew were taken up into the fresh air in a semi-conscious state.

The *Krab*'s instructions were to lay her mines in a mile long line off the lighthouses at Rumeli and Anatoli which mark either side of the northern end of the Bosporus, giving a mine spacing of about 100 feet. During the approach to the mining area Fanshaw sighted a Turkish patrol craft but did not attempt to attack for fear of compromising the minelay which began just after 8.00 pm. The operation was completed in 35 minutes, though not without some problems with both trim and the complicated system for carrying the mines aft and then launching them. The *Krab* then returned safely to Sevastopol where the officers were all decorated or promoted, as were some of the crew. Fanshaw himself wrote of the patrol:

> The submarine had many design faults which it was difficult to take account of during its construction and which had a great effect on this prolonged and serious voyage. Furthermore it is not yet fully complete in all respects. Nevertheless, thanks to the resourcefulness, complete calmness and hard work of the crew, who eliminated many of the shortcomings, the operation was successfully carried out.

The *Krab* herself went into refit until August having more of her design faults corrected, but apart from a local minelay off the Crimea in September she carried out no more operations in 1915. The mines she had laid were discovered the following day and sweeping had been completed by 16 July, though the gunboat *Isa Reis* hit one of the mines on the 11th and was badly damaged at the bow and was towed back to Constantinople.

There was one new development in the naval war in the Black Sea which had till then been dominated by the threat posed by the heavy guns and high speed of the *Goeben* and the overcautious Russian response. In June 1915 the first of the German U-boats, the *UB7*, arrived at Constantinople, badly in need of a thorough overhaul. These small UB boats were thought to be more suitable for work in the Black Sea than south of the Dardanelles, special importance being given to attacking the Russian ships and submarines in the Zonguldak area where their presence was affecting the supply of coal even if they were having little actual success in sinking the colliers. Leutnant Werner took the *UB7* through the Bosporus on 5 July, his orders were ambitious; first to go to an area between the mouth of the Danube and Odessa where Russian shipping might be surprised by her presence, then to cruise on the route between Sevastopol and Zonguldak, and finally to return via Zonguldak where it was hoped both Russian destroyers and submarines might be met. The first phase passed without incident, nothing being sighted, not even any of the ships covering the move of the *Imperatritsa Mariya*, but on the 15th while lying in Zonguldak taking in fuel sent from Constantinople three Russian destroyers appeared and began to bombard the town and port, causing minor damage to some of the ships berthed there, including the oiler. The *UB7* immediately left but was unable to get within range for a torpedo attack before the Russians steamed away. Werner completed his patrol and returned to Constantinople on the 22nd.

Late in August the *Skat* went twice to Zonguldak and the *Nalim* once, both submarines having to be towed to their area by a destroyer, and then only being able to spend one day on patrol. It was hardly worth the effort and the two submarines spent the rest of the year on defensive patrols from either Sevastopol or Batum. At about this time the *Som* and *Shchuka* were considered to be of no value in the Black Sea and were transported overland to the Baltic where they were also found to be of no operational value.

A regular supply of coal from the Zonguldak area was essential for the operations of the German-Turkish fleet and it was perhaps fortunate for Souchon that a number of German merchant navy masters of the Norddeutscher Lloyd shipping company had been sent to Turkey in 1911 to help reform the Turkish merchant marine. They were now employed as Harbour Masters at Zonguldak, Eregli and other ports along the coast where they organised the coal convoys back to Constantinople. Yet, despite their importance, a Turkish report in March 1915 stated that the proximity of the mines to the port was such that a Russian landing party could have destroyed them easily in a short action, and that the Turks had then no means of re-opening them. The defences of the port consisted of 4 x 105 mm and 6 x 76 mm field guns, badly sited according to the German port commander, aided by only 200 *Gendarmarie*. The wonder is that the Germans were unable to convince the Turks to reinforce this vital area, and that the Russians did not attack.

A routine convoy consisting of the German *Eresos*, the Austrian *Illiria* and the Turkish *Seyhan* and escorted from Zonguldak by the cruiser *Hamidieh* and two destroyers on 5 September developed into a minor action when they were first attacked by the Russian destroyers *Bystry* and *Pronzitelny*. The Russians first drew the Turkish escort away from their charges, putting the cruiser's two 150mm guns out of action in the process, then using their superior speed turned back towards the merchant ships. Seeing that the Russian destroyers approaching at speed the merchant ships turned and headed to the shore where they beached, being unsuccessfully attacked by the *Nerpa* as they went by and were destroyed by gunfire when ashore. Two of the ships were subsequently refloated but the Turks had to face the loss of over 10,000 tons of coal. Meanwhile the *Goeben* had been drawn out in support of the virtually defenceless cruiser, but the Russian destroyers had departed by the time she reached the area. It was not the best of days for the *Nerpa* for having missed a chance at the colliers and earlier having been out of position for an attack on the *Hamidieh* she was then caught on the surface by the *Goeben* who at a range of nearly nine miles fired a salvo of five 280mm at the boat while diving. However, to compensate she did then sink a tug and a lighter loaded with coal in the vicinity of the original action.

Both the *UB7* and *UB8* were sent out from Constantinople in early September to operate off the Crimea and Odessa. The former torpedoed the British registered steamer *Patagonia* (6,000 tons) off Odessa, leaving the ship lying in shallow water with her upperworks showing to mark the passing of the U-boat. Meanwhile the *UB8* found four small sailing ships, three of which she destroyed by fire, having forced them to heave to with a shot from the 37mm gun which had been fitted while in Constantinople for just such an occasion. After this the *UB8* had to dive hurriedly and was then hunted for some hours by a force of ten destroyers. Later von Voigt tried to use the gun for bombarding certain shore targets, but it was too light for effective use, and then the fourth sailing vessel, which had been abandoned when the submarine dived earlier to avoid the Russian destroyers, was seen and finally destroyed. A third U-boat, the *UB14*, was sent to the Crimean coast in early October and sank the small Russian steamer *Katya* (500 tons), and the larger *Apsheron* (1,850 tons) near Sevastopol. As he withdrew to seaward von Heimburg was able to see a number of destroyers searching for him but no contact was made. As the submarine was loosing oil it was decided to break off the patrol and return to Constantinople, calling first at the Bulgarian port of Varna.

The entry of Bulgaria into the war on the side of Germany and Turkey scarcely altered the balance of naval power in the Black Sea. At this time the Bulgar fleet consisted of a training ship of no military value and six small French built torpedo boats of 100 tons displacement, and armed with 2 x 37 mm guns and 3 x 45 cm torpedo tubes. They had a defensive value only and offensive operations were not to be considered. During the earlier Balkan wars the Bulgars had shown no real inclination to fight a war at sea, and though at various times there had been proposals to strengthen the fleet with additional ships, and even submarines, the plans came to nought as a navy was considered an unnecessary expenditure and there was little enthusiasm for it in the country. The main benefit to the Germans was to be the use of the port of Varna, just south of the border with Romania and close to the mouth of the Danube. Even before the Bulgars entered the war the *UC13* (Kirchner) was sent there on 30 September to liaison with the local commander. A good berth for the submarines was found in nearby Euxinograd, while the crews were to based ashore in part of the Royal castle.

The *UB8* arrived in Varna to begin operations on 16 October. The first patrol based on an intelligence assessment of Russian shipping leaving the Danube was abandoned as the submarine could not reach the area in time because of a bad storm. The *UB7* arrived in Varna on the 25th.

Two days later the Russian fleet arrived to bombard the port. The new battleship *Imperatritsa Mariya* led three older ships, two cruisers, destroyers, minesweepers and two seaplane carriers – the Russians hoping to make a simultaneous attack from sea and air. Both German submarines left harbour as soon as information was received of the Russians' approach, the berths at Euxinograd proving their value in allowing the boats to get to sea quickly. Both submarines manoeuvred to attack the Russian line but their periscopes were sighted and they were heavily fired on, though without causing any damage. The *UB8* was unable to fire before the Russians turned to break off the action. The *UB7* fired one torpedo at the last ship in the line, the *Pantelimon* – better known as the 'Battleship *Potemkin*' and the scene of a famous mutiny in 1905. The range had been 950 yards and the submarine crew all heard an explosion but no results could be seen. In fact the torpedo had not hit, but had exploded prematurely leaving the battleship unscathed. Though the bombardment lasted for an hour there was little military damage in the port to show for the considerable expenditure of ammunition.

The *UB8* was in need of a refit and returned to Constantinople in mid November, her sister submarine staying another month during which time she carried out one patrol. The area off the mouth of the Danube surprisingly yielded no targets.

The *UC13* left Constantinople on 12 November for a patrol which was to take her across the Black Sea to the North East coast, yet it is hard to see just what it was hoped that this submarine – would achieve. Existing records indicate that no mines were laid – the prime purpose of this class of submarine – and with no torpedo tubes she was forced to rely on a single 57mm (6pdr) gun which had been specially fitted in Constantinople. On leaving the Bosporus she first went up the coast to Euxinograd, then across to Sinope on the Anatolian coast riding out a strong gale which badly affected her compass while on passage. It was the first submarine that had been seen in Sinope and before leaving Kirchner actually dived in the harbour for the benefit of the local inhabitants. Off Tuapse she stopped and boarded two sailing ships, destroying them with an explosive charge as well as setting them on fire. A third ship, a tanker, was run aground and abandoned when the submarine approached. Kirchner then ran down the coast and actually entered Sochi harbour where, despite intense fire from small arms, two of several sailing ships lying in the harbour were set on fire and destroyed. Returning to the Bosporus Kirchner spent two days in Zonguldak before proceeding on the last leg home. Once again heavy seas were met and although the *UC13* was dived to ride out the storm they were forced to surface before the weather moderated because of the lack of oxygen after too long dived. In difficult conditions the submarine went aground near the mouth of the Melen river on 29

November. When daylight came she was seen to be lying in heavy surf about 50 yards from the shore.

All the crew of the *UC13* were safely taken off as was most of the movable equipment from the submarine. On 10 December two Turkish gunboats, the *Taskopru* and *Yozgat*, were sent out to recover the survivors and their equipment but ran into three Russian destroyers and were sunk. The Russians, however, failed to see the submarine which was in any case beyond salvage.

For the submarines, 1915 had not been a momentous year in the Black Sea. By the end of the year the German submarines were beginning to make their presence felt and forcing the Russians to take notice of their potential, while the Russian boats had hardly shown the aggressive spirit so necessary to make an impact on the Turkish coastal shipping which had suffered more from the raids by the Russian surface ships. The opening of the new year was marked by the final withdrawal from the Gallipoli peninsula of the British and French armies, freeing Turkish forces to be deployed in the Caucasus while the Russians continued to harry the coastal shipping along the Anatolian coast.

The *Nerpa* was the first Russian submarine to be in action in 1916 when on 21 January she sighted 21 sailing vessels off Zonguldak. She attempted to take the largest in tow but was driven off by fire from the coastal batteries and her prize sank. The other submarines all were active in the first three months of the year, the *Tyulen* having a prize schooner sink attacking a small steamer from a range of just over half a mile. Once again the damaged vessel managed to reach the shore and was salved days later. The *Morzh* also became the target for shore batteries and was attacked several times by aircraft.

The Russian submarines were slowly becoming more efficient. On 1 April off the entrance to the Bosporus the *Tyulen* fired two torpedoes at the steamer *Dubrovnik** (4,232 tons) which was being escorted with a cargo of coal, scored one hit and forced the ship ashore. A fortnight later the same ship was attacked again by the *Morzh* and again hit by a torpedo. On the 3rd the *Tyulen* met with a group of schooners each carrying about 50 tons of coal and destroyed 11 of them by ramming and gunfire while the rest were forced ashore. The *Morzh* was constantly active close inshore and on four successive patrols was attacked by seaplanes as a consequence, one bomb which dropped close to the submarine damaged one of the torpedoes carried in the Drzewiecki drop collars. Her commanding officer pleaded in vain to be fitted with an anti-aircraft gun instead of these torpedoes which could so easily prove lethal to the submarine. During May both the *Nerpa* and *Tyulen* continued the new found aggression, the latter towing a large brigantine loaded with kerosene back to Sevastopol while between them the two boats destroyed three ships, two tugs and 21 sailing craft.

---

* Not to be confused with the steamer sunk in the Adriatic. This vessel (sometimes known as *Dutor*) was also Austrian and had been trapped in Constantinople on the outbreak of war.

Although the successful conclusion of the campaign against Serbia had opened up direct communications between Germany and Turkey the main worry in Constantinople at the start of 1916 was the supply of coal. Operations by the Russian destroyers, and submarines, against supplies of coal from Zonguldak had lead to severe shortages. At a crisis conference in early January attended by Enver Pasha it was assessed that stocks of coal in Constantinople were down to 13,500 tons of Cardiff coal and only 900 tons of coal from Zonguldak, while there were only 14 sea-going colliers capable of carrying over 500 tons left. Even a brief sortie by the *Goeben* had only a temporary effect and the small German submarines had to be deployed in an attempt to stop the Russians. Consequently Admiral Souchon had asked for one of the larger U-boats to be sent to the Black Sea, a request which was fully supported by Enver Pasha and the Turkish Government. It was a request that was initially turned down by Berlin on 11 January, but after Souchon had pointed out the urgency of the situation the *Admiralstab* agreed to send the old *U21* in early March, subsequently changed after more signals from Souchon to the *U33* which was expected to leave Pola on 21 February.

Meanwhile the small submarines already at Constantinople had not been idle with the *UB7*, *UB8* and *UB14* all at sea. From Zonguldak the *UB8* went to Varna where she began the task of training a crew of Bulgars to take over a submarine. In early February the *UB14* found herself in a good attacking position on the Russian cruiser *Kagul*, but was unable to fire as her conning tower broached in heavy seas. She was then off the port of Zonguldak when a Russian force led by the battleship *Imperatritsa Mariya*, and including two seaplane carriers, arrived on the 6th to carry out a bombardment and simultaneous air attack. During the attack the *UB7*, which had also been sent to the area, managed to pass under two destroyers which were circling the carriers while they hoisted out their seaplanes and then fire a torpedo at the *Imperator Alexander*. Unable to see through the periscope because of the actions of the Russian destroyers Leutnant Werner heard the torpedo explode and claimed a hit, though in fact the explosion was premature, as had happened earlier off Varna. The subsequent hunt was aided by one of the seaplanes which tried to mark the submarine's position with smoke floats, though Werner was able to leave the scene undamaged.

Both sides continued with minelaying, and the *Krab*, by then commanded by Senior Lieutenant Mikhail Parutsky, made her first patrol of the year on 9 March when she left Sevastopol to lay mines off the Bosporus, an attempt which was foiled by the bad weather, the attempt not being repeated when the weather eased. For the Germans only the *UC15* (von Dewitz) was available for minelaying, operations being delayed first by a shortage of mines and then by the need for the submarine to return to Varna to make good damage suffered in heavy seas. She eventually laid her first field of 11 mines directly off the entrance to Sevastopol on 24 March. Thick fog prevented an immediate repeat of the operation but a month later she laid another 11 mines near

Sevastopol, a field which subsequently accounted for the loss of the Russian destroyer *Zhivuchi*. A third operation in May took place in the channel between Odessa and Nikolaev where the Russian *Mercury* (3,905 tons) was sunk in June.

The large *U33* eventually arrived at Constantinople on 11 March and was followed by the *U38* on 23 May, the deployment of both boats being only temporary until some of the UBII class could be sent. Gansser's readiness for his first Black Sea patrol was coincidental with the opening of a Russian offensive in the Caucasus towards Trebizond on 26th which was supported by units of the fleet, and the submarine was sent to the area. The following day he sighted the Russian flagship but was not able to get within torpedo range. On the 30th he sighted what he took to be a large transport at anchor close inshore in Surmena Bay, to the east of Trebizond. Gansser fired a stern torpedo at 600 yards which hit, the ship breaking in two after a heavy explosion, and sank within minutes. It was the hospital ship *Portugal*. Russian sources claim that 90 were killed including 15 nurses, yet Souchon defended Gansser's actions in a report to Berlin.

> (Sighted) close under the coast completely darkened except for a white light at the masthead. At daybreak she was seen to be heavily laden towing several lighters with numerous crews which after anchoring were brought alongside. The commanding officer held the ship to be a hostile transport and proceeded to attack. On nearer approach she was seen to be painted grey with a narrow red band, and flew the Russian merchant flag at the stern. The Red Cross and her name were nowhere to be seen. . . . the resultant explosion must without doubt have been caused by a large quantity of explosives in the ship.

During the same patrol he sank a sailing ship by gunfire and went on to shell the town of Sukhum, north of Batum, and also finished off the minesweeper *T233* which had been left burning by the *Breslau*. On a second visit to Surmena Bay on 4 April to attack two transports the submarine was rammed by the torpedo boat *Strogi* bending the after periscope and forcing the submarine to return to Constantinople.

On 9 May Enver Pasha made a fresh appeal for more submarines to be sent to the Black Sea to help against further Russian advances from the Caucasus, the more so as the *U33* was still under repair. Reluctantly the *Admiralstab* agreed to send the *U38*, still commanded by the famous (or infamous) Valentiner. The intention was that she would remain only until the new *UB42* was ready. He arrived in Constantinople on 23 May. During the *U38*'s time in the Black Sea she sank a mere four ships totalling just under 5,000 tons, the largest being a Russian transport, the ex-British *Rockcliffe* (3,073 tons). By the time the *UB42* reached the Aegean fresh minefields off the Dardanelles made the attempt to reach Constantinople too hazardous, and she returned to Cattaro. She was more successful on a second attempt and arrived safely on 16 August,

although by then Valentiner had in turn left on the 11th. The *U33* remained in Constantinople until mid-November when she too returned to Cattaro. The original decision to send them to aid the Turks had been made for political rather than sound military reasons, and their absence from the Pola flotilla was a clear loss to *Handelskrieg* while these two experienced submarines were tied down in the Black Sea where their actual effect on the Russians was minimal.

Following the *UB42* the *UB44* sailed from Cattaro on 4 August but never reached Turkey, and its fate is unknown. The *UB45* arrived on 12 August while the *UB46* did so on 7 October. The *UC23*, commanded by *Kapitänleutnant* Kirchner who had gained experience in the *UC13*, completed Souchon's reinforcements in December. Although four boats had arrived at Constantinople during 1916, another four were lost, all due to mines. The *UB7* left Varna on 27 September and was never seen again, the *UB45* was mined off the same port on 6 November, the *UC15* was another that disappeared without trace after leaving Constantinople on 15 November and the *UB46* was mined off the Bosporus on 7 December. For all that the successes of the U-boats in the Black Sea during the year were meagre, just ten ships of less than 17,000 tons, with one other sunk by submarine laid mines. The *UB8* was handed over to the Bulgarian Navy on 25 May 1916 at a ceremony in Euxinograd and became known as Submarine Torpedo Boat *18* (though just why this number was chosen is not clear!). The commanding officer, Lieutenant Nikola Todorov, had already spent time in the

The Bulgarian submarine No. 18, ex-German UB8, which was transferred on 25 May 1918. The photograph shows the boat out of the water for routine hull cleaning at Varna. (Bulgarian Naval Museum)

submarine and in training at Kiel. The *UB7* had also been destined for the Bulgar navy but was sunk before the transfer was due and no replacement was available. Meanwhile No.*18* was employed on coast defence duties off the Bulgarian coast. One unsuccessful attack by this submarine is recorded when on 25 September she fired at a Russian destroyer shelling the coast.

Perhaps the most important event for the Russians was the arrival of Vice-Admiral A V Kolchak to relieve the ageing Eberhard as Commander-in-Chief on 16 July. Kolchak, still in his early forties had already made a name for himself in the Baltic as an energetic and forceful commander and his appointment owed much to the fact that he was popular with the Tsar who hoped he would bring the Black Sea Fleet to a major victory. His future fame, though, lay not with the fleet but as one of the many leaders of the White Russian forces after the Revolution.

For the Russian submarines the year continued with minor successes against the small coastal shipping, mainly in the area between Zonguldak and Constantinople, but also further eastwards on the Anatolian coast and off the Bulgar coast. The strength of the flotilla was reinforced by the arrival of the *Kit* which carried out her first operational patrol at the end of June, during which a schooner was destroyed and the submarine was attacked by seaplanes. All achieved some success, even the old *Skat* on one patrol from Batum destroyed some small vessels with her gun. The *Morzh* was the only one to sight the *Goeben*, but once again was not able to gain a firing position on the mighty battlecruiser. The *Nerpa* was lucky in that she was attacked with two torpedoes by the *UB7* (*Leutnant* Hans Luthjohan) off the Bosporus. One torpedo hit the hull just abaft the conning tower but failed to explode. In total during 1916 the Russian submarines accounted for 45 vessels sunk or run aground and five captured.

The *Tyulen* had perhaps the most spectacular success of the year. She carried out six patrols during the second half of the year, and during the third on 11 October she met with the transport *Rodosto* (6,000 tons), a German owned steamer chartered to the Turks since September 1914. The ship was intercepted at night near the coast not far from the Bosporus, the submarine opening fire with both her 76 mm and 57 mm guns, while the Rodosto replied with her single 57 mm gun which had been taken together with the four man gun's crew from the *Breslau*. The Turkish vessel was eventually abandoned by her crew, on fire and with her boilers damaged. A prize crew was put aboard which got the ship going again and the fires under control. She was then escorted by the *Tyulen* back to Sevastopol. Senior Lieutenant Kititsyn in command of the *Tyulen* was awarded the Order of St George for his skill and bravery.

The *Krab* continued her accident-prone career during the second half of 1916, but few operations were possible. After a passage from Sevastopol which was an engineering nightmare of breakdowns 60 mines were successfully laid off the Bosporus on the night of 18/19

June, the return passage being marked with further engine breakdowns. A second operation was planned for August with the mines to be laid off the northern entrance to Varna. Sailing had to be delayed when a mine became misaligned and wedged in the mining rails while loading, part of the system having to be dismantled to free it. Then the submarine ran into bad weather: as usual the engines failed, the acid from the battery cells started to leak and there was trouble with one of the pumps. The operation was abandoned and escorted by the destroyer *Zavetni* the submarine sought shelter in Constanta. However, with fresh orders to lay this field it was decided to tow the submarine to a point about 20 miles from the area, leaving her to dive and proceed independently only for the last short distance. Even then, with damage to the mining gear only half the mines could be laid. Nevertheless, this field cost the Bulgars the torpedo boat *Shumni* sunk and another damaged. On return to Sevastopol the submarine was taken in hand for a major refit, and did not become operational again.

By August Romania felt ready to enter the war on the side of the Entente, and on 27th declared war on Austria and Germany. Before doing so the Romanian Government had sought an assurance from the Russians that the Black Sea Fleet would guard not only the Danube estuary but also the whole of their Black Sea coast, the Romanian fleet of one old gunboat, eight patrol boats, with some other even smaller ships being unequal to the task. The Russians sent a force led by the old battleship *Rostislav* and including the two submarines *Karp* and *Karas*. Another vessel that is believed to have been sent at this time was a midget submarine, one of three ordered by the Army's Engineers in 1912 for local defence of Kronstadt. They were Holland type submarines of 33/44 tons each, with two 457 mm torpedo tubes and a crew of four. Their 50hp diesel engines were a constant source of breakdowns while their batteries were of limited capacity. Even the army realised the uselessness of these boats and hurriedly gave them to the Navy, one being sent to the Arctic and one to the Black Sea. Known only by their numbers the intention was to use '3' for attacks on the Austrian Danube Flotilla monitors, but whether this was ever attempted is not known. What is known is that the hull was captured by the Austrian Army at Reni on 12 March 1918. Her subsequent fate is unknown although plans did exist to take the submarine to Vienna where she was to be put on show as part of the drive to raise money in war loans. In any case the rapid collapse of the Romanian army led to the withdrawal of Russian naval units from the Danube area.

Over the winter of 1916-17 the mighty Empire of the Tsar simmered with a mood of intense dissatisfaction which prevailed among the middle and working class. In March food shortages in the capital, Petrograd, led to an outbreak of rioting and the growing restlessness of the troops of the garrison were merely the spark that ignited the gunpowder of revolution. The sailors of the Baltic Fleet at the naval base of Kronstadt soon joined in and within days the Tsar had abdicated, leaving a new liberal Government led by Prince Lvov. At first the Black

Sea Fleet was largely unaffected by the breakdown of discipline so prevalent in the Baltic, partly because of distance from the capital and the events there, partly because the fleet was actively engaged in operations rather than lying ice-bound in harbour and partly due to the influence of the unloved but efficient and successful Commander-in-Chief, Admiral Kolchak. But progressively, discipline deteriorated over the months and operations by the fleet during 1917 became less frequent and more badly managed, particularly after Kolchak's removal in the middle of the year.

During 1917 the submarines, with the exception of the *Krab*, were regularly sent out for their patrols around the Bosporus and off Zonguldak. The loss of the *Morzh*, which had sailed from Sevastopol on 11 May, was particularly felt among the Russian submariners, the more so as the cause was never established. and it may well be that she was destroyed by one of the many Russian mines off the Bosporus. It was at this time too that shortages of spares and skilled labour began to affect the operations of both the destroyers and submarines and forced a break in submarine operations that lasted for three weeks. A final addition was made to the strength of the flotilla when the *Gagara* became operational in August.

In June the *Kashalot* tried to introduce a new element into submarine operations when operating near Cape Kerempe. A part of the crew were formed into a landing party to deal with some Turkish gun positions. However, such an innovation was not a success and the landing party was forced to withdraw under intense machine gun fire having suffered casualties. Later the same month the *Nerpa* had a last chance to attack the *Breslau* but the opportunity was lost as the cruiser altered course as the submarine was about to fire. Once again, Kititsyn – now promoted to Captain 2nd rank – was able to capture a Turkish steamer and take it in prize to Sevastopol, but time was then running out and the last success before the Armistice was by the *Gagara* when she drove a steamer ashore by gunfire on 25 October. In all the Russian submarines had carried out 29 patrols during 1917 with the loss to the enemy of 92 assorted ships claimed as either sunk or captured, though many of those claimed a sunk were merely run ashore and were refloated again by the Turks within a day or so.

The first German patrol in the Black Sea in 1917 was not carried out until 30 May when the *UB14* (*Leutnant* Bodo Elleke) left Constantinople to land some agents on the Caucasus coast who were to contact nationalists in Georgia, and then went on to capture and scuttle the sailing ship *Kerasunda*. When the *UB42* (*Leutnant* Cassius von Montigny) went on patrol on 8 October she too landed agents and weapons on the Caucasus coast, sank a transport and then shelled the port of Tuapse before returning. A second group landed from the same submarine later in the month were captured by Russian patrols.

Both submarines were active in support of the *Breslau* along the coast towards the Caucasus front in November, but by then the Russians had virtually ceased operations and nothing was seen. The final success in this area came on 22 November when the *UB42* hit the transport *Sirakuzy* with a torpedo and then destroyed by gunfire a three masted sailing vessel.

While the Russian fleet had fought on in the Black Sea events elsewhere in Russia had inexorably moved towards defeat and revolution had become more widespread. The nation was war-weary, the army in disarray. Vice-Admiral Kolchak was deposed on 19 June by an assembly of delegates from the soldiers' and sailors' councils. He was replaced by Vice-Admiral Lukin, who in turn was soon replaced by Rear Admiral Nemetic. In October Lenin and the communists took power, the CENTROFLOT (Central Committee of the Black Sea Fleet) authorised no further operations on 16 November and on 15 December the Russians signed an armistice with the Germans.

CHAPTER THIRTEEN

Final Echoes

After three years in Turkey which were marked by his ability to keep his ships intact and remain a threat which tied down a considerable number of the Entente's ships and by his diplomatic ability to sustain the Turkish Navy, Vice-Admiral Souchon was recalled to Germany at the end of 1917 to take over command of a squadron of the High Seas Fleet. He was replaced by Vice-Admiral Hubert von Rebeur-Paschwitz. By the beginning of 1918 with the defeat of the Russians and the consequent ready availability of coal it was decided that the *Goeben* and *Breslau* should sally forth into the Mediterranean. Arrangements were made to widen the gaps in the protective minefields off the Dardanelles and illuminate them with newly positioned search lights while the two German ships, four Turkish destroyers and the *UC23* were made ready for sea.

In the months since the withdrawal of the army from the Gallipoli Peninsula the fleet based at Mudros had been drastically reduced in size as units were withdrawn for duty elsewhere, duty considered to have a higher priority on their services. Remaining were just two pre-dreadnought type battleships, the *Lord Nelson* and the *Agamemnon*, each armed with 4 x 12 inch and 10 x 9.2 inch guns. However, they were capable of only 18 knots, at best, and were still too slow to overtake the German ships at the reduced speed of 20 knots to which time and war damage had reduced them. Also present at either Mudros or Imbros were an elderly French cruiser, some monitors and destroyers as well as units of the RNAS. The British too had had a change of command, the Aegean Squadron now being under Rear Admiral Arthur Hayes-Sadler, the change taking place only days before the Germans were to emerge from the Dardanelles. Like the earlier escape of the two German ships in 1914 the consequences were hardly a triumph for the Royal Navy. The result was that on the morning of 20 January 1918 the monitors *Raglan* and *M28* were sunk while lying at anchor at Imbros, the one battleship at Mudros failed to get to sea before the enemy had returned while the other was away in Salonika with Hayes-Sadler himself. The one submarine available at Mudros, the *E12* (Lieutenant Commander F. A. Williams-Freeman), had a fractured shaft between the diesel engine and the electric motor, a defect not uncommon in this class but one which seriously reduced their surface speed and their ability to charge while under way. The German sortie was only aborted not because of any action by the British ships but because of mines. The *Breslau* sank after hitting five mines, while the *Goeben* herself was damaged by three more.

Returning up the Dardanelles the *Goeben* went aground off the Narrows. There she remained until the afternoon of the 26th when with the help of the Turkish battleship *Torgud Reis* she was freed and returned to Constantinople. In the meantime she had been shelled unsuccessfully by the monitor *M17* and then repeatedly bombed, being hit by only two small bombs which did little damage. As soon as it was known that she was aground Williams-Freeman had urged that he be allowed to try and torpedo her. This was not allowed on the grounds that the *E12* was not fully operational 'in view of the additional risk he would have to take with only one engine available for [battery] recharging purposes', though it was hardly to be expected that Williams-Freeman would be so foolhardy as to try and surface to recharge while still inside the Straits. By the 22nd two other submarines were at Mudros, the *E2* (Lieutenant P H Bonham-Carter) had arrived from Malta while Lieutenant Commander G S White had brought the *E14* from Corfu. The *E2* had the handicap of only one bow tube (the *E14* had two), while Bonham-Carter was new and his crew inexperienced.

It was thus left to the *E14* to try and reach the Narrows and torpedo the German ship, but it was the evening of the 27th before White sailed from Mudros. He reached the Narrows early next morning, but by then the German ship was long gone. Fortune continued to ignore the British and the veteran submarine was detected, blown to the surface and destroyed. Only nine of her crew were rescued to be taken prisoner, the gallant Lieutenant Commander White was not among them. He was subsequently awarded a posthumous Victoria Cross.

Despite the defeat of the Russians the Black Sea area was to be a problem for von Rebeur-Paschwitz for the remainder of the war. Under the terms of the Treaty of Brest-Litovsk, which the Germans had forced the Russians to sign on 3 March, the Germans agreed to recognise an independent Ukrainian state. On the other hand for the Entente their concern centred on the Russian fleet, for if the Germans took it over and manned it then the balance of naval power in the Mediterranean was threatened, the more so if a sortie from the Dardanelles led to a junction with the Austrians sailing from the Adriatic. It was considered that the Germans could probably commission two dreadnoughts, including the recently completed *Volya*, three pre-dreadnoughts, three cruisers, 16 destroyers and six submarines, It was to be a wildly optimistic estimate.

Internal unrest in the Ukraine coupled with the failure of the new state to provide the grain and other supplies demanded by the Germans led to a resumption of the German advance. At the end of March they entered Nikolaev and took over the warships building there and on 19 April entered the Crimea. By the end of the month German troops were in the Russian fleet base at Sevastopol.

By then Vice-Admiral N P Sablin, previously the Chief of Staff, was nominally the Commander-in-Chief, and it was to him that the all powerful Commissars and Fleet Committee turned to save them and the fleet. His first act was to hoist the Ukrainian flag and send envoys to the advancing Germans to inform them that the fleet belonged to the Ukrainian State which they professed to acknowledge. To no avail, the Germans wanted both the port and the ships. So under fire from German artillery Sablin took two battleships, ten destroyers and some smaller vessels to Novorossisk in defiance of the Germans, leaving behind four other battleships with some destroyers and the submarines. The Germans claimed that this was in breach of the Treaty and demanded their return, backing their orders to the extent that the *Goeben*, still with the mine damage of January un-repaired, was sent to the area in a show of strength. Even so the Russian ships at Novorossisk still represented – on paper at least – a superior force to anything the Germans or Turks could send against them. It was, perhaps, the German threat to resume their advance into Southern Russia that swung the argument to sail for Sevastopol. While openly Moscow told the ships to return they also sent secret orders to scuttle. After considerable argument among the Sailors' Council Captain Tikhemieff, of the *Volya*, Sablin being in Moscow clarifying his orders, took his ship together with three destroyers and three other ships to Sevastopol on 18 June. The remainder scuttled themselves.

For the remainder of the war there was considerable activity to see what ships could be made seaworthy and for which crews could be found. The Turks and Bulgars sought to have some of the ships allocated to them, but the Germans refused mainly for the lack of suitably qualified personnel to man the ships without affecting the strength of their allies' existing fleets. Even the Austrians had offered to man some of the submarines for use in the Mediterranean, an offer which the *Admiralstab* accepted if the Austrians manned three of the submarines, though the boats would remain under the command of German officers and would fly the German ensign. Nothing more was heard of the proposal. The Germans did however get some of the ships into commission and manned by German crews. The submarine *Gagara*, numbered as *US4*, carried out sea trials while the *Utka*, given the number *US3*, was scheduled for trials on completion. Even so, the number of ships which could even start trials was far short of the dangerous number which so worried the Admiralty.

In Pola *Kapitän zur See* Pullen was seriously concerned about how long his Austrian allies were going to remain in the war. He was concerned that should Austria sue for a separate peace then the surrender of the German submarines might become a condition of any armistice. Accordingly on 24 October he sought permission from the *Admiralstab* to withdraw his submarines from the Mediterranean, approval being received the next day. He was ordered to observe strict secrecy but Pullen felt bound to let the Austrian Commander-in-Chief, Admiral Horthy, and the senior Austrian officer at Cattaro, *Linienschiffskapitän* Seitz, know what was intended. Evacuation of the flotilla offices at Pola began on 28th and at Cattaro on the 30th. Between the 29th and 31

October 13 U-boats* all left for Germany, while two more who were on patrol, the *U34* and *UC73* received their orders to leave patrol and head for Germany. Pullen was concerned for the *UC74* which was then off Asia Minor as she had insufficient fuel to reach Germany, in fact her commanding officer *Leutnant* Adelbert von der Luhe opted for internment in Spain. Those U-boats which were unable to make the voyage back to Germany were blown up or wrecked at their Austrian bases: the *U47*, *U65*, *U73*, *UB48*, *UC25*, *UC34* and *UC53* were scuttled at Pola, the *UB129* was abandoned at Fiume, the *UC54* at Trieste and *U72* at Cattaro. Also destroyed were two small torpedo boats, the *A51* and *A82*, which had acted as despatch vessels for the German flotilla.

Although Pullen had issued instructions that merchant ships were not be attacked on the way home the last British merchant ship to be attacked was the *Sarpedon* on 7 November. In an attempt to catch the U-boats known to be making for home special patrols were organised across the Otranto and Gibraltar Straits, but there was only one success. The *U34* (*Leutnant* Johannes Klasing) was sunk by the Q-ship HMS *Privet* as she attempted to pass through the Straits of Gibraltar on the night of 8 November. The *U35* was another that did not return to Germany, her commanding officer opting for internment in Spain as the famous submarine was in too poor mechanical state to face the long voyage.

One of the German submarines passing through the Straits of Gibraltar had an encounter with the British submarine *J1* (Lieutenant Commander F Kennedy) which was unique in the history of submarine warfare. The *J1* was based on Gibraltar carrying out anti-submarine patrols in the eastern Atlantic and western Mediterranean. But the *J1* was different from all other submarines. Her previous commanding officer, Commander R B Ramsey had proposed that the boat be fitted with 'four 200lb naval bomb stick throwers' abaft the conning tower. The idea was taken up but the weapons were fitted internally just forward of the steering gear and were launched through two vertical cylindrical tubes, which like torpedo tubes had outer and inner watertight doors. Once loaded, and with the outer door opened, the charge was literally dropped out having been released by a trigger mechanism, the *J1* herself escaping from the effect of the explosion by going at her full speed of 17 knots. Orders for loading and firing were passed from the bridge by means of an instrument similar to an engine telegraph, the actual loading and firing party of Stokers being under the direction of the Chief Stoker. About 20 charges were carried. On the 9 November Kennedy sighted a surfaced U-boat which he identified as a UB type, unable to close to fire torpedoes he surfaced and opened fire with his gun at 8,000 yards. After only two rounds the U-boat promptly dived and the *J1* made her historic depth charge attack when running over the spot many minutes later. Only one charge was dropped for fear of

* *U35, U38, U63, UB49, UB50, UB51, UB105, UB128, UC20, UC22, UC27, UC52* and *UC67.*

cracking the battery cells, and it is not surprising that the attack was unsuccessful, the U-boat must have been a long way from the datum by then. The target cannot be identified for certain but well have been the *UB51*.

The U-boats did not leave the Mediterranean without a last demonstration of their powers. After passing the Straits of Gibraltar the *UB50* (*Leutnant* Heinrich Kukat) encountered the pre-dreadnought battleship HMS *Britannia* off Cape Trafalgar and sank her with two torpedoes on 9 November. The old battleship took nearly three hours to sink and when Kukat raised his periscope to observe his handiwork he was promptly engaged by the battleship's secondary armament. Among those who saw the survivors arriving at Gibraltar was Karl Dönitz, the former commanding officer of the *UB68* and then en route to Britain and a PoW camp.

If the men of the Mediterranean U-boat flotillas expected a hero's welcome on their arrival in Germany they were to be cruelly deceived. They arrived in good order and with pennants denoting their tonnage sunk flying from their periscopes but found the ports of Kiel and Wilhelmshaven in the grip of mutiny and with the red flag flying from most of the ships. Germany herself was on the brink of seeking an armistice.

HMS Britannia *sunk on the 9 November 1918, two days before the armistice, by* UB50 *off Cape Trafalgar.* (IWM Q.38360)

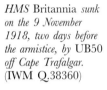

While the Germans were busy withdrawing their submarines from the Mediterranean, the British had made a significant reinforcement to their flotilla with the arrival in November 1918 of the new *M1*, com-

manded by Commander R B Ramsey, recently of the *J1*. The first of
a proposed class of four the *M1* was remarkable for the 12 inch gun
mounted forward of the conning tower, the largest gun ever mounted
on any submarine. Although the gun had a maximum range of about
20,000 yards it was never really considered that a submarine firing only
single shots and with poor spotting facilities would be effective at that
range. Rather, it was intended as a substitute for the erratic performing
torpedo. A single 850 pound shell fired at short range, where the flat
trajectory would ensure a hit, was considered to be an effective way of
dealing with many targets and the number of shells that could be carried was many times the number of torpedoes. By the time the *M1* was
completed there little for her to do in Home Waters and she was sent
to the Mediterranean more in the hope that some operation could be
found for her than with a specific objective in view. Among the crew
there were rumours of a bombardment of Pola, or Constantinople. The
latter, with its implied passage through the Dardanelles in such a large
boat where the large gun could have easily become foul of the many
nets was viewed with some apprehension by the crew, though by the
time she sailed from England the surrender of both Austria and Turkey
rendered such speculation unnecessary.

In mid-September troops from Salonika opened an offensive which
forced the Bulgarians to seek an armistice on 29th. Elsewhere the
British army maintained the pressure on the Turks and a month later
on 30 October they too signed an armistice onboard HMS *Agamemnon*
at Mudros. One of the terms was the *Goeben* should be handed over and
the German crew made PoWs. By then the facade of the previous four
years whereby the ship was really part of the Turkish navy was made
into fact when von Rebeur-Paschwitz hauled down his flag and handed over to his Turkish deputy, Rear Admiral Arif Pasha. The Germans
slipped away to Odessa onboard the steamer *Corcovado* from where the
found their way home by rail.

The armistice terms also provided for an occupation of the
Dardanelles and extensive clearance of the many minefields was begun
at once. Even so it was 11 November before the task was completed to
allow safe passage of ships up to Constantinople. The following day
Admiral Gough-Calthorpe led a combined allied fleet of British,
French, Italian and Greek ships, including HMS *Adamant* and the submarines *E11*, *E21* and *E25*, up the Straits passed the scenes of the fighting in 1915 anchoring off the Turkish capital or in the Gulf of Ismid
on the 13th.

The final days in the Adriatic may be said to belong to the Italians.
The bulk of the Italian submarines were by then based at Brindisi
though a few continued to patrol from Venice. For them the greatest
hope was for a chance to meet the Austrian battleships should they venture out from behind their protective minefields. Elements of the Italian
navy had long been considering other ways of reaching the Austrian
ships as they lay protected by mines, nets and booms. The first idea was
the *Grillo*, a sort of naval tank fitted with lateral caterpillar chains for

climbing over the net booms and armed with two 45cm torpedoes. Two of these craft, the *Cavalletta* and *Pulce*, attacked Pola on the night of 13 April but had to be scuttled. A second attack on the 14 May by the *Grillo* was also unsuccessful, the craft being scuttled, later to be raised by the Austrians.

Not put off by these failures the submarine *Argo* was then taken in hand at Venice for conversion into an 'assault submarine'. She would carry frogmen who would exit from the submarine to cut through the nets. It was then planned for up to forty MAS boats, each with two torpedoes, to enter the main harbour area where they would torpedo the Austrian ships at anchor.

While the *Argo* was being converted two other Italian naval officers came up with another imaginative idea. Engineer Lieutenant Commander Raffaele Rosetti and Surgeon Lieutenant Raffaele Paolucci developed the first human torpedo. They had taken the B57 14 inch torpedo and fitted it with two 170 kg mines. The torpedo, powered by a compressed air engine with an endurance of around 10 miles at 3-4 knots, was controlled by two divers who clung to it and guided it towards the target. Each mine was attached to the hull of the target by large magnets, and was provided with a timer to allow the men to get clear before any explosion. The device was known as the *Mignatta*.

After extensive trials and training in the Venetian lagoon the two officers were given permission to make their attack on Pola and left on the night of 31 October. Towed first by the torpedo boat *65PN* to just off the island of Brioni they were then towed by a motor torpedo boat to just outside the breakwater at Pola. They penetrated the net defences despite the presence of patrols, down a lane of Austrian ships which they found to their surprise to be floodlit. They placed one mine on the hull of the flagship, the *Viribus Unitis*, before being discovered, but managed to scuttle their craft before being picked up and taken onboard the battleship.

Once onboard they announced that they had mined the ship. The result was electrifying. *Linienschiffskapitän* Vunkocic de Podkapelski, the captain, gave the order to abandon ship and the Italians found themselves going back over the side in a general '*sauve qui peut*'. Their freedom was short lived for they were again picked up and returned to the *Viribus Unitis* where the atmosphere was hostile and they were accused of a hoax. Doubts as to what should be done with the two Italians were resolved at 6.30 am on 1 November when the mine detonated. Rosetti and Paolucci found themselves back in the water while the battleship rolled over and sank in 14 minutes. The second mine also found a target having drifted until it struck the old liner *Wien* which had been used as an accommodation ship by German submarine crews.

Rosetti and Paolucci's operation had been well conceived and executed and displayed the Italian talent for midget submarine operations which would be so well demonstrated in the next war. But in sense it was a futile exercise for the day before, on 31 October, the Austrian Navy had ceased to exist. Faced with the break up of his Empire the

Emperor Karl had turned the fleet over to the South Slav National Council at Agram. All officers and men who were not of Slav nationality were allowed to go home, and at 4.0 pm on the 31st the Imperial Ensign was lowered for the last time to be replaced by the red white and blue flag of the new Jugoslav state. Admiral Horthy, together with most of the German, Czech and Hungarian elements in the fleet went home. Horthy's replacement as Commander-in-Chief of the new Jugoslav fleet was Vunkovic de Podkapelski, an appointment that lasted less than 24 hours for he chose to stay with his sinking flagship and was one of some 400 men lost with the ship. Celebrations honouring their new status had been rife in the fleet that night, there was little or no preparedness and no watertight security which accounts for the state of panic and the rapidity with which just one charge sank this large ship.

Armistice negotiations had in fact already been started between Austria and the Entente and it will always be a matter for debate as to how much the Italians knew of the situation at Pola. Austria's military situation was dire, their troops were on the retreat on most fronts and the news that Austria had actually asked for an Armistice came as no surprise to the Allied War Council meeting outside Paris. Armistice terms for Austria had already been agreed by the Entente Powers and the naval element was harsh. The three remaining *Tegetthoff* class battleships were to be surrendered along with three light cruisers, nine destroyers, numerous other vessels and all submarines built between 1910 and 1918, together with all German U-boats in Austrian waters or under Austrian command. This last provision was one that Pullen had feared and had already taken the steps to negate. All remaining Austrian ships were to be immobilised in their harbours and placed under the supervision of the victors. The ships named in the surrender documents, however, were to be steamed to Venice for formal surrender to the Italians.

The armistice was signed at 3.0 pm on 3 November, coming into effect 24 hours later. In the event there was no formal surrender for the Austrian fleet at Venice because there were insufficient crews left to man the ships. Instead, plans were made to occupy the various Austrian bases and almost immediately the Allies began to fall out one with another. Commodore Kelly had wanted to ensure that the entry into the Austrian bases was made by ships of all navies steaming together in a display of unity. In this he was supported by the French, but found that the Italians had other ideas. The Italians had territorial ambitions in the area and did not want the presence of British or French or even American units. Accordingly Pola was occupied by the Italians on 4 November before Kelly knew what was happening. Only at Cattaro was there a semblance of unity when on 9 November the British cruiser HMS *Glasgow* in company with the French *Waldeck Rousseau* and the Italian *Carlo Mirabello* entered the harbour together. Even here the Italians were not disposed to being co-operative and within hours were the cause of a major row with the French over the fate of the Austrian ships.

Austrian U-boats interned at Pola in November 1918.

The cause of the disagreement was the former French submarine *Curie*, captured by the Austrians in December 1914 and renamed *U14*. The French set about reclaiming her back into the fold but the Italians objected and struck a raw Gallic nerve. The Italian argument was that the submarine was an Austrian unit and her fate should be left to the peace conference to decide and until then she should remain with the other Austrian submarines and be disarmed. This was obviously unacceptable to the French and it is surprising that the Italians should have tried such an argument. Telegrams went back and forth until the French emerged the victors and the French colours were again hoisted on the *Curie* on 18 November. She continued to serve until 1929 when she was broken up.

Thereafter relations between the former allies disintegrated rapidly in the Adriatic. The Italians had occupied Pola, the Americans were in charge at Spalato where two Austrian pre-dreadnoughts briefly flew the Stars and Stripes as the USS *Radetzky* and *Zrinyi*. At Cattaro the French assumed control. Britain had no sphere of influence and the Admiralty were reluctant to become involved in any disputes in the area. Kelly noted that 'since the armistice the Italians have been carrying out a war of conquest with a zeal that is worthy of a better cause', and that Admiral Umberto Cagni, the Senior Italian Officer at Pola had 'more than his share of the wisdom of a serpent'.

With the arrival of the allied fleet off Constantinople the next consideration for Gough-Calthorpe was the German ships in the Black Sea and the ships of the ex-Russian fleet, whether they flew the Ukrainian flag, the German ensign or were under the control of the Soviets. Already the British and French were committed to supporting the

Two German UB type submarines secured alongside the former Russian dreadnought battleship Volya *at the end of the war in 1918 with the White Ensign flying over the German ensign. The outboard boat is UB137. The identity of the inboard boat is unknown but the number UN43 ('un boat) has been painted on the conning tower.* (TNSM)

White Russian forces in the north around Archangel and Murmansk, in the far East at Vladivostok and in the Caspian around the port of Baku. Now that aid was to be extended. The full extent of operations in the War of Intervention, as it is sometimes called, is beyond the scope of this book, but the immediate despatch of forces to the south of Russia is of interest in completing the story of submarine operations in the war.

With Austria out of the war the *E46* at Brindisi was ordered to load with mines and in company with the *H2* and *H4* sailed 7 November to join the fleet off Constantinople. The mines were intended to be laid off one of the Black Sea ports to guard against a sortie by the Red Fleet though such an action was unlikely taking into account the prevailing state of efficiency and discipline onboard all the Russian ships. For the *E46* (Lieutenant L Ashmore) and the two H class submarines it was an usual trip for not only were they routed through the Corinth Canal but it was virtually peacetime conditions for the first time in over four years; not to be always warily on guard at sea, with the chance of every man's hand against them, which was the normal lot of any submariner in war, was a blessed relief. Lying at a buoy in Mudros harbour in pouring rain and a rising gale the submariners heard the news of the end of the war with Germany and having received orders to 'splice the mainbrace' they celebrated as best they could. A week later they sailed again to join the fleet in the Sea of Marmara. The next stage came on the 19 November when the Admiralty signalled Admiral Gough-Calthorpe that 'It is desirable that large British forces should enter the Black Sea as soon as convenient in order to impress not only the Ukrainians but also General Denikin and his forces'. When the British squadron, including a force of 500 Royal Marines, finally reached Sevastopol their first task was the evacuation of the German forces in the area. A French force was similarly sent to Odessa. Among the ships in the harbour at Sevastopol were four German U-boats, the White Ensign being hoisted on two of them while the Tricolour was hoisted on the others.

Crews then had to be found to sail the British U-boats back to Constantinople. These were found from the submarines present in the Marmara and from the 'Spare Crew' in the *Adamant* the one commanded by Lieutenant Ashmore, the other by Lieutenant Rushbrooke. The two prize crews sailed for Sevastopol in the *Adamant* accompanied by the *E21* which was carrying the fuel for the U-boats. The British boats were the *UB42* and *UC37*, while the French were allocated the *UB14* and *UC23*. Ashmore relates how that on arrival they carefully examined their boats for booby traps but found none. They also found that the *UC37* was in a much worse state that the corresponding French boat, and that as the French had not then arrived to claim their prizes the British officers, on a first come first served principle, appropriated the best boat for themselves by the simple expedient of switching ensigns. It was not to be, for after furious French protests the ensigns had to be exchanged once again. Before sailing the two British officers were in more mischief. In place of the 'UB' and 'UC' on the conning towers they substituted 'UN' since during the war the Germans were

seldom referred to as anything but 'Huns'! All was well until the new lettering was noticed by a senior officer and Commander Benning, the senior submarine officer, had to make belated explanations which were luckily accepted in good humour.

Numerous Russian submarines were found to be in Sevastopol. During 1918 most of them had flown the Ukrainian flag at one time or another. While the Germans had tried to get four of them into an operational state: the *Utka* had carried out trials as the *US3*, the *Gagara* had started trials as the *US4*, the *Burvestnik* and *Orlan* were to have followed. Yet murder of the officers and desertions by their crews left the whole flotilla with but 28 officers and a few Petty Officers, commanded by Commander Pogeretsky, an able officer and the holder of the British DSO. The state of the submarines themselves was pitiful with the ravages of revolution providing little opportunity for maintenance and the Germans having done an effective job of looting before they left. By the time British arrived in Sevastopol this devoted band of submariners were doing their best to keep their boats in some sort of order. The *Tyulen* being in the best state whilst in the battery shed there was a large store of carefully maintained cells for submarine batteries.

The first British ship to arrive in Sevastopol had been the cruiser HMS *Canterbury* (Captain Percy M Royds), on 24 November. The orders given to Captain Royds were to take the battleship *Volya* under the British flag it being thought that she was in German hands, as indeed she had been only 24 hours earlier. By the time the *Canterbury* entered Sevastopol she was once more flying the Tsarist St Andrew's flag. Nevertheless, a British party was sent over and hauled down the Russian flag and requested the Russian Admiral and the crew to leave the ship. It was a tactless act of rigid obedience to orders and a bitter humiliation to the loyal elements among the Russians, the very people the British had been sent to help and support. The submariners were the next to suffer from this same sort of act when the Gough-Calthorpe ordered that all submarines as well as the stored battery cells were to be rendered useless. It was a distasteful task for the British submariners. and though the cells were wrecked the submarines were merely immobilised by removing the starting switches, with the exception of the *Tyulen*.

Elsewhere support for the anti-Bolshevik forces was found to be lacking while among the French forces around Odessa morale was very low, and there were several incidents of mutiny. Odessa was abandoned to the Red armies and in April Sevastopol was also evacuated. Before leaving the British took 15 submarines out to sea and scuttled them[*]. while four more were handed over to the White forces of General Wrangel[†]. In a surprising turn of fortune Sevastopol and large areas of southern Russia were reoccupied in June before the White forces were again in retreat.

[*] *Kashalot, Kit, Narval, Karp, Karas, Sudak, Skat, Nalim, Losos, Gagara, Lebed, Orlan, Pelikan, Krab* and *AG21.*
[†] *Tyulen, Utka, Burvestnik* and *AG22.*

Linienschiffsleutnant *Georg* Ritter *von Trapp* (right) *dictates the war diary of* U14 *during a Mediterranean patrol in 1917. Evidently attack from the air is not something Trapp is particularly concerned about.* (Kriegsarchiv, Vienna)

The submarine *Nerpa* was to remain in the dockyard at Nikolaev throughout all this period of fighting and was eventually commissioned into the Soviet Navy in 1922. The *AG21* also subsequently entered the Soviet Navy having been raised in 1928 from where she had been scuttled by the British. The first Soviet submarine to be commissioned was the *AG23* which carried out a patrol against White shipping off Sevastopol in November 1920, without any success. It was an operation which was followed by a British protest against similar 'piratical acts' and the Soviets were informed that any of their submarines met with at sea would be treated as pirates! The Soviets also moved four old submarines from the Baltic to the Caspian Sea in 1918, but these boats took no active part in any operations there. With the collapse of the White cause they took their four submarines – which had not achieved anything in the civil war to Bizerta where they were interned and later scrapped by the French.

For the U-boat officers returning to Germany from the Mediterranean the future was bleak with few vacancies in the small navy allowed them under the peace treaty, and of course there to be no submarines. In June 1921 Karl Neumann. formerly commanding the *UC67* was tried for war crimes at Leipzig after the sinking of the hospital ship *Dover Castle* in May 1917, but was acquitted. Neumann was the only U-boat officer of the Mediterranean flotilla to be tried for war crimes. Max Valentiner high on the 'wanted list' for war crimes was never brought to trial for he found sanctuary in Turkey where he started the Turkish navy's submarine school.

The Austrian officers too faced an uncertain future. With the defeat at the end of the war the Empire broke up and was divided among the various nationalist factions. Austrian submariners were then citizens of states far from the sea. Some like Teufl von Fernland lived on their laurels and wrote their memoirs. The most famous, Georg von Trapp, founded the famous Von Trapp Family Singers, immortalised in the film 'The Sound of Music', and was forced to flee to America after Hitler's occupation of Austria.

Before the peace conference could formally end the conflict in the Adriatic the Italians were determined to have their naval victory parade which the chaos of the Austrian surrender had denied them. Accordingly, in March 1919, Italian crews boarded a number of the Austrian ships in Pola, including the battleships *Tegetthoff* and *Erzherzhog Franz Ferdinand*, one cruiser, two destroyers, four torpedo boats and the submarines *U5, U21, U28* and *U40*. Also present was the destroyer HMS *Martin* flying the broad pennant of Commodore Kelly, but that is another story! The force was reviewed by the King of Italy after which the submarines were berthed at St Mark's Square to be gazed at in awe by the public before being towed away to be broken up. Under the terms of the Treaty of San Germain the Italians were assigned eight* of the Austrian submarines which were lying at Pola or Flume, while the French took over the six boats† lying at Cattaro from where they were towed to Bizerta.

With the end of the war the British, French and Italian submarines quickly returned to a peacetime footing. The French went home to Toulon and Bizerta. The British boats took longer to get home. In the haste to demobilise 'Hostilities Only' men from the Royal Navy many of the British submarines were paid off and lay at Malta in 'Rotten Row' before coming home in ones and twos with passage crews, or were

---

* *U1, U2, U4, U11, U15, U17, U27* and *U32.*
† *U22, U29, U31, U41, U43* and *U47.*

even sold for scrap there. For the submariners themselves there were a number of interesting appointments available. Lieutenant Williams-Freeman, for one, commanded a number of motor launches on the Danube serving the Inter-Allied Disarmament Commission. On the night 22 March 1919 he was in Budapest with *ML228* when Bela Kun and the communists seized power. The launch was boarded by Red Guards and Williams-Freeman and the crew were lucky to escape with their lives. He eventually left Budapest after a daring cutting-out expedition was organised using British, French and former Austrian seamen manning ex-Austrian river gun-boats.

Thus a period of over four years of war at sea in the Mediterranean and Black Seas came to an end. Submarine operations were as diverse as the number of Navies involved, all having their successes and failures. For the British the highlight was undoubtedly the campaign in the Sea of Marmara, though even that was not the success which was thought at the time. Conversely, elsewhere the British submariners achieved little. On the other hand the French were unable to cope with the conditions of the Dardanelles but showed considerable flair in the Adriatic, greater success being frustrated by poor torpedo performance. Both the British and French were scathing about the capabilities of their Italian allies, but even this consideration must be tempered by the actions of the Italian midget submarines in the last six months of the war. The Austrians, often regarded as mere puppets of their German partners, were hampered by the lack of large modern submarines capable of reaching out into the Mediterranean as a whole but scored some resounding successes in the Adriatic. The German U-boats mounted a massive campaign against shipping in the Mediterranean, as they did in the Atlantic. It was a campaign which if it had succeeded – and it near-

Sic transit Gloria . . . *six British submarines laid up in* Rotten Row *at Malta awaiting disposal. From left to right:* H2, H4, E11 *(in which Nasmith won the VC),* H9 *and* E2.

ly did but for the late and rather reluctant introduction of convoys – might have had serious consequences for the Entente, especially for Britain. Yet they too had their failures when the same boats were sent into the Black Sea. The Russian submariners failed in their attempts to torpedo the *Goeben* and *Breslau*, or indeed any other warship, but by 1917 were beginning to show their worth in their blockade of the 'coal coast'.

The submarine, untried as a weapon of war in 1914, had started hesitantly but four years later had become a dominant factor in naval warfare.

Bibliography

PUBLISHED SOURCES

Admiralty, *The Mediterranean Pilot, Vol.III (West Coast of Greece and Adriatic Sea)*, 8th Edition, Hydrographic Dept of the Royal Navy, 1957

Admiralty, *The Black Sea Pilot, including the Dardanelles, Sea of Marmara and Bosporus*, 8th Edition, Hydrographic Dept of the Royal Navy, 1930

Aichelburg, W., *Die Unterseeboote Österreich-Ungarns*, (2 vols.), Akademische Druck-u. Verlaganstalt, Graz, 1981

Baumgartner, L., & Pawlik, G., *S M Unterseeboote, Das KuK Unterseebootswesen, 1907–18*, Herbert Weishaupt Verlag, Graz, 1987

Bilzer, F., *Die Torpedoboote der KuK Kriegsmarine von 1875–1918*, H Weishaupt Verlag, Graz, 1984

Chatterton, E Keeble, *Seas of Adventure*, Hurst & Blackett, London, 1931

Conways, *All The World's Fighting Ships, 1906–21*, Conway Maritime Press, 1985

Couhat, J L., *French Warships of World War One*, Ian Allan, 1974

Edwards, Lieut Cdr K., *We Dive At Dawn*, Rich & Cowan, London, 1939

Fraccaroli, A., *Italian Warships of World War One*, Ian Allan, 1970

Gibson, R H., & Prendergast, M., *The German Submarine War, 1914–18*, Constable, 1931

Gould, S W., *Submarine Warfare in the Adriatic*, USNIP, 1944 (pp 683–689)

Grant, R M., *U-boats Destroyed*, Putnam, 1964

Grant, R M., *U-boat Intelligence, 1914–18*, Putnam, 1969

Greger, R., *The Russian Fleet, 1914–17*, Ian Allan, 1972

Greger, R., *Austro-Hungarian Warships*, Ian Allan, 1976

Guleryuz, A., & Langensiepen, B., *The Ottoman Navy, 1839–1923, Vol.I*, Kampmeier Druck & Verlag, Hamburg, 1989

Halpern, Paul G., *The Anglo-French-Italian Naval Convention of 1915*, The Historical Journal, 1970 (pp 106–129)

Halpern, Paul G., *The Naval War in the Mediterranean, 1914–18*, United States Institute Press, 1987 (also by Allen & Unwin, London, 1987)

Halpern, Paul G., (ed.), *The Keyes papers, Vol. I*, The Navy Records Society, 1975

Halpern, Paul G., (ed.), *The Royal Navy in the Mediterranean, 1915–18*, The Navy Records Society, 1987

Hough, R., *The Great War at Sea, 1914–18*, Oxford University Press, 1983

Hough, R., *Former Naval Person*, Weidenfeld & Nicolson, 1985

Hurd, A., *Italian Sea Power in the Great War*, London 1918

Kemp, Paul, & Jung, P., *Five Broken Down B Boats: British Submarine Operations in the Northern Adriatic, 1915–17*, Warship International, 1989

Keyes, Admiral of the Fleet Sir R., *Naval Memoirs*, Butterworth, London, 1934–35

Lorey, H., *Der Krieg in den turkischen Gewassern, Vol. I*, Berlin, 1928

Marder, A J., *From the Dreadnought to Scapa Flow*, (5 vols.), Oxford University Press, 1961–70

Martiny, Nikolaus von, *Bilddokumente Aus Österreich-Ungarns Seekrieg, 1914–18*, Akademische Druck-u. Verlagsanstalt, Graz, 1973

Pavlovich, Rear Admiral Professor N B., (ed.), *The Fleet in the First World War, Vol. I, Operations of the Russian Fleet*, Amerind Publishing, New Delhi, 1979

Roskill, S., *Churchill and the Admirals*, Collins, 1977

Rössler, E., *The U-boat*, Arms & Armour, 1981

Schupita, P., *Die KuK Seeflieger; Chronik und Dokumentation der Österreich-Ungarischen Marineluftwaffe*, Berard und Grafe Verlag, Koblenz, 1983

Sokol, H., *Österreich-Ungarns Seekrieg, 1914–18*, (2 vols.) Akademische Druck-u. Verlagsanstalt, Graz, 1967

Spindler, A., *Der Handelskrieg mit U-Booten, Vols. I & II*, Berlin, 1932–4

Stoker, H G., *Straws in the Wind*, Herbert Jenkins, 1925

Thomazi, A., *La Guerre Navale Dans L'Adriatique*, Payoy, Paris, 1925

Ufficio Storico Della R. Marina, *La Marina Italiana Nella Grande Guerra, Vol. III*, Valechi-Firenze, 1938–42

Vat, Dan van der, *The Ship that Changed the World*, Hodder & Stoughton, 1985

Wilson, M R., *The British B Class Submarines, Warships Nos 17 & 18*. Conway Maritime Press, 1980

Wilson, M R., *Destination Dardanelles*, Leo Cooper, 1988

Winton, J., *Convoy*, Michael Joseph, 1983

Zalessky, N A., *Krab – The First Submarine Minelayer in the World*, Shipbuilding Publishing House, Leningrad, 1967

UNPUBLISHED SOURCES

Admiralty, The Naval Staff Monographs, No. 21, *The Mediterranean, 1914–15*, March 1923

Ashmore, Vice-Admiral L H., *Russian Scrapbook, 1915–19*

Chrisman, H., *Naval Operations in the Mediterranean in the Great War, 1914–18*, Stanford University PhD dissertation, 1931

Public Record Office, London

ADM 137/2076-77 – Commodore (S) War Records, Vols. 10 & 11
ADM 137/2120-22 and 2126 – Taranto Base Records, Vols. 5, 6, 7 & 11
ADM 173 (Series) – Submarines' logs

APPENDIX A

Major Warships Sunk by Submarines in the Mediterranean

Date	Name (Nationality)	Type	Cause	Sub (Nat.)
13 Dec 14	*Messudieh* (Turk.)	BB	T	*B11* (Br.)
27 Apr 15	*Leon Gambetta* (Fr.)	CC	T	*U5* (A-H)
25 May 15	*Triumph* (Br.)	BB	T	*U21* (Ger.)
27 May 15	*Majestic* (Br.)	BB	T	*U21* (Ger.)
7 Jul 15	*Amalfi* (It.)	CC	T	*UB14* (Ger.)
18 Jul 15	*Giuseppe Garibaldi* (It.)	CC	T	*U4* (A-H)
8 Aug 15	*Heireddin Barbarossa* (Turk.)	BB	T	*E11* (Br.)
8 Feb 16	*Amiral Charner* (Fr.)	CC	T	*U35* (Ger.)
27 Feb 16	*Russell* (Br.)	BB	M	*U73* (Ger.)
27 Dec 16	*Gaulois* (Fr.)	BB	T	*UB47* (Ger.)
4 Jan 17	*Peresviet* (Rus.)	BB	M	*U73* (Ger.)
9 Jan 17	*Cornwallis* (Br.)	BB	T	*U32* (Ger.)
19 Mar 17	*Danton* (Fr.)	BB	T	*U64* (Ger.)
14 Dec 17	*Chateaurenault* (Fr.)	CC	T	*UC38* (Ger.)
1 Nov 18	*Viribus Unitis* (A–H)	BB	(note 1)	*Mignatta* (It.)
9 Nov 18	*Britannia* (Br.)	BB (note 2)	T	*UB50* (Ger.)

T = Torpedoed
M = Mined

Note 1. Sunk by torpedo warhead clamped to the hull by crew from midget submarine.
Note 2. Sunk outside the Mediterranean by a submarine of the Mediterranean flotilla on passage back to Germany.

Major Warships Damaged by Submarine attack in the Mediterranean

Date	Name (Nationality)	Type	Cause	Sub (Nat.)
21 Dec 14	*Jean Bart* (Fr.)	BB	T	*U12* (A–H)
9 Jun 15	*Dublin* (Br.)	LC	T	*U4* (A–H)
15 May 17	*Dartmouth* (Br.)	LC	T	*U25* (Ger.)
1 Oct 18	*Weymouth* (Br.)	LC	T	*U31* (A–H)
10 Oct 18	*Voltaire* (Fr.)	BB	T	*UB48* (Ger.)

Submarines Sunk by Submarine Attack in the Mediterranean

Date	Name (Nationality)	Type	Cause	Sub (Nat)
10 Jun 15	*Medusa* (It.)	*UB15* (Ger.)		As *U11* (A-H)
5 Aug 15	*Nereide* (It.)	*U5* (A–H.)		
25 May 17	*UC24* (Ger.)	*Circe* (Fr.)		
19 Jun 17	*Arlane* (Fr.)	*UC22* (Ger.)		
16 Apr 18	*H5* (It.)	*H1* (Br.)	Accident	
23 May 18	*UB52* (Ger.)	*H4* (Br.)		
6 Jul 18	*U20* (A–H)	*F12* (It.)		
20 Sep 18	*Circe* (Fr.)	*U47* (Ger.)		

Characteristics of Austrian Submarines

Submarine	First of class Launch	Length	Displacement Surface/Dived	Torpedo Tubes	Armament	Speed Endurance	Surface Endurance	Dived	Remarks
U3	Aug 08	139 ft	240/300 tons	2 x 45 cm	None	12/8½	1,200 miles at 12 knots	40 miles at 3 knots.	U4 similar.
U5	Feb 09	105 ft	240/273 tons	2 x 45 cm	None	10¾/8	800 miles at 82 knots	48 miles at 5 knots	U6 and U12 similar.
U15	Apr 15	91½ ft	125/140 tons	2 x 45 cm	None	6½/5½	1,650 miles at 5 knots	45 miles at 4 knots	Also: U10 (ex German UB1), U11 (ex German UB15), U16 & U17.
U20	Sep 16	127 ft	173/210 tons	2 x 45 cm	1 x 66 mm plus 1 MG	12/9	1,700 miles at 8 knots	40 miles at 6 knots	Also: U21, U22 & U23. Havmanden type.
U27	Oct 16	121 ft	264/301 tons	2 x 45 cm	1 x 75 mm plus 1 MG	9/7½	6,250 miles at 7½ knots	20 miles at 5 knots	Also: U28 to U32 and U40 and U41. Similar to German UB II.

Characteristics of British Submarines

Submarine	First of class Launch	Length	Displacement Surface/Dived	Torpedo Tubes	Armament	Speed Endurance	Surface Endurance	Dived	Remarks
B Class	25 Oct 04	142 ft	287/316 tons	2 x 18 inch	None	13n	1,300 miles at 9 knots	50 miles at 4½ knots.	Petrol engine.
E Class and AE2	14 Feb 11	178 ft	655/796 tons	4 x 18 inch (see remarks)	Various	14/9½	3,000 miles at 10 knots	99 miles at 3 knots	One extra bow tube in *E9* and later. No beam tubes in *E46* which carried 20 mines.
H Class	16 Apr 15	150 ft	355/467 tons	4 x 18 inch	None (see remarks)	13/9	2,800 miles at 10 knots	130 miles at 2 knots	1 x 6 pdr gun fitted on arrival in the Mediterranean.
J Class	6 Nov 15	275 ft	1,204/1,820 tons	6 x 18 inch	1 x 3 inch	19/10	2,500 miles at 19 knots	55 miles at 5 knots	Also fitted with depth charges (*J1* only)
M Class	9 Jul 17	295 ft	1,594/1,946 tons	4 x 18 inch	1 x 12 inch 1 x 3 inch	15/8	2,500 miles at full power	10 miles at full power	

Characteristics of French Submarines

Submarine	First of class Launch	Length	Displacement Surface/Dived	Torpedo Tubes	Armament	Speed Endurance	Surface Endurance	Dived	Remarks
Saphir	6 Aug 06	147¼ ft	39 V 425 tons	6 x 45 cm	None as built	11½/9	2,000 miles at 7 knots	100 miles at 5 knots	Also: *Turquoise.*
Pluvoise	27 May 07	167¼ ft	398/550 tons	1 x 45 cm plus 6 external	None	12/8	1,500 miles at 9 knots	50 miles at 5 knots	Also: *Cugnot, Floreal, Fresnel, Gay-Lussac, Monge, Papin.* Bow torpedo tube removed from all but five boats by 1914, including *Floreal* and *Monge.* Steam engines for surface running.
Circe	13 Sep 07	154½ ft	351/491 tons	6 x 45 cm (all external)	1 x 47 mm	12/7½	2,160 miles at 8 knots	98 miles at 3½ knots	Became Austrian *U14.*
Brumaire	29 Apr 11	170 ft	397/551 tons	1 x 45 cm plus 6 external	None as built	13/8½	1,700 miles at 10 knots	84 miles at 5 knots	Also: *Bernouilli, Coulomb, Curie. Faraday, Foucault, Joule* and *Le Verrier.*
Archimede	4 Aug 09	197 ft	598/810 tons	1 x 45 cm plus 6 external	None	15/10½	1,160 miles at 10 knots	100 miles at 42 knots	Steam propulsion on surface.
Mariotte	2 Feb 11	210¼ ft	530/627 tons	4 x 45 cm plus 2 external	None	14¼/11	1,050 miles at 10 knots	100 miles at 5 knots	

Characteristics of German Submarines

Submarine	First of class Launch	Length	Displacement Surface/Dived	Torpedo Tubes	Armament	Speed Endurance	Surface Endurance	Dived	Remarks
U21	Oct 12	210½ ft	650/837 tons	4 x 50 cm	1 x 88 mm	15½/9	9,700 miles at 8 knots	80 miles at 5 knots	U19–22 class the first diesel powered boats in the German Navy.
U32–39	7 Jan 14	2,3 ft	685/878 tons	4 x 50 cm	2 x 88 mm	16½/9½	8,790 miles at 8 knots	80 miles at 5 knots	
U63–65	Feb 16	224¼ ft	810/927 tons	4 x 50 cm	2 x 88 mm	16½/9	9,170 miles at 8 knots	60 miles at 5 knots	
U72	Oct 15	186¼ ft	755/832 tons	2 x 50 cm 2 x 100 cm mine tubes (34 mines)	2 x 88 mm	10½/8	7,880 miles at 7 knots	83 miles at 4 knots	Known as the UE 1 class (minelayer). U73 similar.
UB1	Jan 15	92 ft	127/142 tons	2 x 45 cm	1 MG	6½/5½	1,650 miles at 5 knots	45 miles at 4 knots	UB I type. Also UB3 to UB15.
UB42–47	Aug 15	118½ ft	272/305 tons	2 x 50 cm	1 x 50 mm	9/6¼	6,940 miles at 5 knots	45 miles at 4 knots	UB II type.
UB48	Jan 17	181½ ft	516/651 tons	5 x 50 cm	1 x 88 mm	13½/7½	9,040miles at 6 knots	55 miles at 4 knots	UB III type. Also higher numbers to UB129.

Submarine	First of class Launch	Length	Displacement Surface/Dived	Torpedo Tubes	Armament	Speed Endurance	Surface Endurance	Dived	Remarks
UC12	Apr 15	111½ ft	168/183 tons	None	1 MG	6¼/4/5	780 miles at 5 knots	50 miles at 4 knots	UC I type minelayer with chutes for 12 mines. Some temporarily for store carrying. Some boats fitted
UC20	Feb 16	162 ft	417/480 tons	3 x 50 cm	1 x 88 mm	11½/7	9,430 miles at 7 knots	55 miles at 4 knots	UC II type mine-layer with chutes for 18 mines. UC22 to UC74 similar.

Characteristics of Italian Submarines

Submarine	First of class Launch	Length	Displacement Surface/Dived	Torpedo Tubes	Armament	Speed Endurance	Surface Endurance	Dived	Remarks
Medusa	Jul 11	147½ ft	252/705 tons	2 x 45 cm	None	12/8	1,200 miles at 8 knots	50 miles at 6 knots	Also: *Argo, Jaiea, Jantina, Salpa* and *Zoea.*
Nereide	Apr 13	134¼ ft	225/320 tons	2 x 45 cm (see Remarks)	None	13/8	1,000 miles at 10 knots	14 miles at 7 knots	Also: *Nautilus.* Built with external tube on forward casing which was removed on completion.
G. Pullino Ferraris.	Jul 13	138½ ft	345/405	6 x 45 cm	1 x 57 mm and 1 x 47 mm	14/9	2,700 miles	170 miles at 8 knots	Also: *Galileo* at 22 knots
Balilla	4 Aug 15	213¼ ft	728/825 tons	4 x 45 cm	2 x 75 mm	14/9	3,500 miles at 10 knots	85 miles at 3 knots	Originally ordered by Germany as the *U42.*
Mignatta	1918	15 ft	(see remarks)			3 to 4 knots		8–10 miles at 3–4 knots	Consisted of a B57 torpedo with hand holds for the crew of 2, carrying two 117 kilo charges. Only two built.

Characteristics of Russian Submarines

Submarine	First of class Launch	Length	Displacement Surface/Dived	Torpedo Tubes	Armament	Speed Endurance	Surface Endurance	Dived	Remarks
Losos	1905	65½ ft	105/122 tons	1 x 381 mm	1 Machine gun	8½/6 kts	585 miles	42 miles	Also *Sudak*.
Karp	1907	130 ft	207/235 tons	1 x 457 mm		10/8½ kts	1,250 miles	50 miles	Also *Karas*.
Morzh	28 Sep 13	220 ft	630/760 tons	4 x 457 mm	1 x 57 mm 1 x 47 mm	10½/8 kts	2,500 miles	120 miles	Also *Nerpa* and *Tyule*.
Narval	1914	230 ft	621/994 tons	4 x 457 mm	1 x 75 mm 1 x 63 mm	10/9 kts	3,000 miles	120 miles	Also *Kashalot* and *Kit*.
Krab	1 Sep 12	173 ft	512/740 tons	2 x 457 mm	1 x 75 mm	11½/7 kts	1,700 miles	82 miles	Carried 60 mines.
Bars	2 Jun 15	223 ft	650/780 tons	4 x 457 mm	1 x 63 mm	18/10 kts	400 miles/17	25 miles/9	Also *Burvestnik*, *Gagara*, *Lebed*, *Orian*, *Pelikan*, and *Utka*.
AG21	1917	151 ft	355/433 tons	4 x 18 inch	1 x 47 mm	12/10 kts			Bought from USA and re-assembled in Russia.

Index